A STRANGER
IN MY OWN BODY

A STRANGER
IN MY OWN BODY

Atypical Gender Identity
Development and Mental Health

Edited by
Domenico Di Ceglie

with
David Freedman

Foreword by
John Money

London
KARNAC BOOKS

First published in 1998 by
H. Karnac (Books) Ltd.
58 Gloucester Road
London SW7 4QY

British Library Cataloguing in Publication Data

A C.I.P. record for this book is available from the British Library.

ISBN 1 85575 183 6

Edited, designed, and produced by Communication Crafts

Printed in Great Britain by BPC Wheatons Ltd, Exeter

10 9 8 7 6 5 4 3 2 1

To my parents,
who tried to foster in me openness, curiosity, and compassion

ACKNOWLEDGEMENTS

First of all I would like to acknowledge my and the contributors' debt to the young people and their families on whose experience this book is based.

I wish to express my gratitude to Anton Obholzer, Chief Executive, Tavistock & Portman NHS Trust, to Robert Hale, Director, Portman Clinic, to the staff of the Portman Clinic for their generous support for this book, and to all the authors for agreeing to collaborate in this project. Among the many people who contributed to the development of my ideas over the years, I am particularly indebted to Edna O'Shaughnessy, Ronald Britton, and Nicholas Temple. I would also like to thank Liam Hudson for his encouragement in the initial phase of the work and his helpful suggestions on chapter two, The Royal College of Psychiatrists for Appendix 1, my secretary Susan Nollet for her enduring patience over the manuscript, and Eric and Klara King for their kindness and attention to detail. My thanks to my family for their support and putting up with my late evenings. Last, but not least, a special thank you to David Freedman, who has assisted me in the editorial work and has made it, dare I say, an enjoyable experience.

CONTENTS

LIST OF CONTRIBUTORS

Susan J. Bradley Psychiatrist, The Hospital for Sick Children, Professor, Department of Psychiatry, University of Toronto, and Consultant Psychiatrist, Child and Adolescent Gender Identity Clinic, Clarke Institute of Psychiatry, Toronto, Ontario, Canada.

Caroline Brain Consultant Paediatric Endocrinologist, St George's Hospital, and Gender Identity Development Unit, Portman Clinic, London, UK.

Susan W. Coates Associate Clinical Professor of Medical Psychology, Department of Psychiatry, College of Physicians and Surgeons, Columbia University, and Faculty, The Columbia University Center for Psychoanalytic Training and Research, New York, USA.

Leo Cohen Clinical Psychologist, Department of Medical Psychology, Vrije Universiteit, Amsterdam, the Netherlands. Formerly President of the Dutch Rorschach Society.

Peggy Cohen-Kettenis Head of Clinical Psychology and Psychotherapy Department, Child and Adolescent Psychiatric Clinic, University of Utrecht, Holland.

Domenico Di Ceglie Consultant Child and Adolescent Psychiatrist, Adolescent Department, Tavistock Clinic, and Director, Gender Identity Development Unit, Portman Clinic. Honorary Senior Lecturer, Royal Free Hospital School of Medicine, London, UK.

David Freedman Freelance researcher, health and social policy.

Barbara Gaffney Senior Child and Adolescent Psychotherapist, Pathfinder NHS Trust, and formerly Gender Identity Development Unit, Portman Clinic, London, UK.

Karine George Headteacher, Westfields County Junior School, Yateley, Hampshire, UK.

Richard Graham Consultant Child and Adolescent Psychiatrist, Watford Child and Family Clinic and Borehamwood Child and Family Clinic, Hertfordshire, UK.

Richard Green Consultant Psychiatrist, Research Director and Head, Gender Identity Clinic, Charing Cross Hospital, London, and Senior Research Fellow, Institute of Criminology, University of Cambridge, UK.

Peter Hill Professor of Child and Adolescent Psychiatry, Department of Mental Health Sciences, St George's Hospital Medical School, London, UK.

Leslie Ironside Principal Child Psychotherapist, Child and Family Consultation Clinic, Brighton, UK.

Allison James Reader in Applied Anthropology, University of Hull, UK.

Mary Lightfoot Formerly Principal Clinical Social Worker, Gender Identity Development Unit, Portman Clinic, London, and formerly Social Work Team Manager, Child and Family Psychiatry Clinic, Croydon, UK.

John Money Professor of Medical Psychology and Professor of Paediatrics, Emeritus, Psychohormonal Research Unit, The Johns Hopkins

University School of Medicine, The Johns Hopkins Hospital, Baltimore, Maryland, USA.

Mary Sue Moore Clinical Lecturer, Psychology Department, University of Colorado, Boulder, USA, and Honorary Senior Psychotherapist, Child and Family Department, Tavistock Clinic, London, UK.

Mauro Morra Psychoanalyst. Formerly Consultant Child and Adolescent Psychiatrist, Burnt Oak Child Guidance Clinic and Edgware Hospital, London, UK. Formerly Visiting Professor, Department of Psychiatry, University of Genova, Italy.

Paulina Reyes Senior Child and Adolescent Psychotherapist, Pathfinder NHS Trust, London, and formerly Gender Identity Development Clinic, Department of Child Psychiatry, St. George's Hospital, London, UK.

Hartwin Sadowski Lecturer in Child and Adolescent Psychiatry, Tavistock Clinic and Royal Free Hospital School of Medicine, London, UK.

Adrian Sutton Consultant in Child and Family Psychiatry and Psychotherapy. Honorary Lecturer, University of Manchester, Manchester, UK.

Fiona Tasker Lecturer in Psychology, Birkbeck College, University of London, UK.

Judith Trowell Consultant Child and Adolescent Psychiatrist, Child and Family Department, Tavistock Clinic, and Honorary Senior Lecturer Royal Free Hospital School of Medicine. Chair, Young Minds, London, UK.

Stephanie H. M. van Goozen Senior Research Psychologist, Child and Adolescent Psychiatric Clinic, University of Utrecht, Holland.

Jane Whittaker Clinical Tutor and Honorary Senior Registrar, University Department of Child and Adolescent Psychiatry, Royal Manchester Children's Hospital, Manchester, UK.

Gianna Williams Consultant Child and Adolescent Psychotherapist, and Chair, Eating Disorders Workshop, Adolescent Department, Tavistock Clinic, London, UK.

Peter Wilson Child Psychotherapist. Director, Young Minds, London, UK.

Bernadette Wren Consultant Clinical Psychologist, Gender Identity Development Unit, Portman Clinic, London, UK.

Kenneth J. Zucker Head, Child and Adolescent Gender Identity Clinic, Psychologist-in-Charge, Child and Family Studies Centre, Clarke Institute of Psychiatry, University of Toronto, Toronto, Ontario, Canada.

FOREWORD

John Money

Freud would in all likelihood have been terminologically mystified by a book about gender identity and its atypical development, for, until sixteen years after his death in 1939, human beings did not have gender as a personal attribute (Money, 1995): they had only sex. From the study of hermaphroditism, also known as intersexuality, it became evident that sex is not a unitary but a multiple attribute, and that a person's societal role as male or female may be discordant with the sex of the chromosomes, gonads, hormones, genital anatomy, and body morphology, singly or severally. The term coined for the societal role as male or female was "gender role" (Money, 1955), to which "gender identity" soon became added.

The term "gender" rapidly became assimilated into the vernacular as well as the professional language. It acquired two incompatible meanings: one as a simple synonym for sex, the other as sex socially constructed with biology omitted. This omission of biology paved the way for a resurgence of the shop-worn nature/nurture dichotomy, even as it became increasingly evident that the correct paradigm is nature/critical-period/nurture.

Nature needs nurture, and vice versa. Neither can exist without the other. This new paradigm diffuses through most, if not all, of the chapters of this book on the atypicalities of gender development and mental health. Its diffusion is sparse with respect to aetiology, as knowledge of the origin of gender typicality and atypicality is still woefully incomplete. Hence, with respect to diagnosis, more attention is given to nurture than to nature; this applies similarly in the chapters on intervention and case management. Commendably, however, the book avoids the blithe assumption that development of gender atypicality can easily be changed. On the contrary, various case examples illustrate the policy of accepting the way things are, and of not doing harm by trying to do good coercively. The bravest chapter in this regard is that of Peggy Cohen-Kettenis, who reports on the outcome in the Netherlands of early hormonal intervention in selectively screened cases of transsexualism in adolescence, before the discordant secondary sexual characteristics of the natal sex have developed in full. In other chapters, intervention is weighted in favour of talking treatment, and less in anticipation of a curative than an ameliorative or rehabilitative effect.

The book includes contributions, predominantly from the United Kingdom and Europe, from leading clinicians and researchers in the field of child and adolescent gender identity problems and mental health. It takes a broad approach to the subject by including chapters on eating disorders, child abuse, and intersex disorders, and by highlighting their relationship to atypical gender identity development. It shows the value and originality of a multidisciplinary approach to these issues.

Phenomenologically, this is a very important book: it draws the attention of health care personnel, teachers, media people, and parents to the phenomena of gender identity development, which have a very long history of virtually total neglect. Like all other aspects of development, gender identity can in a variety of ways become derailed. All too often, the response of adults has been to blame the victim and to punish or criminalize the derailment. Halt! says this book. It is time to approach gender identity in the non-judgmental way of science.

PREFACE

In no other area of human development is the relationship between the mind and the sexual body so central as it is in gender identity development. Difficulties in this area can cause great distress to children, adolescents, and their families and may require the intervention of mental health professionals. Gender identity issues can generate strong controversy and a great deal of anxiety amongst professionals and in society.

This book brings together the contemporary thinking of an international group of clinicians, researchers, and professionals from different disciplines and is based primarily on a selection of papers presented at a conference on the same topic held at the Tavistock Centre, London, in November 1996, but with additional original contributions. It presents a dialogue amongst the various perspectives that can be taken about atypical gender identity development and their relevance to mental health in children and adolescents. The book is aimed at a multidisciplinary professional readership and interested lay people.

Given the variety of views presented and the different frameworks used by different authors, the terminology used in the book is at times redefined by each author in order to be consistent with their particular framework. Some chapters have more theoretical content than others, while an entire section is devoted to case illustrations and detailed experiences. Some contributions come from professionals who are specialists in the field, whereas others are from experienced professionals who have encountered a case involving an atypical gender identity development for the first time in their working lives; faced with the new experience, they try to apply their expertise to this area of work.

I very much hope that, by facing the tensions generated at the boundaries between these different perspectives, new ideas and new models will emerge to help us increase our understanding of this area of human development, to the benefit of the children, adolescents, and families facing these complex problems.

A STRANGER
IN MY OWN BODY

CHAPTER ONE

Development and mental health: the issue of difference in atypical gender identity development

Peter Wilson

People who are different—who appear, behave, or think in ways that are not congruent with the majority with whom they live—raise questions about the nature of normality or of health. By virtue of their difference, they represent a threat to others. For the most part they are required to conform; rarely are they adequately understood.

There is, of course, nothing exceptional in this state of affairs: groups and societies are forever tussling in one way or another to deal with the differences within them and hold on to their own essential equilibrium and identity. There are different levels of tolerance for different kinds of differences—and, by and large, the more complex a group or society is, the greater the range of tolerances found. However, there are some differences that present particular challenges. Some may be political or religious in nature, but invariably it is those that have a sexual quality about them that raise the largest concern. In our society, we struggle, for example, with issues about homosexuality, teenage sexuality, extra-marital casual sex, and so forth—against an underlying pressure towards adult heterosexual monogamy. When it comes to responding to individuals whose view of their gender role and identity is manifestly discrepant with the evidence of their physical bodies and appearances, most groups or societies are at a loss. So fundamental is the need for clarity about who is male and who is female that those who demonstrate apparent unclarity (or indeed express a perplexing certainty) are viewed with alarm.

Children and young people who present with unusual gender identities set a major challenge to the groups and societies in which they grow up. By virtue of their unique and peculiar self-convictions, they stand out as odd, beyond conventional understanding. Their plight is perilous, testing the patience of those around them. Yet it is in the nature of their gender convictions that they persist in believing or behaving in the way that they do—and demand that the group or society in which they live pays respect and attention to who and what they are.

The developmental influences in gender organization are complex; clearly more research is needed to understand the interplay of genetic, biological, familial, psychological, and social factors in the developmental process of atypical gender identity organization. Through the combined forces of these various factors, children with particular and unusual gender identities produce for themselves and for others a situation of extraordinary and distinctive difference. They are unquestionably at variance with other people and within themselves; inevitably they enter a social world in which they are perceived as unfamiliar, out of step—a species apart to be mocked or bullied. This, of course, can do little to assist them in their development, but—whatever the response—these children raise difficult questions for themselves and others about how best to respond to their gender identity and how to deal with it. Is their difference to be seen as abnormal, as pathological, as something to be changed, eradicated, or "treated" in some way? Or should it be viewed as a manifestation of a unique developmental process, to be understood, fostered, protected, and adapted to? These questions can readily lead to polarized positions, and clearly there are no straightforward answers—but they do create problems, especially when, for example, a teenager's convictions demand physical interventions to change sex in a way that is irreversible.

The DSM–IV diagnostic criteria for Gender Identity Disorder (APA, 1994) are quite clear: a strong and persistent cross-gender identification; a persistent discomfort with one's sex or sense of inappropriateness in the gender role of that sex; a disturbance that is not concurrent with a physical intersex condition; a disturbance that causes clinically significant distress or impairment in social, occupational, or other important areas of functioning. There is enough here to describe and define a genuine state of disorder, and to justify an intervention of some sort to reduce discomfort and distress, improve functioning, and facilitate development (in the sense of restoring some degree of fluidity).

The task of intervention is formidable, involving a wide range of psychological, social, and physical responses, dependent on a full assessment of the individual child and the family. Much can be done to improve the child's environment and to gain greater understanding of associated and emotional difficulties, and the possibilities exist in some cases to alter the characteristics of the body. All such therapeutic activity is designed to reduce the anguish, confusion, and isolation of the child and his or her family—and, in effect, to mitigate the harmful effects of the child's essential state and experience of difference. In so far as it is the predicament of the child's state of difference that is problematic—that it is the child's extraordinariness that arouses such negative social responses—these therapeutic endeavours are clearly necessary. However, it is important, in carrying out any kind of intervention, to hold in mind two key considerations: firstly, the developmental context and, secondly, the mental health context in relation to the paradox of such difference.

The developmental context

The essential questions that need to be answered during the course of assessment and treatment of a child or adolescent with a gender identity developmental problem are (1) how different is he or she from other children and adolescents, and (2) how open to further development is he or she? We know, for example, that such children and adolescents, despite (and perhaps because of) their difference are but part of the wide generality of young people, all of whom are absorbed in one way or another in the mysteries of their own identities and sexualities. They may have unusually strong beliefs, all the more striking because of the discordance with the evidence of their bodies, but in many respects they share in the unease and uncertainty of all young people in the course of growing up. It is in the process of child and adolescent development that there is an ongoing fascination with the questions that arise about their bodies, their genders, and their selves. There is no adolescent who does not worry about the size or shape of his or her body, who does not compare it with others, and who does not wonder what he or she should do with it by themselves or with others. There is no child or adolescent who is not learning about the nature of masculinity and femininity and building some inner sense of himself or herself as male or female. At the core of this enquiry is a basic narcissistic preoccupation with the essence of oneself. This is difficult and complicated, for it embraces all the thoughts and memories that young people have about their natures and relationships with others: Who am I? How coherent am I (how well do I hold together)? How valued am I (by myself and by others)? How well do I stand up in relationship to other people? How like or unlike am I to them (and how likeable and unlikeable am I)? These are key questions about the nature of self and the issue of distinctiveness—how separate, individual, and, above all, different am I? The word "differ" derives from the Latin word *differe*, which means "to bear" or "to carry apart". The young person asks, how can I bear myself apart from others? It is through answering this question that children and adolescents build a sense of themselves and mark out their identities—different from their mothers, their fathers, their grandparents, their siblings, their peers, and so forth—and, in so doing, they seek their own difference, their own personal integrity, their sense *of* themselves that makes sense *to* themselves.

Development, then, involves the discovery of mind and body, which is fundamentally concerned with the emergence of differences. Whether at an intellectual, cognitive, physical, social, or emotional level, development consists of varying processes of differentiation—between different parts or elements within the individual and between the individual and others. Erikson (1963) emphasizes the epigenetic course of development, underlining its sequential nature, a series of rising steps, each state building on the developmental achievements of those that went before. As he sees it, the adequacy of development at one developmental state fortifies movement onto the next; inadequacy may not stop development from proceeding, but it may leave areas for future developmental vulnerability. Throughout his writing, Erikson stresses the uniqueness of individual development—the timing and intensity of development varying considerably from one person to another—and the importance of mutual regulation between the individual's internal developmental momentum and the surrounding environment. He writes that society, in principle, tends to be so constituted as to meet and invite this succession of potentialities for interaction and attempts to safeguard and encourage the proper rate and the proper sequence of their enfolding.

Development is thus clearly a highly complex phenomenon—a gradual process of differentiation, an unfolding of abilities and potentialities—always in a social context and driven by the imperatives of maturation and by the assertion of the individual's self. It is not, by its very nature, an easy or comfortable process. It contains inevitable dilemmas and unpredictabilities. It also carries with it at any given point of time a particular contradiction. The individual in the midst of the movement and fluidity of development needs at the same time to mark out moments of achievement of new integration. The contradiction resides in the coincidence of fluidity and fixity. The growing individual needs, for example, to be able to say, in effect: "Today I have discovered something new about myself that is real and significant, but at the same time it is changing and disappearing and making way for something new." A great deal depends on the capacity of the individual to tolerate and cope with this tension, to build a sense of identity and yet to keep the processes of development open and not foreclose on further possibility through defensive fixation.

It is in this context of developmental preoccupation and the general capacity for growth and differentiation that children and adolescents with gender identity problems need to be considered. Their differences can be set alongside a continuum of variation in adolescent sexual development and their convictions and assertions understood and assessed in the midst of the process of change that is characteristic of child and adolescent development.

The mental health context:
the paradox of difference

Mental health is a notoriously difficult concept to define. All too often it is confused with its opposite, mental illness. Alternatively, it becomes a vehicle for idealistic and moralistic notions of virtue and beauty. The mentally healthy individual comes to be seen, almost in statuesque form, as the epitome of perfection. At one level, mental health can be defined simply in terms of the sound-ness and the well functioning of the mind. Difficulties arise, of course, as to what it is that constitutes such soundness. In recent attempts to reach a definition (NHS Health Advisory Service, 1995), the mental health of children and adolescents has been un-derstood in terms of a series of capacities: first and foremost, a capacity to develop (psychologically, emotionally, intellectually, and spiritually) and then to initiate, develop, and sustain mutually satisfying personal relationships; to become aware of others and be empathetic; and to use psychological distress as a developmental process so that it does not hinder further development. Implicit in all of this is a sense of movement and openness—to develop, ini-tiate, become aware, and so forth. Mental health, like physical health, is not static: it ebbs and flows, functions well and not so well, and carries at any given time its own imperfections and stick-ing points.

There is clearly a close link between the concepts of mental health and development, not least in the capacity to be receptive to new experiences, to learn, and to seek integrity. It is in this respect that a paradox needs to be held in mind, a paradox that resides at the centre of the meaning of mental health itself: for in the midst of a mental illness or mental health problem, there may be a mentally healthy process in operation. There is, in short, health in illness. If we take this through to the fundamental problem of the difference of the child and adolescent with a gender identity problem, we can gain some fuller understanding of the function of that difference; that is to say that, in being so different, the child exposes him/herself to mental health problems, yet safeguards his or her mental health, through maintaining his or her difference (and his or her integrity).

What is clear and unequivocal in the children and adolescents who have gender identity problems is the strength of their assertions and beliefs about themselves. Out of the diverse developmental processes that have produced their gender identity, they create their own certainties about themselves. Most definitions (e.g. Stoller, 1968a) of gender identity emphasize the sustaining and persisting quality that characterizes young people's perceptions of themselves as male or female. Such persistence, of course, can be problematic, unrelenting, and distressing. Equally, however, it can maintain a self-conviction that represents, in effect, the only meaningful conclusion for the individual in making sense of the many developed mental processes that have occurred throughout his/her life. There may be no other way, for example, that a boy with a significant hormonal imbalance who has been raised as a girl by his grandmother and subsequently traumatized by her death can experience himself at a certain point in his development other than as a girl. Such a conviction stands at the core of his mental health; he is holding on to a belief that is integral to his developmental experience and is not to be relinquished, whatever social advantages there may be.

In many respects, this is not dissimilar to the beliefs, assertions, and behaviours that many children (not only those with gender identity disorders) hold on to, often against the convenience of others, in order to keep faith with their own experience and to hold open possibilities for their "true self" to be developed (Winnicott, 1960). The obdurate disobedience of a child in school, the determined refusal of the anorectic to eat, the unrelenting self-destructiveness of the drug-taking adolescent—all can be seen as representing a vital position, standing up for something important for themselves that is consistent with their experience of what has happened to them. Their development may temporarily be stuck, but it can be said that their mental health resides in their capacity to be true to themselves and to the reality of their own development—and not simply in terms of superficial happiness or conformity.

This is, then, a conception of mental health that allows us to see the possible strength and soundness of the nature of gender identity differences that in many other respects may be problematic and give rise to problems. Such a conception may, of course, be seen as fanciful, denying the desperateness of the distress of many young people and ignoring the anxieties that surround them. It may also be seen as anti-therapeutic, resistant to the demands from young people and professionals for immediate and dramatic intervention. It is, however, a conception that is founded on an understanding of the complexity of development and of an understanding of the nature of mental health. The primary therapeutic aims outlined by Domenico Di Ceglie in chapter twelve (see also Di Ceglie, 1995) clearly reflect this understanding—notably in fostering recognition and non-judgemental acceptance of the gender identity problem, activating interest and curiosity, allowing mourning processes to occur, and, most importantly, enabling the child and the family to tolerate uncertainty in the area of gender identity development (in particular, in allowing for the possibility of change in the course of further development). Perhaps the essence of mental health and of development is the capacity to keep possibilities open, to refuse to foreclose on their development, and to maintain respect for self-integrity.

CHAPTER TWO

Reflections on the nature of the "atypical gender identity organization"

Domenico Di Ceglie

The recognition in the late 1950s that there is a facet of personal identity called gender identity has had widespread repercussions in our understanding and attitudes towards unusual developments in our relationship to the body. A new *Weltanschauung* about psychosexual development could be constructed, and it became possible to conceptualize atypical experiences in the areas of sexuality which had been poorly understood thus far. In this chapter, I review the history of the concepts of gender role, gender identity, and core-gender identity. I propose the term *atypical gender identity organization* (AGIO) to define an internal psychological configuration whose phenomenology is represented by the typical characteristics of a gender identity disorder. This phenomenology includes atypical variation in the following areas: gender identity statements, dressing, toy and role playing, peer relations, mannerisms and voice, anatomic dysphoria (i.e. intense dislike of their sexual bodies), and rough and tumble play, as described by Zucker and Bradley in their book *Gender Identity Disorder and Psychosexual Problems in Children and Adolescents* (1995).

I then outline an interactive approach in the formation of the atypical gender identity organization, within a psychodynamic framework of development, and finally discuss the implications for therapeutic strategies.

Historical notes

The concept of gender identity made its appearance in the early 1960s as a result of the clinical work of Robert Stoller. It was preceded by the term "gender role" described by John Money in an article in the *Bulletin of the Johns Hopkins Hospital* in 1955. Money wanted to differentiate a set of feelings, assertions, and behaviours that identified the person as being a boy or a girl, or a man or a woman, from the contrasting conclusions that one could have reached by considering only their gonads. In the vast majority of the cases described, gender role was consistent with the gender in which they had been reared. Stoller (1986) defined gender identity as: "A complex system of beliefs about oneself: a sense of one's masculinity and femininity. It implies nothing about the origins of that sense (e.g. whether the person is male or female). It has, then, psychological connotations only: one's subjective state."

The definition of gender identity made it possible to further the thinking about human conditions in which the external reality of the body and the inner subjective perception do not match. In some cases, a harmonious relationship between the internal representation of the body and the body itself has not been achieved, with a consequent feeling of estrangement within oneself. These are conditions where atypical gender identity development occurs. In the early 1980s, the clinical category of "gender identity disorders" appeared for the first time in the American DSM psychiatric classification.

In adulthood, we encounter human conditions described by the words transsexualism, transvestism, homosexuality, and bisexuality. These conditions are experienced and described as different from each other and discrete, or, phenomenologically, they appear to be different entities, and people who have these unusual experiences are also clear about their own sense of belonging to one or the other grouping.

In 1964 in his paper "The Hermaphroditic Identity of Hermaphrodites", Stoller proposed the concept of *core-gender identity*. He saw it as "produced by the infant–parent relationship, the child's perception of its external genitalia, and a biologic force which results from the biologic variables of sex (chromosomes, gonads, hormones, internal accessory reproductive structures and external genitalia)". He also added that "while the process of developing gender identity goes on intensively at least until the end of adolescence, the core-gender identity is fully established before the fully developed phallic stage" (1964b, p. 453). He later described it as a *psychic structure* that was unchangeable after the age of 2 or 3 years and largely due to the sex in which the children were reared.

Stoller concluded that transvestic men are people who wish to be female and "their transvestism is an acting out of this wish but they know that they are not (female). Their core gender identity is male; that is, they know their bodies are male, that they have been assigned since birth to the male sex". One might say that in particular circumstances transvestic men wish to be in a female role and their cross-dressing is necessary to confirm a transitory sense of femaleness.

Homosexuals have a largely male or female gender identity and gender role, but these people feel sexually attracted to people of the same sex. Bisexual people feel sexual attraction towards both sexes.

Transsexuals perceive their gender identity as incongruous to their body, and they wish to develop a gender role consistent with their gender identity; however their sexual preferences can vary in that they can be heterosexual or homosexual in relationship to the gender that they perceive themselves belonging to.

If one takes a developmental perspective, a more complex picture emerges. The antecedent to these conditions is commonly an atypical gender identity development, with some or all of the features of a gender identity disorder. The earlier we come in contact with the children showing these types of problems, the more difficult it is to predict the eventual outcome of their gender identity development. A developmental perspective introduces an element of flexibility and greater variability in the developmental pathways of children with gender identity disorders.

AGIO and an interactive approach

Since the early work of John Money and Robert Stoller, further clinical and developmental research has indicated that the picture is more complicated. The work of Imperato-McGinley (Imperato-McGinley, Peterson, Gautier, & Sturla, 1979a) has shown that core-gender identity is not firmly linked to the sex of rearing but that change in the physical characteristics of the body at puberty led in this group to a change of their sense of gender identity. These people did not present the transsexual outcome one might have expected when the reality of their body changed. How to account for this change is complex. Imperato-McGinley stresses the importance of hormonal influences on the sense of gender identity. However, another explanation could rely on the capacity of adaptation of these people to the changed external appearance of their bodies. At the beginning of chapter six, Allison James describes the rearing practices of the Inuit and highlights how some children are raised in a cross-gender role for particular social reasons, and how, in some cases, the children adapt themselves to the gender in which they have been raised in spite of their biological sex. What makes some people more psychologically adaptable than others is an interesting issue. Research on how people respond differently to traumatic situations may throw some light on this adaptability.

A case referred to our Gender Identity Development Unit illustrates the complexity between child rearing and gender identity development.

"Christine" was referred at the age of 12 by a child psychiatrist because when she was asked if she was a boy or a girl she used to reply: "I don't know." Christine was believed to be a boy at birth. Her mother had reported that she had even seen a small penis soon after the birth of her baby, and she had then developed a view that the penis had retracted as a result of a black magic spell by her mother-in-law. She had then persisted in treating her child as a boy, always expecting her to turn into a boy at some point. Her husband had colluded with his wife's false belief. Christine was called by a boy's name, was dressed as a boy during childhood, and was repeatedly told by her mother that she was a boy. At the clinic, we offered this girl individual therapy and we saw the parents separately. Social services had been involved for many years in this case as there had been a risk for some time that her mother would take her to her country of origin and arrange for her to undergo some surgical procedures. In spite of this extraordinary upbringing, Christine did not present an established gender-identity disorder. She admitted to having been confused as a child, but when puberty started it strongly confirmed her view that she was an ordinary girl and that her mother had psychological problems because she was convinced that her daughter was a boy.

This clinical case shows that intense psychological pressure cannot on its own determine the course of the gender identity development. We have here a protracted traumatic experience or chronic emotional abuse from which the child emerges fairly unscathed in her gender identity development. A totally different outcome could have occurred with a more vulnerable child. In the case of Christine, the powerful projection from the mother could probably be recognized by the child as a view—but not the only one—about her gender. This led to a temporary sense of inner confusion from which she could emerge when her own views based on reality testing at puberty became stronger and clearly separate from those of her mother. I want to propose here that Christine's capacity for symbol formation, as described by Hanna Segal in her paper "Notes on Symbol Formation" (1957), is what made her less vulnerable to an adverse situation. This capacity would underpin both her ability to explore her own body and different gender roles within her social environment, and escape from being entangled in her mother's projections. Similar considerations might be applied to the understanding of different responses by children to strong parental expectations about career choices and therefore the development of professional identities. I want to emphasize here the interactional nature of internal and external factors in determining gender identity development.

The concept of "core-gender identity" does not lend itself to describe the multiplicity of psychological constellations involved, particularly in atypical gender identity development.

In Stoller's view, core identity is a psychic structure with concrete qualities and therefore unchangeable. In my view, this is true in some conditions but not in others. The term *typical or atypical gender identity organization* seems more suited to a multidimensional understanding of this phenomenon. I use here the term "organization" in a similar way to John Steiner's usage in *Psychic Retreats* (1993). Steiner adopts the term "pathological organisation of the personality" to denote "a family of defensive systems which are characterised by extremely unyielding defences and which function to help the patient to avoid anxiety by avoiding contact with other people and with reality". He describes "psychic retreats as states of mind in which the patient is stuck, cut off, and out of reach, and he (the analyst) may infer that these states arise from the operation of a powerful system of defences" (p. 2). In the development of the AGIO there are aspects similar to the ones described by Steiner; however, I would like to stress the importance of two other components to its formation. First, the AGIO has the function of ensuring a sense of psychic survival in the face of an experience of psychological catastrophe and chaos in early infancy; second, it could be a way of integrating biologically based atypical experiences and perceptions in the area of sexuality. This second component has to be postulated on the basis of recent biological research and the study of children's responses to traumatic situations.

Recent research findings

Hereditary (Bailey & Pillard, 1991) and genetic factors (Hamer, Hu, Magnuson, Hu, & Pattatucci, 1993) have been linked to the development of homosexuality in men. The contribution of these factors to the development of gender identity disorders in children is unclear, and further research is needed. Hormonal influences on the brain during critical periods of foetal life have been suggested. Androgens might masculinize the brain at a critical period of foetal life. In humans, it has been found that the third interstitial nucleus of the anterior hypothalamus is larger in the male. LeVay (1991) has shown that in the brain of homosexual men this nucleus is similar in size to that of women and about half the volume of that in heterosexual men. A difference has also been identified in "the bed nucleus of the stria terminalis" of the brain between male-to-female transsexuals and non-transsexual males (Zhou, Hofman, Gooren, & Swaab, 1995). These data need replication. The psychological implications of these differences in terms of changes in specific psychological functions are unclear. A fuller discussion of these research data is given by Caroline Brain in chapter five.

Traumatic experiences, gender identity, and brain development

Clinical and research experience today are pointing towards a multifactorial/interactional causation of the AGIO. This perspective would include the presence of predisposing biological factors. There may be a number of pathways leading to the formation of the atypical organization in which some factors play a major or lesser role. In this section, I want to focus on the role of traumatic experiences in early childhood, as they seem to play a relevant part in a number of cases. In a recent paper, "Childhood Trauma, the Neurobiology of Adaptation, and 'Use-dependent' Development of the Brain: How 'States Become Traits'", Perry, Pollard, Blakely, Baker, and Vigilante (1995) describe how infants and young children respond to traumatic events. They suggest that children tended to respond differently from adults, whose main response is the well-known "flight/fight" reaction. Children instead will use what Perry et al. call the *sensitized hyperarousal response* or *the dissociative response*. They define dissociation as "disengaging from stimuli in the external world and attending to an internal world. Daydreaming, fantasy, depersonalization, derealization, and fugue states are all examples of dissociation" (p. 280). I would like to hypothesize here that, within the "dissociative continuum" as a response to trauma, the child, given certain conditions as in the cases I describe later, can have a sudden illumination or revelation, a new self-concept—"I am Mummy" or "I am Daddy" and, by extension, "I am a woman" or "I am a man"—which seems to deal omnipotently with the external threat and to ensure psychic survival. The internal reality has been changed in order to reduce the power of the external one. From then on, this facet of internal reality will predominate over the external one, the body, establishing supremacy of the mind over the body as far as gender is concerned.

Perry et al. also state that "our clinical experience suggest that the younger the individual is, the more likely he or she is to use disassociative adaptations over hyperarousal responses" (p. 282). The other important contribution that these authors make by reviewing current research literature is that during a critical period in the developing brain, mental states—such as hyperarousal or dissociative states—organize neural systems, thus leading to the creation of traits. It is therefore reasonable to speculate that when the response to traumatic experiences has lead to the formation of an AGIO in early childhood, this can become an *established trait*, along with other traits deriving from the traumatic experience. This neurobiological state may also explain the impermeability of certain atypical organizations to change.

The leap from biological differences and altered psychic functions affecting early infantile interactions with the parents or other care-givers to atypical gender identity formation remains, however, complex and somewhat mysterious. What follows is an attempt to describe some of the features of the AGIO.

Clinical features of AGIO

The clinical significance of the concept of AGIO lies in its ability to be examined in relation to a number of clinical features that are relevant to clinical management.

1.   Rigidity—flexibility

A psychotherapeutic exploration over a period of time may determine how rigid the organization is, or how liable to evolution in the course of development. In only some cases can it be seen to possess the structural qualities of Stoller's core-gender identity: an unshakeable system of beliefs.

2.   Timing of the AGIO formation

In a number of cases it will be possible to determine when the first signs of the atypical organization became apparent. Atypical organizations that develop very early in the child's life may be more likely to become rigidly structured than organizations that develop later in response to some traumatic experience.

3.   Presence or absence of identifiable traumatic events in the child's life in relationship to the AGIO formation

The following clinical vignette illustrates this point:

"Julie" was referred at about the age of 15 as she had a gender identity disorder and wished to become a man. During the interview it emerged that before the age of 6 or 7 there had been no clear features of a gender identity disorder. When she was 7 years old, her mother gave birth to a baby boy who was severely disabled. It was one or two years after this family event that Julie started to express a wish to be a boy, wished to play with boys, refused to wear female clothes, and refused to play with dolls and began to dislike her feminine body. In this case it seemed that a masculine identification was a response to her mother's distress following the birth of the disabled baby boy and, perhaps, to her own feelings towards him which could not be acknowledged but led her to take his place. Traumatic events could also have affected the child before birth indirectly through a traumatic experience affecting the mother or the family during foetal life.

4. *Where the formation of the AGIO can be located*
on the continuum from the paranoid–schizoid position
to the depressive position

Within a psychoanalytic developmental framework, deriving from the work of Klein and Bion, we can speculate on the nature of the mental state during which the AGIO was formed, and its implication for the clinical features. In the Klein/Bion framework, mental processes can occur under the predominance of two modes of psychic functioning: the paranoid–schizoid position and the depressive position. These are not intended only as developmental stages but are conceived of as two states of mind between which the individual can oscillate in particular circumstances, although developmentally the paranoid–schizoid position precedes the depressive position. From the point of view of the development of an AGIO, we could then infer that an organization that is formed under the predominance of the paranoid–schizoid position will be characterized by the massive use of projective identification, splitting processes, loss of contact with external reality, limited capacity to symbolize, very low tolerance of frustration, and uncertainty in the acquisition of knowledge. The resulting features of the organization would be a high level of rigidity and an inability to integrate and process information coming from an external reality, such as the body, leading to a serious disorder of body image. There would be no room for change or adaptation—one possibility only can be entertained.

On the other hand, if the AGIO has developed under the predominance of the depressive position, it can result in a more flexible structure, ambivalence over gender identity can be achieved, and sexual ambiguity can be present. Conflicts can be symbolized, and there is more room for entertaining various representations of the self and the object. An example of sexual ambiguity is Michelangelo's statue of "The Night" in the Medici Chapel in Florence (see cover illustration). The body of The Night is here represented with masculine and feminine features. It is interesting that Michelangelo used this as a representation of the night, as this could be associated with dreaming; this sculpture could, therefore, be seen as similar to a visual image in a dream.

AGIO: psychodynamic frameworks

In this section I would like to describe two psychological constellations that characterize AGIO. The evidence for this derives from research findings and clinical experience. However, I think that they ought to be seen as hypothetical models proposed in an attempt to understand the nature of atypical gender identity development.

Coates and Person (1985) have clearly also shown how a large proportion of boys with a gender identity disorder show clinical signs of separation anxiety disorder. Coates has also described how the child, in order to deal with separation anxiety, develops what she calls "the reparative fantasy" in a feminine identification with the mother (Coates, Friedman, & Wolfe, 1991). In her view, genetic factors may contribute through their influence on the child's temperament to this development. Our clinical experience supports the view that separation anxiety may play an important role in the development of the AGIO. These boys seem to experience separation from the mother or any other attachment figure as a psychological catastrophe, and they fear psychic disintegration and chaos. This may have its basis in an unsatisfactory relationship with the internalized breast and, in particular, temperamental characteristics such as inability to tolerate frustration. Within a Kleinian framework, splitting processes are employed by the infant to cope with frustration and psychic pain. If they are used in an excessive way, they lead to the constitution of a splitting between an idealized or satisfying breast and a persecutory depriving breast, which can, in turn, be perceived as damaged as a result of the infant's angry attacks. With the development of a relationship to all objects, this split may persist, leading to an idealized all-gratifying image of the mother from one side and a persecutory, denigrated, and damaged image from the other.

In a situation where the boy with this psychological make-up is exposed to repeated separation from an attachment figure or to threats of it leading to an insecure attachment, he may cope with the fear of psychological catastrophe by identifying through the mechanism of projective identification with the all-gratifying idealized image of the mother. In this way, he becomes the mother, with the consequence that there is nothing to fear and a great sense of relief. Psychic survival is assured but at a cost of disavowing some aspects of reality and, in particular, the male body. It is unclear why the child would find this to be a particular solution to his fear of disintegration. It could well be a chance phenomenon within a predisposing background, but it is quite unpredictable. If this event occurs within the domain of the paranoid–schizoid position, the process will have psychotic qualities. There will be no possibility for symbolization, and the identification will have very concrete qualities. Only one possibility can be entertained, and no other representation of oneself would be possible. We may hypothesize that if this process occurs during a critical period of development in the early years, this psychotic experience can be sealed, and then the development is affected by the sequelae of a psychotic process that has occurred early in life. There will be difficulties in negotiating a triangular relationship in the oedipal phase, as illustrated by Ronald Britton in his chapter "The Missing Link" in The Oedipus Complex Today (Britton, Feldman, & O'Shaughnessy, 1989). The possible formation of specific neural systems would make the AGIO an established trait.

In the alternative situation where processes of this kind take place within the domain of the depressive position, similar identificatory processes can occur. However, because there is more capacity for alternative representations and identifications, there is more flexibility, and perhaps feminine identification can be used in a more transient way. The need for these identifications may well increase under stress or the threat of impending separations.

A clinical vignette will illustrate the role of separation anxiety.

"Nicholas", aged 5, was referred by the court following the divorce of his parents and a dispute about custody between the parents. He had a well-established gender identity disorder and both parents were accusing each other of having caused Nicholas's gender identity problems. The father accused the mother of having influenced the boy by exposing him to a homosexual relationship, while the mother was accusing the father of having implanted the idea that he was a girl by buying him female clothing and stereotypical feminine toys.

During the assessment interviews, Nicholas could not separate from his mother to be assessed on his own. During one interview, I wondered with the parents if Nicholas would find it easier to come on his own if he was allowed to dress as a girl. Nicholas, who was playing on his own, apparently unaware of what was happening around him, suddenly became alive and said that the next time he would bring a white bridesmaid's costume that his father had bought for him, and he seemed to indicate that that would enable him to part from his parents. Later in the interview, it transpired that during some access visits to his father he used to be left on his own, and this frightened him. He then could easily recognize that dressing as a girl gave him a great sense of relief and he could be on his own without being frightened. Another factor involved in this case was his mother's suffering from a congenital physical disease which made her severely disabled in the lower part of her body while she had a particularly beautiful appearance in the upper part of her body. This aspect partially contributed to a splitting of her image into a damaged vulnerable one on one side and an idealized gratifying one on the other. This child also suffered from encopresis and school-refusal. He had problems in the expression of his aggressive impulses, which he probably considered responsible for the damage to his mother. The splitting and disowning of his aggressive feelings relieved him from his sense of guilt and reinforced his identification with a gentle, protective, and feminine image of himself.

In the case of a girl, the psychic constellation that seems to occur can be described as follows. The girl has a perception of the mother as vulnerable, weak, and in danger. Her role in life is to protect this damaged mother. She feels, however, that in order to do this she has to be a male. The nature of the threat to the mother and her survival is variable. In some cases, the threat may come as a result of the child witnessing verbal or physical violence from father towards mother, coupled with the experience of the mother as unresponsive, depressed, and damaged. In these circumstances, a masculine identification with physical masculine characteristics becomes the solution to enable psychic survival. In the mind of the child, being a man ensures the survival of the mother and also protects her from the possibility of the same destiny falling upon herself. It seems that at the height of a traumatic experience, a solution is found by the child along the line of a wish so well expressed by Beatrice in Shakespeare's "Much Ado About Nothing":

> Beatrice: "Is't not approved in the height a villain that hath slandered, scorned, dishonoured, my kinswoman? Oh that I were a man! What! bear her in hand until they come to take hands, and then with public accusation, uncover'd slander, unmitigated rancour—Oh God, that I were a man! I would eat his heart in the market place." [Act 4, scene 1, line 300]

In some cases, instead of a wish, the child presents with an unshakeable belief about gender which contrasts with the reality of the body and is aimed at ensuring psychic survuival.

"Jennifer" was 17 when I saw her following three suicide attempts. She was a female-to-male transsexual who presented with depressive episodes and a number of borderline features. Her mother, who had died just before she had come to see me, suffered depression after her birth, and her father had been physically violent towards her during Jennifer's childhood, until they separated. During her psychotherapy sessions with me, she vividly remembered episodes when her father in fits of temper had kicked her mother, even in her stomach. In one session she admitted, not without a sense of embarrassment and shame, that she had identified with him, an experience that she could not explain. She loved her mother, and her main aim in life was to do something extraordinary that would have made her mother happy. There was no recollection that Jennifer herself had been physically abused by her father, but witnessing violence between her parents had been a traumatic experience during her childhood. One defensive manoeuvre to cope with the fear of damage to her mother and possibly to herself was an identification with a male possessing the strength of a physical masculine structure. This belief, once established, allowed her in an omnipotent way a sense of survival and also the protection of her mother perceived as a damaged object. In this case, another important factor seemed to play a part. After the birth of two older sisters, her mother had a miscarriage of a baby boy. One year later, Jennifer was born. Jennifer seemed to feel that her mother had expected her to be a boy, and in one session she alluded to her mother having "psychic qualities" as if she had been part of a magical experience in which she and her mother could read each other's minds. She had probably received, and made her own, her mother's wish that she were a boy. This wish was probably never consciously expressed by her mother, but remained unconsciously active in the relationship between Jennifer and her mother.

The two years' psychotherapeutic exploration with this patient allowed this partial reconstruction of her childhood relating to her atypical gender identity development to be made. However, any step made towards this understanding led to continuous interruptions in the therapeutic work, which showed her extreme resistance and fears of having the foundation of her gender identity revisited.

Even if she retained some of this understanding, it certainly did not alter her gender identity development—that is to say, the sense of who she was—within the limitation of a twice-a-week psychotherapy. Her AGIO was well established and not amenable to evolution. The timing of its formation was very early in her life, and traumatic events had played a large part in it. Its formation seemed to have occurred under the dominance of the paranoid–schizoid position constituting a rigid nucleus of gender identity on which her development had been based.

Other aspects of her life improved. She did not attempt suicide again, she established herself in a job, and she was more able to establish relationships with other people. One might say that therapy had helped her to reduce the hold of the AGIO on other aspects of her development and of her life.

Therapeutic strategies

As the formation of the AGIO is complex, probably multi-factorial, and in some cases not amenable to evolution at our clinic, we have developed a model of management in which altering the gender identity disorder *per se* is not a primary therapeutic objective. Our primary therapeutic objectives are the developmental processes that, on clinical and research experience, seem to have been negatively affected in the child and the adolescent. These are described in chapter twelve.

It is possible that, by targeting and improving the developmental processes that may underpin gender development, the gender identity disorder itself will be affected in a secondary way and will not lead to an atypical gender identity development in adulthood.

Conclusion

In this chapter, I have illustrated the concept of atypical gender identity organization and discussed possible models to understand it and the relevance of the models to management. The view I have taken is that atypical gender identity development can be construed from a medical perspective as a gender identity disorder, but from another perspective as a process analogous to the development as a vocation, such as an early calling to the priesthood or an enduring and compulsive ambition to pursue particular professional roles.

I would like, therefore, to conclude with a brief story from a book, *Psychoanalysis in a Monastery* (Lemercier, 1966), which may provide a useful metaphor in our work with children and adolescents with gender identity problems.

> Grégoire Lemercier was a Belgian Benedictine monk in charge of a seminary in a monastery in Cuernavaca, Mexico. He had had an interest in undertaking a psychoanalytical experience. He had, however, been firmly discouraged by a well-experienced psychoanalyst. In 1960, he had some visual hallucinations. While in bed awake he saw flashing lights and then, on

the wall of his room, "a rapid succession of human faces. The kaleidoscope stopped on a very beautiful face", and then he cried "my God, why don't you speak to me". He was afraid of going mad (p. 26). He consulted a psychologist who advised him to start psychotherapy. Presumably this was aimed at curing his psychotic symptoms, the hallucinations. Three months later, a cancer was found in his left eye and he was operated on.

Although he had entered psychotherapy with a wrong aim, he persisted and found that a psychological exploration had enabled him to see things within himself better than he had ever done before. I assume that he had conflicts about his religious choice which could not be fully acknowledged. His psychotherapeutic experience reinforced his idea that the people entering the seminary to become monks might benefit by a psychological exploration regarding the motives of their vocation and that this could be an eye-opening experience. After all, in the Catholic church being ordained as a monk is an irreversible step! So in the early 1960s the monastery undertook an experience of group psychotherapy with a male and a female psychotherapist.

The results of this experiment are interesting. A large number of monks—about two-thirds—left the monastery, but one-third persisted, became ordained monks, and continued a stable religious life. Gregoire Lemercier himself eventually left the order a few years later.

The key aspect of the experience in the monastery was that a psychotherapeutic exploration led to a change in some people but not in others, as far as their religious identity was concerned. How to deal with the psychological, family, and social problems linked with a vocation is the common issue between the experience in Cuernavaca and the therapeutic work with children with an atypical gender identity.

CHAPTER THREE

Associated psychopathology in children with gender identity disorder

Kenneth J. Zucker

Introduction

In this chapter, I focus on research that has examined associated psychopathology in children with gender identity disorder (GID). At the outset, it should be explained why such research is potentially important for the understanding of children with GID. First, understanding the nature and patterning of associated psychopathology may be helpful in clarifying aetiological factors with regard to GID; second, such work, even if inconclusive regarding aetiological matters, may still have relevance for clinical care. I should emphasize that we have done somewhat more work on this topic with regard to boys than to girls with GID.

Nature of the sample

Let me begin by describing the overall sample of children with GID that we have worked with. Between 1978 and 1996, 253 boys and 40 girls were referred to our Child and Adolescent Gender

26

Identity Clinic, which is a sex ratio in referral rates of 6.3:1. At referral, the mean age of the children was about 7 years, with a range of 3 to 12 years. Their mean full-scale IQ was at the high end of the average range, with a range from Intellectually Deficient to the Very Superior. Parents' social class was, on average, middle-class, with a range that fully covered the socioeconomic spectrum. About two-thirds of the children lived with both of their parents; the remaining third came from single-parent or reconstituted families (Zucker, Bradley, & Sanikhani, 1997). Relative to the general population, there was a disproportionate number of referred boys who had been adopted in the first year of life (7.6%), mainly at birth (Zucker & Bradley, in press).

Associated psychopathology

In studying associated psychopathology in the children, we have employed different assessment techniques. Some of these have been collected on the entire sample, whereas other measures have been used in only more focused samples (Table 3.1). Table 3.2 shows how the study of associated psychopathology might be conceptualized *vis-à-vis* GID.

TABLE 3.1

Associated psychopathology in children with gender identity disorder: some assessment measures

1. Child Behaviour Checklist (Zucker & Bradley, 1995)

2. Teacher's Report Form (Zucker & Bradley, 1995)

3. Structured Maternal Interview for Separation Anxiety Disorder (Zucker, Bradley, & Lowry Sullivan, 1996)

4. Quality of Peer Relationships (Zucker et al., 1997)

5. Rorschach (Ipp, 1986; Kolers, 1986)

6. Feelings, Attitudes, and Behaviour Questionnaire for Children (unpublished)

7. Quality of Attachment (Birkenfeld-Adams, 1998)

TABLE 3.2

Possible relations among gender identity disorder, general psychopathology, and parental influences in boys

---

1. Gender identity disorder ———> general psychopathology

2. Parental influences ———> general psychopathology ———>
   gender identity disorder

3. Parental influences ———> general psychopathology

   Parental influences ———> gender identity disorder ———>
   general psychopathology

Note. From Zucker & Bradley (1995).

The first model in Table 3.2 holds that the child's marked cross-gender behaviour is the target of social ostracism, particularly by peers, which is the mechanism that leads to the display of general psychopathology.

The second model in Table 3.2 implicates the role of parental influences, such as psychiatric disorder, erratic child-rearing practices, and marital discord, in the child's gender development. In general, this view considers the genesis of the GID in the context of more global problems in the child's development and familial psychopathology. Coates and her colleagues (e.g. Coates & Person, 1985; Marantz & Coates, 1991), who have discussed this view in some detail, have advanced a specific hypothesis, namely that separation anxiety—which is activated by uneven maternal availability—plays a pivotal role in the development of GID in boys. According to Coates and Spector Person (1985), severe separation anxiety precedes the feminine behaviour of the boys, which emerges in order "to restore a fantasy tie to the physically or emotionally absent mother. In imitating 'Mommy' [the boy] confuse[s] 'being Mommy' with 'having Mommy.' [Cross-gender behaviour] appears to allay, in part, the anxiety generated by the loss of the mother" (p. 708).

The last model in Table 3.2 suggests that parental influences play a role in both the general psychopathology and the GID, but that different aspects of parental behaviour are involved. In this view, the relation between parental influences and general psychopathology in boys with GID could be explained, for example, by aspects of parental functioning that are, diagnostically speaking, non-specific, such as marital discord and psychiatric disorder. Other parental variables, such as reinforcement or tolerance of cross-gender behaviour and atypical psychosexual parental traits, which may be diagnostically specific, lead directly to the GID, which, in turn, is associated with general psychopathology through the mechanism of social ostracism.

Although this last model suggests that GID and general psychopathology may be influenced by distinct parental influences, it could also be argued that these two facets of parental influence may be related; for example, parents with extensive marital discord or personality disorder may be less mobilized psychologically to intervene in their child's cross-gender behaviour, which increases the likelihood of subsequent exposure to social ostracism.

Several key findings are summarized below.

Parent- and teacher-report measures
of general behaviour problems

On measures such as the Child Behaviour Checklist (CBCL) and the Teacher's Report Form (TRF), clinic-referred boys and girls with GID show significantly more general behaviour problems than their siblings and non-clinic ("normal") children. Compared to demographically matched clinical controls, they show similar levels of behaviour problems. On the CBCL and the TRF, boys with GID have a predominance of internalizing behavioural difficulties whereas girls with GID did not. The following case vignettes are illustrative.

> "Charles" was 8 years old, with an IQ of 106. He was referred at the suggestion of a friend of his mother, who had been an employee at our Institute and knew about our clinic. He lived with both of his parents and a younger sibling. On the Hollingshead classification (see Glossary), the family's social-class ranking was a III.

On the CBCL, Charles's mother identified 40 items as characteristic of his behaviour, which summed to 51 and fell in the clinical range. The Internalizing T score (71) was in the clinical range and was substantially higher than the Externalizing T score (58). The ratings provided by the father, however, contrasted sharply with those provided by the mother. He identified only 23 items as characteristic of Charles's behaviour, which summed to 23 and was well below the clinical cut-off. Both the Internalizing T score (57) and the Externalizing T score (53) were below the clinical cut-off.

The maternal CBCL profile of a markedly internalizing youngster was very consistent with clinical observation. In our view, the paternal profile seemed to underestimate the difficulties that Charles was experiencing, which seemed related to the father's general style during the assessment, which was to minimize any concerns about Charles in particular or the family in general. During the initial assessment with the family, Charles spent the first forty-five minutes of the interview sitting on the arm of his mother's chair, on her lap, or behind her. He seemed to have a strong need to be in close proximity to his mother, and several members of our team commented that his behaviour was reminiscent of Harlow's classic photographs of frightened rhesus macaque infants.

Apart from his cross-gender identification, Charles's mother commented during an initial intake telephone interview that he was "very insecure". There was a two-year history of encopresis, and Charles talked about "hating school" because of peer teasing. He also worried that, if he attended school, he might "miss something" at home and someone might come there and hurt his mother. He did not like to be separated from her, and he worried that she might die if she went away on a trip. On the way home after the initial interview, Charles said to his mother that he was "holding a lot of things in" that he had never told anyone, including fear of his stuffed animals and of his closet door when it was ajar. He also said to his mother that he thought the assessment had to do with his parents wanting him to be "sent away". This seemed related to his literal interpretation of comments that his mother would make to him when she became frustrated with his behaviour: "Maybe go live with someone else . . . we'll let someone who doesn't have anything come and live in your room."

Charles was felt to be anxious and withdrawn during psychological testing. His fingernails were noted to be extensively bitten. His eye contact with the female examiner was poor. On the Rorschach, he provided only 11 responses, which was consistent with his constricted psychological state.

The DSM-III-R diagnoses were functional encopresis (secondary type) and separation anxiety disorder.

* * *

"Eva" was 6 years old and lived with a younger sibling and her parents. The referral was initiated by her mother, who had been episodically concerned about her gender identity development. On the Hollingshead, the family's social-class ranking was a I.

On the CBCL, Eva's mother identified 38 items as characteristic of her behaviour, which summed to 38. This fell somewhat below the clinical range; however, the Internalizing T score (67) was in the clinical range and was somewhat higher than the Externalizing T score (60).

The CBCL profile of an internalizing youngster was consistent with clinical observation. Eva was described by her mother as "sensitive" and "quick to tears". Eva's mother also felt that she had low self-esteem and was very sensitive to comments made by other children. On school days, she tended to be clingy and tearful and was avoidant in new situations where she might be singled out. There had been a three-month wait before Eva could be seen. During this time, there had been several extensive telephone discussions with her mother. In these conversations, her mother made no mention of what proved to be a severe marital crisis—Eva's parents had separated briefly because of an event involving her father. In the course of the assessment, Eva's father blocked every effort to explore the marital relationship and commented bluntly that it had no bearing on her development. He seemed to minimize the extent of Eva's gender dysphoria and refused to return after the initial visit. However, Eva's mother continued to attend the assessment sessions, although she would not permit Eva to be seen for psychological testing. During the initial interview, Eva fought back tears when the interviewer gently commented on the parents' "separation".

Because the parents were reluctant to let us assess Eva comprehensively, only a provisional DSM-III-R diagnosis of adjustment disorder with depressed mood was given.

* * *

"Sammy" was 8 years old, with an IQ of 94. At the time of the assessment, she lived in a residential treatment setting. On the Hollingshead, her social-class background was a V.

On the CBCL, Sammy's child care worker identified 84 items as characteristic of her behaviour, which summed to 141, well within the clinical range. Both the Internalizing T score (79) and the Externalizing T score (89) were also well within the clinical range.

Apart from her marked cross-gender identification, Sammy manifested pervasive socioemotional disturbance. Her life had been characterized by extreme instability. Her mother had come from a very disturbed family and had spent many years under the care of child welfare authorities. Around the time of Sammy's birth, she had been an amphetamine addict, a heavy user of barbiturates, and a prostitute. Sammy's father was her mother's pimp. Her parents never lived together. When Sammy was 2 years old, her mother felt unable to cope with parenting and turned her care over to her father. He would permit her mother to see Sammy only if she had sex with him. When living with her father, Sammy was surrounded by older half-brothers from his previous liaisons and, according to reports from other agencies, was subject to severe physical abuse. On numerous occasions, she also saw her father physically abuse her mother. When she was 5, she was in her father's apartment when his current partner shot him in the face with a revolver. She was then taken into care. At the time of our assessment, Sammy was in terror that her father might find her and take her away again, and she ruminated about finding a gun so that she could protect herself.

The DSM-III-R diagnoses were functional enuresis (nocturnal), oppositional-defiant disorder, and overanxious disorder. A reactive attachment disorder was also queried. Sammy showed profound impairment in her personality functioning that strongly suggested the risk for later character pathology.

Separation anxiety

Boys with GID have also been found to show high rates of separation-anxiety traits (Coates & Person, 1985; Zucker, Bradley, & Lowry Sullivan, 1996). The following case vignette is illustrative.

"Darnell" was a 5-year-old boy with an IQ of 128. He was referred by a child psychiatrist who had previously assessed and treated an older brother for symptoms suggestive of oppositional-defiant disorder and a "difficult temperament". Darnell was born at a time when his parents were experiencing increased marital discord, which was characterized primarily by increasing withdrawal on his father's part. There was little overt marital discord. His father spent long periods of social time away from the family and experienced a strong absence of sexual desire, including impotence, towards his wife, who reported that her previous sexual relationships had always been fulfilling. Darnell's parents separated a couple of times before his second birthday and separated for the last time when he was 2 years old. Darnell's mother was a sensitive parent, accomplished in her profession, and free of gross psychopathology; by her late childhood, however, the quality of her family's life had been adversely affected by her father's emergent alcoholism.

For most of Darnell's life, the routine of his family was extremely stressful. He experienced several changes in baby-sitters, his father's prolonged absences, and frequent brief separations from his mother, whose profession required her to be away from the family for several days at a time. Darnell's mother described him as sensitive and having considerable difficulty separating from her (e.g. at nursery school). She felt that he had low self-esteem, manifested, for example, by frequent self-deprecatory remarks (e.g. "I hate myself").

Darnell's cross-gender behaviour began in the context of the chronically stressful family situation. When Darnell was 4, his mother became involved with another man (whom she eventually married), who reported that when she was out of town because of her work as a flight attendant, he would come home from work and often find him cross-dressed. That Darnell's cross-dressing and other feminine behaviours increased during his mother's absence was, therefore, fairly compelling, at least as judged by the observations of his stepfather-to-be. By age 4, Darnell had developed an intellectual interest in geography, often looking at globes or maps of the world. During the assessment, the interviewer commented to him that by learning about the world, he was able to "keep track of . . . mom". Darnell smiled and nodded affirmatively.

Quality of mother–child attachment

Birkenfeld-Adams (1998) assessed quality of attachment to the mother in young boys with GID, ages 3 to 6 years, and found that the majority (73%) were classified as insecurely attached, a rate comparable to that of an internal clinical control group and of other studies of clinical populations (e.g. Greenberg, Speltz, DeKlyen, & Endriga, 1991). Birkenfeld-Adams also found evidence for more signs of separation distress on the Separation Anxiety Test (Klagsbrun & Bowlby, 1976) in both the GID and clinical control boys than in the normal control boys. We have also assessed quality of attachment in ten girls with GID; all of the girls were classified as insecurely attached (unpublished data).

These data suggest that boys and girls with GID show signs of insecure attachment to the mother, which is consistent with observations of family psychopathology that it is likely to interfere with the quality of mother–child relations (e.g. Coates, 1985). The findings are also interesting in light of the fact that younger children with GID have significantly less general behaviour problems on measures such as the CBCL and TRF than school-age children with GID.

Poor peer relationships

The quality of peer relations was measured from five CBCL items that, on the basis of content validity, seemed most relevant to peer group relations: "Doesn't get along with other kids" (Item 25); "Gets teased a lot" (Item 38); "Not liked by other kids" (Item 48); "Prefers being with older kids" (Item 63); and "Prefers being with younger kids" (Item 64).

From these items, we attempted to devise a scale that might be a reasonable index of poor peer relations. For comparative purposes, we included data for these items from the male ($N = 108$) and female ($N = 80$) siblings (4–12 years of age) of the probands. From the maternal data, we calculated the internal consistency of the five CBCL items. Visual inspection of the data suggested that Items 25, 38, and 48 best indexed the construct of poor peer relations, whereas Items 63 and 64 lowered the scale's internal consistency. Accordingly, we created a scale using Items 25, 38, and 48, which yielded a Cronbach's alpha of .81 (with Items 63–64 included, Cronbach's alpha was reduced to .70). The mother–father correlation for the scale was .66 ($N = 312$, $p < .001$).

The hypothesis was that gender-referred boys would have poorer peer-group relations than the gender-referred girls, on the grounds that cross-gender behaviour in boys is subject to more social disapproval than it is in girls (Zucker, Wilson-Smith, Kurita, & Stern, 1995).

A 2 (group: gender-referred and siblings) × 2 (sex) analysis of covariance (ANCOVA) was performed on our scale of poor peer relations. The covariate was the sum of items scored as either a 1 or a 2 on the entire CBCL minus the sum of Items 25, 38, and 48.

Table 3.3 shows the mean scale score as a function of group and sex. The ANCOVA revealed a main effect for group, $F(1, 412) =$

TABLE 3.3

Maternal ratings on scale of poor peer relations as a function of group and sex[a]

Group	M	SD	N
Gender-referred			
Boys	1.99	1.77	200
Girls	1.72	1.53	29
Siblings			
Boys	0.62	1.14	108
Girls	0.75	1.11	80

[a]Absolute range, 0–6.
Note. Data from Zucker et al. (1997).

16.1, $p < .001$, and a group × sex interaction that approached significance, $F(1, 412) = 2.95$, $p = .087$.

The group main effect indicated that both the gender-referred boys and girls were judged by their mothers to have significantly poorer peer relations than their siblings. The marginal group x sex interaction was explored further with simple effects analysis. The gender-referred boys tended to have significantly poorer peer relations than the gender-referred girls ($p = .093$), but there was no significant difference in peer relations between the male and female siblings. The gender-referred boys had significantly poorer peer relations than the male siblings ($p < .001$), but there was no significant difference between the peer relations of the gender-referred girls and the female siblings ($p = .17$).

The following case vignette is illustrative.

"Norton" was 10 years old, with an IQ of 81. He lived with his lower middle-class parents and an older sister. Apart from his cross-gender behaviour, which had been of long-standing duration, he also had some notable academic learning problems, had been previously diagnosed with Attention Deficit/ Hyperactivity Disorder, and was on Ritalin.

His parents requested an assessment at the present time after previous involvement at another agency had not resulted in any major changes in Norton's cross-gender behaviour. Social ostracism was of particular concern, as it appeared to be getting worse. In the neighbourhood, Norton had no close friends. At school, he was called "fag, gay, stupid". When asked why he was called stupid, Norton commented "I'm not that good at maths". Norton knew what the words "fag" and "gay" meant—"like you kiss another boy or you sleep with another boy". Norton was fairly demoralized about his peer relations: "They don't care about me, they don't like me, they never do anything for me." He talked about feeling "unappreciated", and he acknowledged having revenge fantasies after episodes of teasing. The girls at school were much more rejecting of Norton than they had been in the past—several girls tried to convince him, but to no avail, that he was really now too old to be playing with them and that he should learn how to play with the other boys. Norton's parents noted that he had never had a close friend and that he complained of loneliness. Because of the teasing, the parents contemplated withdrawing Norton from school and teaching him at home.

Our data on poor peer relations differed somewhat from those reported by Green and colleagues (Green, Williams, & Goodman, 1982; Green, Williams, & Harper, 1980). In Green's study, feminine boys appeared to have poorer same-sex peer relations than did masculine girls. Because our measure was different from that employed by Green, it is, of course, difficult to make direct comparisons. Nevertheless, our results for the gender-referred boys were quite consistent with Green's findings, but our data for gender-referred girls were more equivocal (particularly as judged by the very strong group main effect). It may well be the case that the route of entry into the respective studies accounted for the difference—our sample of girls was a clinical one, whereas Green's sample of masculine girls was recruited via newspaper advertisements, so it is conceivable that our sample consisted of a more extreme group of cross-gender–identified girls.

Reasons for associated behaviour problems

At present, reasons for the associated behavioural psychopathology described here have been best studied in boys with GID (Zucker & Bradley, 1995). It is positively associated with age, which may reflect the results of increasing social ostracism, particularly in the peer group (Zucker & Bradley, 1995). It is also associated with a composite index of maternal psychopathology, which may reflect generic, non-specific familial risk factors in producing behaviour problems in general (Zucker & Bradley, 1995). The predominance of internalizing psychopathology may reflect familial risk for affective disorders and temperamental features of the boys. The extent to which aspects of the behavioural psychopathology may actually induce the emergence of the GID itself remains unresolved (see e.g. Coates & Person, 1985).

In summary, our data, as well as the work of others, suggest that children with GID show a variety of other behavioural difficulties, which, in their own right, are worthy of serious therapeutic attention. The presence of these other psychological difficulties makes it only the more difficult in formulating and implementing a therapeutic plan of action that will address not only the GID itself but these associated problems as well (see also chapter twelve).

CHAPTER FOUR

The complexity of early trauma: representation and transformation

Susan W. Coates & Mary Sue Moore

I n this chapter, we describe the case of "Colin", a 3½-year-old boy, who suffered significant trauma of a non-sexual nature which occurred in the context of his primary attachment relationship. The case was the subject of an extended previous communication devoted to a psychodynamic understanding of gender identity disorder of childhood (Coates et al., 1991). Here we present the case as seen through the particular lens of trauma, rather than with special reference to issues of gender. Colin's traumatization can be conceptualized as having two different components, one entailing the precipitous loss of the emotional availability of his primary caretaker and the other entailing physical confrontations, experienced as potentially life-threatening, when he tried to re-establish contact with her. Beyond this, the case also touches on the issue of the cross-generational transfer of trauma.

This chapter is reprinted from *Psychoanalytic Inquiry*, Volume 17, Number 3, 1997, with the kind permission of Analytic Press.

To be noted at the outset is that neither what has been documented of Colin's traumatization nor the cross-generational issues involved in it were sexual in nature. Our hope is that by identifying the salient features of Colin's traumatic reactions, we will provide a basis for appreciating traumatization as a general process, especially when it occurs at a very early age and most especially when the traumatizing agent is the child's primary attachment figure (cf. Main, 1991; Carlson & Cicchetti, 1989). This, hopefully, will afford a more direct means of comparison to cases of sexual abuse that occur under the same or roughly the same conditions, that is, when the abuser is a primary attachment figure and when the abuse occurs early, roughly between 2 and 3 years of age.

We define trauma as an overwhelming threat to the survival or integrity of the self that is accompanied by annihilation anxiety. Such a threat can be registered even in the neonate. Infants abused within days of birth show powerful fear and avoidant responses to the specific abuser, both at the time and in subsequent encounters (Gaensbauer & Harmon, 1982; Sander, 1987). When such emergency defensive reactions persist, they can interfere with the subsequent development of a flexible range of age-appropriate defence mechanisms and, ultimately, with the further development of the self.

Among the general features associated with trauma that will be evident in the discussion of Colin's case are the following:

- the transmission of intense, unmetabolized affect as an aspect of trauma;
- the multiple uses of imitation as means of managing traumatic experience;
- the development of distortions in the self-structure as the result of imitation;
- an impairment in the differentiation of self and other;
- an impairment in symbolic capacity, and in the ability to play;
- repetitive re-enactments of the trauma;
- the preservation of a physiological memory of the trauma quite independent of representational memory;
- an increase in characterological sensitivity;

• the adoption of a hypervigilant stance;

• the development of role-reversed behaviours in the primary attachment relationship.

In discussing Colin's treatment, we make special reference to his drawings. We have found the drawings of children with traumatic early histories to be of particular relevance in the understanding of the impact of the trauma on the child's development (Hammer, 1958; Moore, 1990, 1994; Terr, 1988, 1990). Drawings are often a powerful expression of the traumatic memories, and the most accessible for use by the therapist. Hammer (1958) cites studies by Zucker (1948), stating that drawings are "the first to show incipient psychopathology and the last to lose signs of illness after the patient remisses". He quotes from Stern (1952): "It seems that the affect emanating from a picture reaches into the unconscious more deeply than does that of language, due to the fact that pictorial expression is more adequate to the developmental stage in which the trauma occurred" (p. 629). In addition, drawings of the human figure collected throughout an intensive psychotherapeutic treatment reflect changes in the self-state of the child and reveal adaptive developmental changes related to the age-appropriate use of symbolic capacity in the service of defensive organization (Burgess & Hartman, 1993; Moore, 1994; Robins, Blatt, & Ford, 1991).

Colin was referred at the age of 3½ to a mental health practitioner by his nursery school teacher because of his inability to get along with other children. If he did not get his way, he would hit them or else he would scowl, cross his arms, and turn his face to the wall. Moreover, from the perspective of the nursery school, his current behaviour appeared to be a marked change from the time that he had been evaluated for entrance into the nursery programme nearly eight months earlier. Both the marked change and the inability to contain aggression against peers are significant indicators of distress that could result from a number of different causes.

In the initial contact, it was discovered that Colin had an extensive history of cross-gender interests and behaviours that had begun a year earlier, and he was thus referred to a gender identity centre for further evaluation and treatment. At the time of his evaluation, which occurred during the latter part of his third year, the following behaviour was evident. He openly stated that he wished to be a girl and that he hated being a boy. He believed that he was born a girl and that, if you wore a girl's clothes, you could really become a girl and "not just for pretend". Since the age of 2½, he had regularly dressed in his mother's clothes and would spend long periods of time cross-dressing while observing himself intently in front of a mirror. He was intensely interested in jewellery and make-up; he repetitively stroked the hair of Barbie dolls and had a marked interest in heroines (not heroes) in fairy tales such as Snow White.

In an initial interview, Colin appeared eager to talk, but he was peculiarly uninterested in toys and appeared to have no interest in playing. Throughout the interview, he seemed hypervigilant and his gaze was riveted to the eyes of the two interviewers, who were both female; he studied their faces as if he were intensely attempting to understand their every expression. Of particular note was his expressed concern about "ladies with angry eyes". He talked about how afraid he was of a girl in his class who had angry eyes, and he proceeded to imitate her for the interviewer. He could not say any more about this anxiety but was noted to watch the interviewers' eyes intently throughout the interview.

In many ways, Colin's initial presentation was of a precocious, compliant, over-attuned adult; he responded to meeting with two new adults in a singularly un-childlike way. Of considerable import was the fact that he engaged in no spontaneous play. He exhibited none of the ordinary joyfulness of a child his age and showed no exploratory behaviour or curiosity in the new environment which included a playroom for children. He was, however, very aware of unfamiliar noises. Typical of traumatized children in general was the fact that he maintained a hypervigilant stance in relation to the new adults throughout the interview, was unable to play, and showed a constricted range of affect and responses to a new environment. (For a more detailed discussion of the play of traumatized children, see Terr, 1983.)

In addition, Colin was very attentive to his mother (Mrs S) and preoccupied with her well-being. He was overtly solicitous of his mother, asking her, for example, "Mommy, are you okay?" His attentiveness to her—"That's a pretty dress, Mommy"— and her response to that attentiveness was reversed in terms of the ordinary roles of child and parent. This role-reversed stance suggested that his attachment relationship had been highly stressed. Where the child is securely attached, he or she is not ordinarily solicitous of the parent to this degree. In fact, in longitudinal research the pattern exhibited by Colin is most often seen in cases where the attachment bond was frankly disorganized at earlier ages, that is, when for whatever reason the child was simply unable to maintain a coherent set of behaviours with regard to the attachment figure (Main & Solomon, 1990).

Colin had several significant sensory sensitivities. For example, he would cry when he heard loud sounds such as the doorbell. He was also very sensitive to colour. In fact, in the initial evaluation he immediately noticed and commented on the fact that the two interviewers were wearing similar shades of blue. Such an observation from a 3-year-old is quite unusual. Such heightened sensory sensitivities are, in fact, typical of boys who develop gender identity disorders, as is a shy, behaviourally inhibited temperament. Incidentally, to avoid misunderstanding, it should be pointed out that this constitutional sensitivity and reactivity is not necessarily sex-linked, nor does it constitute an innate tendency towards "femininity". Rather, its contribution to the aetiological picture can best be understood in terms of a heightened need for attachment and a greater vulnerability to disruptions in attachment relationships (Coates & Wolfe, 1995).

Colin was the only child of middle-class parents. His mother had initially been reluctant to become pregnant because she believed that she would not be very good at being a mother. She thought she would be much too impatient. In time, her husband persuaded her to try to become pregnant, and the pregnancy and birth were uneventful. Colin's parents reported further that he did well in the first year of life. His mother described him as a very easy baby who would just "drink in" the world around him, and she remembered feeling quite disappointed when he weaned himself at the age of 8 months.

Colin's arrival significantly altered the dynamics of the family. During the immediate postpartum phase, his father began to feel unimportant and he withdrew. He was surprised to discover how left out he felt while Colin was breast-feeding, despite the fact that he had eagerly anticipated becoming a father. From his perspective, he was disappointed in his relationship with Colin. Colin did not seem responsive to him. During the subsequent months, the father found himself inexplicably becoming suddenly destructive of property; for example, he destroyed a picnic table in a sudden burst of anger. He was confused by this behaviour and had no understanding of what initiated these uncharacteristic episodes.

The family was an extended one. Colin's maternal grandmother moved into the apartment next door to assist in caring for Colin. But Mrs S experienced her mother's assistance as hypercritical, intrusive, and undermining, and daily there were heated verbal fights between the two women. The history revealed that Mrs S's mother had never fully recovered psychologically from a miscarriage she had had when Mrs S was 2 years old. In the year after Colin's birth, Mrs S also felt abandoned by her husband. Despite all this stress, Mrs S remembers Colin at age 1 year as a "laughing baby" with an easygoing temperament, who was loving and "always happy".

As Colin moved out of infancy into toddlerhood, Mr S seemed to distance himself further, not only from his wife but from his son as well. His chief preoccupation as a parent was that Colin should "do his own thing" and develop a sense of his own "power". What this meant in practice, however, was that he set no limits on Colin's behaviour whatsoever. He appeared to have no concern about his son's inappropriate expression of aggression, even when the aggression involved physical assault upon himself. Colin at one point took a toy train and hit his father in the face with it; in response, his father physically withdrew but made no attempt to set any limits on the behaviour.

Shortly after his second birthday, his family planned a five-day trip abroad, but Colin became ill before their departure. Colin and his mother stayed behind, and his father and his grandmother who lived next door both left for Europe. During their absence, as the mother reported, Colin became inconsolable: "He cried until his father and grandmother returned." During the evaluation, the mother denied having been upset herself. Later, however, during the course of treatment, she recalled being very angry and disappointed. The purpose of the grandmother's trip had been to see the mother's brother, and this replicated a painful scenario frequently experienced in the mother's childhood where the sickly brother received the lion's share of their mother's attention. Colin's mother was hurt and furious at this latest repetition.

Both parents agree that Colin's behaviour changed at this point in time. He became more anxious, was now markedly clingy, and became extremely sensitive to all separations. His parents saw him as changing from being sensitive and creative to being overly sensitive.

Mrs S, concerned that Colin "did not have enough companionship", decided to have a second child. She also was eager to repeat her earlier pleasurable experiences with Colin as an infant. However, this time her pregnancy ended in tragedy: amniocentesis led to the foetal diagnosis of Down's syndrome. The amniocentesis also revealed that the foetus was a female. During the three-week waiting period prior to an abortion, Mrs S developed elaborate fantasies about this girl child. She named the foetus "Miriam" after a revered teacher and felt grateful for the waiting period prior to the abortion because this allowed her "to get to know Miriam". She had fantasies of sewing dresses for the child and of giving her to her mother so that "she would have something to live for". Moreover, although her husband experienced a pronounced grief reaction following the abortion, Mrs S did not. Though she felt chronically depressed and anxious thereafter, Mrs S did not connect these feelings with the loss of the baby.

Colin's cross-gender behaviour began within weeks of the abortion, and it rapidly assumed the driven quality characteristic of children with the full syndrome of gender identity disorder (GID). Colin's mother was unconcerned about this. In the months following the abortion, she came to experience Colin's general hypersensitivity and responsiveness as selectively attuned to herself. "He was always tuned in to my feelings", she would recall later: "He always knew how I felt." She adopted a new nickname for him: "Lovey."

At approximately the same time that the GID emerged, Colin also began to have temper tantrums at home. These arose when he attempted to intrude on his mother's withdrawn, depressed state. Mrs S experienced his tantrums as overwhelming and at these times viewed Colin as if he were a persecutory object. She felt at moments that he was doing her in. It was fully two years into her own therapy, however, before she remembered how strongly she would censure his demands that she spend more time with him. On numerous occasions during the height of her depression, she would grab him around the shoulders and neck and shake him while screaming at him full-face. She recalled that, while shaking him, she looked into his eyes and realized that he was afraid that she might kill him. She began to fear that she might in fact harm him and worried that she was going crazy. We believe that these episodes reactivated unresolved trauma in the mother from her own past (particularly the mother's early memories of her *own* mother's rageful reactions following the miscarriage), and we suspect further that Mrs S's rageful episodes may have occurred in dissociated states.

Recall that in our initial interview Colin was preoccupied with ladies with angry eyes. At home, he was reported to crossdress while standing in front of a mirror making angry eyes. In viewing a subsequent videotape of this behaviour, we were struck with the way that he would make these angry eyes and then back away as if he were studying this troublesome expression. It was while his mother was observing this behaviour with the mirror, which continued into his second year of treatment, that she realized that he was imitating her. At this and other times, it was almost as if he were her primary source of information about her own affective states. It appeared that Colin had comprehended his mother's inner state—or was trying to—but she was unable to comprehend his inner experience.

Continued work in the mother's individual therapy revealed more of the meaning to her of the loss of the female foetus and the fantasy of having a daughter and why this loss precipitated such a significant depression. Most notable was the emergence of a family history of loss of daughters going back two generations. Colin's maternal grandmother was the oldest of seven children; along with a maternal aunt, she was put in charge of raising her younger siblings because her own mother, Colin's great-grandmother, was incapacitated due to depression. When the grandmother was a child, her 4-year-old sister died. According to family mythology, this death occurred because the child did not get proper medical attention; the grandmother held herself responsible. The second loss occurred when, as an adult, Colin's grandmother miscarried a female foetus when Colin's mother was 2 years old. After this miscarriage, the grandmother went into a rageful depression, which continued to the present. It is important to note that, when Colin's mother aborted the female foetus, Colin was the same age she had been when her mother's miscarriage occurred. When the grandmother had been interviewed in relation to Colin's evaluation, she had burst into tears recalling her own miscarriage which had occurred over thirty years ago.

Here we should note that the grandmother's reaction to recalling the loss—that is, her re-experiencing it as though it had just happened and with such intensity that her ability to maintain concentration on the interview was compromised—constitutes a kind of reaction that Main and her colleagues (George, Kaplan, & Main, 1985; Main & Hesse, 1990) have underscored as highly significant when it occurs on the Adult Attachment Interview, a structured interview protocol designed to tap experiences related to early attachment relationships. Briefly, research indicates that lapses in a parent's meta-cognitive monitoring indicative of unresolved grief and trauma are highly predictive of an "insecure–disorganized–disoriented" attachment between parent and child. The inference is that, when the parent becomes similarly distressed by unresolved loss from the past in the presence of the child, the child is placed in an irresolvable paradox, unable to use the parent as a secure base in order to cope with the distressing, but for the child uninterpretable, affective communication. In such situations, the child may become disoriented and the child's attachment behaviours may become disorganized.

The reaction of Colin's mother to the loss of her female foetus similarly appears from the available data to have been one of emotional blockage and depression. Severe depression in the mother is also known to have significant impact on the attachment relationship between mother and child, again with the most common result being the formation of an insecure attachment (Murray, 1991). An insecure–disorganized–disoriented attachment pattern may result if the depression is sufficiently severe (Lyons-Ruth, 1992; Radke-Yarrow, Cummings, Kuczynski, & Chapman, 1985). Thus, in Colin's case, there were indications that attachment relationships in two different generations had probably been compromised by unresolved loss (Main & Hesse, 1990), with first Colin's grandmother's grief disrupting her attachment bond to Colin's mother and then the mother repeating the same pattern with him.

Not only trauma but also wishes for reparation had a multigenerational context. It subsequently emerged in Colin's mother's therapy that as a child she had held herself responsible for the death of her mother's miscarried "baby girl" and for her mother's subsequent depression. Thus, during the pregnancy with "Miriam", the mother had had active fantasies of repairing her own mother's suffering by giving her a daughter so that she would have "something to live for". In the context of the multigenerational transmission of trauma and disorganized attachment, we hypothesize that this wish to make reparation to the grandmother so preoccupied Colin's mother that she ceased to be emotionally accessible to Colin even before the abortion.

In this overall context, let us distinguish two aspects of Colin's traumatization—and two dimensions in his response to it. His adoption of stereotypical cross-gender behaviour can be seen as directly responsive to his mother's withdrawal into her own depression. Not only is identification with the lost object entailed, but there was a reparative wish as well—namely, to help the mother overcome her trauma by giving her the little girl that she, and the grandmother as well, so fervently wished for. His use of imitation was therefore dynamically quite complex, involving an attempt to cognize his situation, stabilize his sense of self, create a means of maintaining contact with his mother, and—not incidentally—repair his depressed mother. We note in particular that his emergent identification with a stereotyped image of his idealized mother (i.e. without aggression and without hostile affect) became an important source of a sense of specialness for Colin, as well as a coping mechanism for dealing with anxiety arising from multiple sources. Thus, he relied on this false-self personification as an active defensive means of managing intolerable affect states. Colin used splitting organized around gender content to preserve his mental representation of his mother and his father. He viewed females and self as primitively idealized and without aggression, whereas he viewed males as aggressive and devalued. This both facilitated the use of dissociation as a means of defending him from his experience of his own aggressive fantasies and, in turn, blocked his identification with his father who, after Colin's birth, began to experience occasional rages which he himself found inexplicable and which were frightening to Colin.

The mother's angry, threatening responses to Colin's temper tantrums, meanwhile, constituted a separate level of traumatization, and Colin's response to the mother's rageful outbursts—his fearful imitation of a lady with angry eyes in the mirror—constituted a distinctly different use of imitation to deal with his experience. From our point of view, the concept of identification with the aggressor only partially captures the meaning of this aspect of Colin's behaviour.

Here let us pause for some general remarks about imitation and the contagion of affect. Recent research demonstrates that, from the first hours of life, the infant is biologically organized to transform a visual perception of a facial expression into a matching proprioceptive experience that results in being able to imitate the facial expression of the other (Meltzoff & Moore, 1977; Trevarthen, 1985). Moreover, Ekman (1983) has demonstrated that in adults the mere imitation of a facial expression results in a physiological arousal pattern—that is, the internal "feelings" known to be associated with that facial expression. Even more striking is the finding of Davidson and Fox (1982) that in 10-month-olds the perception of a specific emotional state in another simultaneously creates a corresponding affective resonance in the infant that can be measured in EEG changes. In these ways imitation is a vehicle for empathy and, eventually, intersubjectivity.

Nathanson (1986), writing in another context, has raised what we see as the critical question. Rather than asking how emotional communication is transmitted, we should, as Nathanson puts it, "consider how such transmission is blocked"—that is, how an empathic wall is constructed in development to protect one from being flooded by the affect of the other.

What defences are available to the infant whose experience of affect is altered from a tolerable affective state into one perceived as a threat to the continued existence of the self? From the early weeks of life, infants have a number of physiological self-regulatory mechanisms available to alter the intensity of incoming experience from the environment (Fraiberg, 1982). These include, among others, extreme or chronic gaze aversion, going limp, rapidly sliding into a sleep state, and affect reversal (Beebe & Stern, 1977; Fraiberg, 1982; Sander, 1977). Clinical research has demonstrated that these extreme responses do not occur in the context of expectable perturbations in the mother–infant relationship (Murray & Trevarthen, 1985; Tronick & Cohen, 1989) but, rather, in the context of massive interpersonal affective distress.

There may well be large individual differences in infant experiences of affect "contagion" that may be mediated both by reactivity thresholds and by focused arousal thresholds (Ghent, 1994). An infant who constitutionally has low sensory thresholds may be particularly open to affective contagion and, besides "drinking in" the world as Colin did, may be that much more vulnerable to the contagion of negative affect. Moreover, one of the consequences of very early trauma, a consequence heightened in a constitutionally sensitive child, is an exacerbation of the normal degree of affective contagion between self and other. The heightened affect contagion may thus inhibit the development of "meta-cognitive thinking" or reflective function—that is, the ability to consider the perspective of the other as different from one's own (Fonagy, Steele, Moran, Steele, & Higgett, 1993; Main, 1991). When a child has experienced repetitive trauma in the context of a primary relationship, a common defensive strategy is to disavow the perception of the parent's toxic behaviour by denying its meaning and fleeing into a manic defence (Winnicott, 1935). This occurs even in the context of remaining highly vigilant to the parent's affect and moods. Such a defensive solution interferes with the development of an integrated capacity to experience the full range of affects, as an aspect both of the self and of the other. In this context, it is important to note again that Colin's personifications of a girl/woman were characterized by a high degree of highly stereotyped soft, gentle, and non-aggressive conceptions of femininity.

When Colin stood in front of the mirror cross-dressed, imitating his mother's angry eyes, however, we believe that he was attempting to understand an experience that he could not assimilate or otherwise metabolize. The fact that the behaviour persisted for almost 2 years after his initial traumatization underscores the degree to which the experience remained unmetabolizable in the specific sense that Colin seemed unable to "locate" the experience in terms of self and other—that is, unable to distinguish who was expressing what towards whom. His persisting imitation of his mother, accordingly, was being employed in both a defensive and a potentially adaptive manner. Emch (1944) views imitation as a mechanism serving "the need to know". She suggests that acting like someone or "becoming" the person allows a child to predict what the person will do so that they will not be taken off guard and hurt by the person. Ghent (1990) extends the concept of "the need to know" to an understanding of the defence of identification with the aggressor. He asks, "Could it be that the child or infant uses his available medium, his quite plastic self" (p. 130) as a way of attempting to perceive and comprehend aggression that is incomprehensible and unmetabolized?

We now consider selective aspects of Colin's therapy. At the beginning of treatment, as we have already noted, Colin had virtu-

FIGURE 4.1.   Princess

ally no capacity to engage in joyful, spontaneous pretend play. He was preoccupied with Barbie and would stroke her hair, repetitively put her clothes on and take them off, and so on, but he had no interest in using her to create narrative play. He would draw pictures of princesses in beautiful costumes over and over again, but would never draw a picture of a male (see Figure 4.1). He was obsessed with whether things were where they were left at the time of his last session and whether the toys were the same ones that were there during his last visit. He was particularly concerned about whether his therapist would be there when he returned. Concerns about object constancy were extremely concrete and preoccupied him for several months.

Ending sessions was very difficult for him. When he was told that there were five minutes left before the end, he would pick up Barbie and stroke her hair or would create images of women by drawing them or constructing them with clay. As therapy progressed, he began to make boys out of clay, but when his therapist announced that the session was going to end he would smash up his models and quickly make a model of a girl. It was as if he needed to restore the image of a female in a highly concrete way in order to tolerate the anxiety of the impending separation.

Again, we should note the dynamic complexity involved in Colin's stereotypical cross-gender preoccupation. Just as fashioning an image of a woman out of clay enabled him to tolerate the anxiety of ending a session, so too did similar behaviours enable him to tolerate anxiety arising in other contexts. In other words, the false-self personification, even though it arose in the traumatic circumstances of emotional abandonment by his mother, continued to function, quite rigidly, as an internal structure to which he could turn to manage anxiety.

We leave as an open question the extent to which the overt or covert development of similar false-self personifications as a means of managing anxiety may be partly responsible for a phenomenon widely noted in the clinical literature: namely, the high degree of stereotypy in the play of traumatized children. In general, the play of severely traumatized children shows a lack of variability or flexibility in play scenarios (Terr, 1983). They do not enjoy creating stories, and reciprocal interactive role-playing is especially difficult for them. Many traumatized children, in fact, cannot "play" in the usual sense of the word. In some cases, traumatized children will rapidly act out a particular scene with dolls or puppets, without words and without pausing to "choose" a story line. These compulsive, joyless, "un-play-like" enactments may be repeated in a single session or over many sessions. In other cases, these stereotypical or repetitive "play" behaviours will occur only in response to certain triggers in the therapy situation, such as the mention of a particular person's name or the sight of a specific evocative "toy", or when approaching the end of the session, or when the therapist announces a vacation. A key to the likelihood that this behaviour is not truly spontaneous play but an enactment of a traumatic experience is precisely the driven, rigidly compulsive, unchanging quality of the behaviour patterns. In some cases, a rigidly maintained "false self" that was developed out of early interpersonal traumatic experience may also serve to reduce the spontaneity in such repetitive un-play-like behaviours.

During the second year of his treatment, Colin continued to be fascinated with drawing glamorous ladies, but he now also became preoccupied with evil witches. For the first time, aggressive themes began to be represented in his drawings of females. He produced pictures of overpowering witchlike women drawn in

FIGURE 4.2.   Mommy

black ink, with fierce frightening angry eyes and elongated claw-like fingernails, whom he identified as "Mommy" not only to his therapist, but also to his mother when he presented her with the pictures after his sessions (see Figure 4.2). This act seemed to express the importance for Colin of having his affective experience comprehended by his mother. During this period in his treatment, there was a marked reduction in his cross-gender behaviour at home and an increase in his capacity to play with his peers.

After two years of therapy, when his cross-gender behaviour was no longer repetitively enacted, he showed a marked increase in his capacity to represent his experience symbolically, both verbally and non-verbally. During this time, one evening at home he drew a series of drawings which he entitled "My Story". He asked his mother to write down a caption that he dictated for each of the nine pictures. The result was a pictorial and verbal narrative (the pictures were published in Coates et al., 1991):

1. The cat is angry that she's turning into a lady. She doesn't know why she's turning into a lady.

2. She's screaming because she's so mad she's turning into a lady.

3. She's crying and sad she's turning into a lady. She already has hair.

4. She's crying and she's almost a lady. She still has her tail.

5. She almost lost her tail.

6. She's screaming so loudly her hair is going up and her tears are going up.

7. She's so mad she bit her tongue and she lost her tears.

8. She's eating her mother and she looks like a weirdo. She's mad but not at her mother. She ate her mother because she's so mad.

9. She's going to the bathroom; she got her mother out and her mother is dead. She's not sad.

The story depicts an experience of being taken over from the outside, resulting in a sense of annihilation of the self as Colin is transformed against his will into another. This experience, first represented in terms of annihilation, becomes fused in the later pictures with imagery expressive of age-appropriate castration anxiety. His profound anguish, pain, and suffering is poignantly expressed. His massive rage is depicted in the primitive incorporative imagery of eating his mother. When he attempts to put this primitive rage into words, there is a breakdown in his cognitive coherence (see Caption 8). What is most striking is that the representation and fantasy of the physical incorporation of the mother leads both to a fusion with her and a destruction of the representation of her as a separate individual while simultaneously leading to the elimination of the affective experience of being sad and, presumably, mad. (We have also wondered to what extent the last drawing, to which Caption 9 refers, might constitute an attempt by Colin to understand his mother's abortion and her subsequent emotional reaction to it.)

It was not until the third year of therapy that Colin first began to draw pictures specifically representing the various aspects of the trauma of his mother "choking" him about the neck and shoulders. These pictures represent important step towards an increasingly differentiated sense of self and other. One picture that he drew early in this sequence depicted two bald female-like figures facing one another, with one seemingly placed inside a mirror facing the other outside it (see Figure 4.3). Strikingly, the image in the mirror is reaching out of the mirror to choke the other, who is drawn with its arms at the sides and is exhibiting no reaction to the hand near its neck. This single drawing represents both the

FIGURE 4.3.   Figures at mirror

identification with the mother and the increasing capacity to experience self and other not only as separate beings, but also as capable of experiencing different affective states at the same time. As there is a shift from a defensive self–other fusion fantasy to a capacity to represent the self and other as separate, there is simultaneously a capacity to represent aggression as originating in one person.

As self–other representations became more individuated, he drew a picture of two figures differing in age and gender, separated in space and looking in the same direction, not face to face. One figure is a youthful male clown; he appears to be laughing while he watches a woman's head being severed at the neck by a large sword. The woman is not looking at the clown. In this depiction, there is an increase in Colin's representation of aggression towards the female. Notably, the content of the aggression is the severing of her head at the neck. It is not clear in the drawing whether the sword was originally held by one of the persons in the drawing. Thus, despite his increased awareness of his own aggression at this stage, he is still unable fully to acknowledge himself as an agent of aggression.

When fantasies of persons in interaction began to emerge in his fourth year of treatment, Colin was 7 years old, and his preoccupying narrative came to involve stories of men rescuing women. He began drawing pictures of a large, angular, angry-looking woman with tears coming out of her eyes, on the verge of falling off a cliff. In each picture, he drew a man running to save her. What made these drawings unlike those he had done initially was that, while they continued to emphasize the aggressive aspects of the woman, they simultaneously depicted her as crying and in desperate need of rescuing. This represented an important increment in Colin's ability to represent both depressive and aggressive feelings. We have wondered whether these fantasies will become developmentally incorporated into a sexual script such that the fantasy of a person in distress may develop an erotic valence for him.

By the end of therapy, the impact of the traumatic experience was no longer so pervasive and compromising of his affective and behavioural flexibility. Colin no longer manifested a gender identity disorder, separation anxiety, notable difficulties with aggression, or difficulties with his peers. He had developed the capacity for spontaneous symbolic play and personally generative fantasy and could sustain and enjoy relationships with peers. Despite the magnitude of change that had occurred in his treatment, unintegrated aspects of his earlier trauma emerged in a follow-up evaluation. During an interview when asked to talk about a range of feelings, including sad, angry, happy, weird, and secret feelings, he asked what weird feelings were and was told that they were feelings that were kind of hard to understand. He responded with instant recognition: "Oh, yes. When my guinea-pigs fight, I get very scared that they are going to kill each other, and I run over to separate them and then my neck gets hot and cold and hot and cold, and Mommy and Daddy say I turn white."

Colin's reaction to the guinea-pigs indicates that he still carries a memory of intense fear linked to feelings of choking around his neck and accompanied by physiological arousal, which can be activated by highly specific stimuli. We observe with interest that the elicitor of the physiological sensations, which we believe to be a residue from his earlier traumatization, is visual and auditory—that is, the sight and sound of guinea pigs fighting—and seems to have an iconic relation to the original traumatic scene. We also note with interest that Colin was not able to link his feelings at the sight of the animals fighting with any conscious memory of his mother or with his earlier fascination with ladies with angry eyes. An aspect of his earlier trauma remains coded procedurally in non-declarative memory and thus remains dissociated despite the many hours of treatment working through this trauma. This, we believe, is typical of trauma in general (Moore, 1997; Terr, 1988; van der Kolk, 1987).

It is an open question whether the physiological arousal, which is part and parcel of Colin's "weird" feeling, creates a potential for later sexualization of the dissociated trauma, just as it remains unknown whether the original arousals in the traumatic encounters were accompanied by any sexual arousal. One also wonders further what complication the development of sexuality at puberty and beyond might bring in terms of activating the traumatic memory. In Colin's case, it might be hard to avoid a reactivation of this memory if there were any pressure on his neck in a sexual contact. A response thus triggered would likely to be dissociative in nature and out of his awareness. One wonders how Colin's oedipal narratives will evolve into adult erotic scripts and whether the thematic qualities of those scripts will serve either to enhance or militate against the possibility that his somatic memory will become sexualized. At present, we just do not know.

When a parent has been the instrument of a trauma to the child, he or she has an important reparative role to play in helping the child work through the trauma, even if he or she is unable to undo all the traumatic effects. The parents' failure to intersubjectively experience, recognize, or comprehend and hold in awareness the traumatic impact on the child undermines the child's development of an authentic sense of self, as well as a coherent and integrated sense of reality in an interpersonal context. The flooding of the child's interior with traumatic levels of parental affect is compounded by the failure of the parent to register the significance of the event for the child. The child, left with an unmetabolizable experience, is much like Colin staring at his reflection in the mirror and making "angry eyes".

Perhaps this is the place to pause and consider Colin's traumatic abandonment by his mother in terms of the multigenerational transmission of trauma. With the death of " Miriam", Colin's mother began to repeat with him the painful experience she had had in her own childhood of being emotionally abandoned by her own depressed mother secondary to the death of a female child. Ever since the pioneering contribution of Fraiberg, Adelson, and Shapiro (1975), psychoanalytically oriented clinicians have been attuned to the possibility of such "ghosts in the nursery"—that is, of maternal childhood traumas being repeated in the lives of their children. More recently, Fonagy and his colleagues (1995) have identified reflective functioning as a potentially significant variable in the cross-generational transfer of trauma. Specifically, where parents are able to reflect psychologically on their own and their parents' experience, this can serve as a significant protector against the transmission of such "ghosts" from one generation to the next (Fonagy et al., 1995; Main, 1991). Judging from her reported behaviour at the time of her abortion, however, Colin's mother was unable to reflect on her own childhood experience, or on her mother's depressed withdrawal at that time. This, in turn, interfered with her ability to understand what Colin was experiencing.

In this context, we note pointedly that, as Colin's treatment progressed, it appeared very important to him to share his memories of his earlier experiences with his mother and to get her to recognize and acknowledge them. This process, we argue, goes beyond "working through" in the usual sense of that term and is part and parcel of a restoration of the derailed attachment relationship in the attempt to foster reflective functioning in both the child and the parent. Undeniably, Colin made steady progress towards greater symbolic representation of his experiences, and much of this progress reflects his own individual treatment. At the time of his referral, he could only imitate his mother's angry eyes. He could neither explain his experience, nor create symbolic representations through drawing or play. But we also note that Colin's progress was both accompanied and significantly facilitated by his mother's concurrent progress, both in terms of her increased understanding of herself and in terms of her ability to understand him (Slade, 1987).

This aspect of Colin's treatment makes it unusual to a certain degree because Colin's mother was equally well motivated in treatment, and she, too, had a profound wish to make reparations.

She put herself at enormous risk in her efforts to help Colin repair his suffering. As her own treatment unfolded, she made significant gains in her ability to grasp her own internal experience as well as the internal experience of her son. Indeed, it was in observing and attempting to understand Colin's continued imitation of angry eyes in the mirror, three years after the fact, that she began to remember her own angry rages at him during her depression following the abortion. Her progress in these respects was promptly reflected in further gains that Colin made, specifically in a dramatic increase in his ability to differentiate self and other and in a significant increase in his ability to represent his own aggressiveness.

Let us conclude with a few brief remarks regarding the representation of trauma, the nature of the therapeutic process, and the special significance of attachment relationships to the child's sense of self.

First, we are struck by the degree to which Colin's representations reflect the reality of his traumatic experience. In his narrative "My Story", he provides a vivid depiction of feeling appropriated and thus annihilated by his mother. Certain elements in the story, such as the loss of the cat's tail or the oral incorporation and subsequent elimination of the traumatizing object, indicate that the trauma has been represented in part through the structures and wishes of various psychosexual stages. But the story as a whole emerges as a representation of having been unwillingly transformed; this story is largely without any wishful elaboration. It is not primarily a story about wishes, but about traumatic impingement ultimately followed by a rageful reaction.

It might be wise to stay with this issue a moment longer, since we have found that it is frequently misunderstood. Colin's representations of his traumatization are accurate only to the extent that any symbolic representation can be. His representations refer to actual events, but they do not constitute a comprehensive, "objective", or positivistic account of those events. Indeed, in "My Story" the event triggering his gender transformation—that is, the mother's withdrawal into depression following her abortion—is not depicted. Also not depicted are the processes of projective identification and selective attunement in the mother, which were also at work. Nor could one deduce any of these events from the story itself, save that something awful happened in relation to the mother and that Colin's response to it involved gender content—and, in Colin's case, one has the advantage of his written captions. Most often, however, children's traumatic representations merge not verbally but pictorially, with little verbal elaboration (Burgess & Hartman, 1993; Schachtel, 1959; Terr, 1990; Wohl & Kaufman, 1985).

We believe that, in order to construct a valid understanding of the relation of trauma to representation, one has to obtain independent information about traumatic events to understand fully a child's depictions and verbalizations of them. But we also believe that once one has obtained such information, the representations of the traumatized child will be seen to contain components that can be best understood as pertaining directly to the actuality of the trauma as the child experienced it. As development proceeds, these components may be joined by wishful elements, to be sure, but to assume at the outset that wish-fulfillment is the dominant organizing principle can and will lead one far away from the child's experience in cases of trauma (Moore, 1994). The change in quality in Colin's drawing, across time, and the complex levels of representation seen, for example, in the "mirror" drawing—integrating elements of graphic re-presentation as well as various symbolic meanings—help us to realize that a single interpretation of children's drawings would be a disservice to the child and to the complexity involved in the construction of all representations.

Beyond being reality-based in the sense just specified, traumatic representations also show a noticeable tendency to endure, this despite further psychic growth. Colin's progress in terms of symptom remission was paralleled by an increasing ability to represent self and other as distinct and, finally, to create narratives about them. Yet here let us call attention to the motif of the neck as a place where injury can occur. This motif, reflective of Colin's actual experience, continues to reappear in Colin's later drawings as he struggles to understand it in terms of his evolving meaning-making systems. Yet the motif itself, once it emerged, remained relatively untransformed and undistorted, as did the actual physical sensations of choking. What changes is not the motif, but the symbolic organization around it. In our view, it remains an open question to what extent the persistence of physical sensations, a characteristic of all trauma, may account for the relative fixity of the symbolic representation.

Now let us turn to another important aspect of therapy. The transformation of representations was but one facet of the restoration of Colin's sense of self, and quite probably it was not the most important one. As we hope we have made clear, it was of the utmost importance to Colin that he get his mother to understand and acknowledge what had happened to him (and also what happened to her). Moreover, this only became possible to the extent that the mother herself began to become aware of her previous depression and her aggression against the child. Colin's sharing of his experience with his mother was essential to his restoring the derailed attachment system with her; and restoring the derailed attachment system was, we believe, indispensable to restoring his sense of self and for his progress in treatment generally. This was a crucial aspect of the work with regard to Colin's experience of his mother's rages. Not until his mother was able to acknowledge this side of herself, and also able to acknowledge its impact on Colin, was he able to confront her with his experience of her without running the risk of retraumatization.

Accordingly, we are led to a third issue, namely to the relation of the self to attachment and, more particularly, to the very special consequences that follow when trauma originates within the attachment relationship. If our understanding of Colin's traumas and of his progress is correct, then there are important implications for the understanding and treatment of sexual abuse. Specifically, when the abusing person is one of the child's primary attachment figures, then the effects of the abuse will be compounded in such a way as to block the pathway to symbolic repair and transformation. This is perhaps the single most devastating consequence of sexual abuse by a primary attachment figure—that is, the difficulty in ever restoring the attachment system, as Colin and his mother did, once this kind of violation has occurred. In particular, the appropriation of the child for the abuser's needs, coupled with the invalidation and denial of the child's experience, would seem to present the gravest obstacle to the kind of reparative work that must done on the attachment relationship if the child is to restore a viable sense of self.

CHAPTER FIVE

Biological contributions to atypical gender identity development

Caroline Brain

The concept of masculine women and feminine men has fascinated historians and physicians alike for centuries. A quote by Ambroise Paré (1510–1590) says: "Some women, having lost their monthly flow, or never having had them, degenerate in to a male type and are called masculine women or in Latin *viragines*, because they are robust, aggressive and arrogant, have a man's voice and become hairy and develop beards, because the blood they (normally) lose every month is retained." This quote, like many others in the literature, is very relevant to the topic of gender identity disorder, as it describes very clearly the process of masculinization occurring in parallel with defeminization. Both of these processes are necessary for somebody of a given gender to change to the opposite gender.

This chapter first gives the background to biological sex, which then allows us to attempt at least to understand how conditions of intersexuality, homosexuality, and transsexuality may occur. It then considers recent research that has provided data to support possible biological contributions to, in particular, atypical sexual orientation and transsexuality.

Biological sex

Jost's original paradigm (Jost, 1947) was that of the chromosomal or genetic sex, determining gonadal differentiation (and hence hormonal sex), which in turn dictated the development of either male or female genitalia and hence phenotypic sex. To this paradigm, Money and colleagues later added psychological sex, which becomes important in cases of ambiguity (Money, Hampson, & Hampson, 1955).

Thus:

Chromosomal (genetic) sex
↓
Gonadal (hormonal) sex
↓
Apparent (phenotypic) sex
↓
Psychological (behavioural) sex

Armstrong developed the concept of a sexual spectrum with man and woman at extreme ends of this spectrum, each being determined by wholly male or female determinants of biological sex (Armstrong & Marshall, 1964). A bimodal distribution between man and woman allows for a mixture of male and female characteristics that enables us to develop the concepts of intersexuality and transsexuality (Figure 5.1). Whilst conditions of intersex imply a discrepancy between chromosomal, gonadal, and phenotypic sex, in cases of transsexuality or gender identity disorder there is an incongruity between the biological sex (which is either wholly male or wholly female) and the psychological sex.

The biological aspects of the paradigm are outlined further below; the psychological aspects are discussed in chapter two.

Chromosomal (genetic) sex

A normal male karyotype is 46 XY and a female 46 XX. The presence of a Y chromosome usually indicates that the undifferentiated gonad will develop into a testes and that the phenotypic sex will be male. In the absence of Y material, the undifferentiated gonad becomes an ovary and the external genitalia develop to produce a

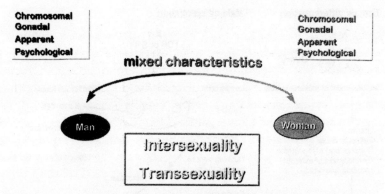

FIGURE 5.1. "Sexual spectrum" with bimodal distribution of male and female characteristics

phenotypic female. A variety of different karyotypes have been described (e.g. XXY, XXXY, XYY, XO, XXX), and, whilst many of these have implications in terms of abnormal pubertal development, there is usually no ambiguity of the external genitalia at birth. In the presence of both X and Y cell lines (e.g. XO/XY moseicism or chimaerism), then a situation of true hermaphroditism may exist with both testicular and ovarian tissue present and with ambiguity of both internal and external genitalia.

Gonadal (hormonal) sex

At conception, the developing embryo contains a pair of undifferentiated gonads. In the presence of a Y chromosome (on which is found the SRY gene) and under the influence of various other genetic sex differentiating factors, these gonads become testes containing both leydig and sertoli cells (Figure 5.2). The latter cell line produces anterior mullerian factor (AMH) which inhibits the development of mullerian ducts that would otherwise form the internal female structures (uterus, fallopian tubes and vagina). At puberty, these cells also function to produce sperm. Leydig cells produce testosterone, which determines the development of the wolffian ducts (epididymis, vas deferens, and seminal vesicle). Testosterone is reduced by the enzyme 5-alpha-reductase to dihydrotestosterone (DHT), which determines the development of the external male genitalia and the prostate. It is significant that

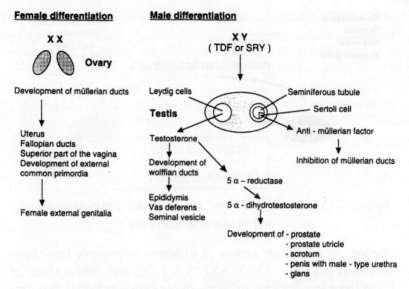

Female differentiation

X X

Ovary

Development of müllerian ducts

↓

Uterus
Fallopian ducts
Superior part of the vagina
Development of external
common primordia

↓

Female external genitalia

Male differentiation

X Y
(TDF or SRY)

↓

Leydig cells

Testis

Seminiferous tubule

Sertoli cell

Testosterone

↓

Development of
wolffian ducts

↓

Epididymis
Vas deferens
Seminal vesicle

Anti - müllerian factor

↓

Inhibition of müllerian ducts

5 α – reductase

5 α - dihydrotestosterone

↓

Development of - prostate
- prostate utricle
- scrotum
- penis with male - type urethra
- glans

FIGURE 5.2.   Gonadal differentiation and influence on the
subsequent development of internal and external genitalia

Reprinted by permission from *Pediatric Endocrinology: Physiology, Pathophysiology, and Clinical Aspects* (2nd ed.), edited by J. Bertrand, R. Rappaport, & P. C. Sizonenko. Baltimore, MD: Williams & Wilkins, 1993. Copyright © Williams & Wilkins.

testosterone is also converted by an aromatase enzyme to oestradiol and that both the aromatase and 5-alpha-reductase enzyme systems are present outside the gonad and specifically are found within the CNS in the area of the hypothalamus.

In the absence of Y material, the undifferentiated gonad becomes an ovary with development of the mullerian ducts and of the female external genitalia (Figure 5.2).

Apparent (phenotypic) sex

The urogenital ridge is identical in both the male and female conceptus. Figure 5.3 shows the differentiation of male and female genitalia under the influence of the differentiated testes or ovary, respectively, and it is clear to see how easily conditions of intersex can arise. Undervirilization of a genetic male may occur if the testes do not develop properly (e.g. dysgenetic testes), if there is a failure in the biosynthesis of testosterone, or in the presence of end organ resistance such as in androgen insensitivity (AIS). In the first two instances, there is inadequate testosterone produced to ensure the development of normal male genitalia. The biochemical effects of testosterone are mediated via interaction with the androgen receptor, and in the third instance there is adequate production of testosterone, but an abnormality of the peripheral androgen

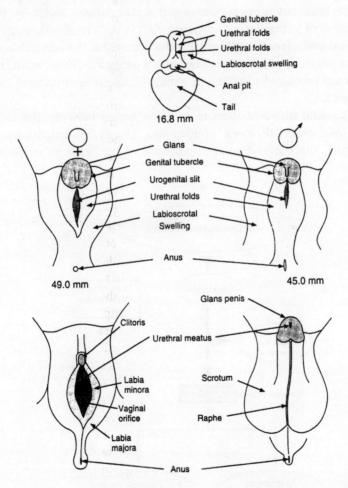

FIGURE 5.3.   Differentiation of male and female external genitalia from a common genital ridge

receptors results in impairment of testosterone action. A complete block in either testosterone production or action results in a female external phenotype.

Virilization of a genetic female can occur with biosynthetic defects in the pathways leading to the production of cortisol and aldosterone within the adrenal gland (e.g. congenital adrenal hyperplasia). Via negative-feedback pathways, the pituitary gland in the brain attempts to increase the low cortisol levels by the secretion of a stimulatory hormone, ACTH. ACTH stimulates both cortisol and adrenal androgen production within the adrenal, and, in the presence of a block in the cortisol pathway, excessive androgens are produced resulting in a male hormone environment (see Figure 5.4).

Gonadal differentiation in humans occurs between the sixth and twenty-fourth week of life, and, clearly, in conditions of intersex, there may be early exposure of the brain to excessive

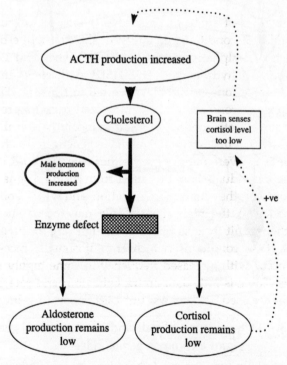

FIGURE 5.4.   Disruption of normal pathways for control of production of cortisol and aldosterone, seen in CAH

androgens in a genetic female, or to insufficient androgen in a genetic male. There is also a postnatal surge of gonadotrophins and hence oestrogen or testosterone, which again may be disrupted in conditions of intersex. At birth, we assign gender and not sex, and it is clearly distressing in cases of genital ambiguity/intersex when gender cannot immediately be determined. By studying individuals with these conditions, we can try to understand the consequences to the developing brain of a reversed hormonal environment. The potential effects on role-play, sexual behaviour, orientation, and gender identity are considered later. One must remember, however, that it is impossible to remove completely the environmental consequences of having been born with ambiguous genitalia, especially if corrective genital surgery is required.

Disorders of intersex

As an illustration of some of the above points, let us consider three examples of conditions of intersex. The first is the biosynthetic defects of 5-alpha-reductase (5α-R) deficiency and 17-beta-hydroxysteroid dehydrogenase (17β-HSD) deficiency. In 5α-R deficiency, testosterone cannot be converted to DHT; in 17β-HSD deficiency, testosterone cannot be synthesized from its precursor androstenedione. Both conditions result in incomplete virilization (or feminization) of the external genitalia in genetic males. In cases where there is a severe deficiency of either enzyme (5α-R or 17β-HSD), these individuals may be raised from birth as females. At puberty, however, they undergo virilization, and within some cultures a change to the male gender role may occur such that they lead their adult lives as males. Although rare in the general population, these conditions (which are autosomally recessively inherited) occur with increased frequency in some highly inbred populations. There is little data on the behaviour and role-play of these children raised as females, but case reports by Imperato-McGinley and co- workers suggest that many of these individuals are considered unambiguously to be females until the time of puberty (Imperato-McGinley et al., 1979a, 1979b).

Environmental and social factors are clearly very important. An isolated community within the Dominican Republic has a high prevalence of 5α-R deficiency (1:90 males) and was described by Imperato-McGinley and co-workers (1979a). Within this society affected individuals were nicknamed *"guevedoche"* ("eggs [testicles/balls] at 12 years": John Money, personal communication, 1998), and they were expected to change their gender role at puberty. They never questioned their core identity as female prepubertally, the subsequent genital and physiological changes under the influence of male sex hormones providing the basis of their change of gender identity (facilitated by culture and their environment). (See chapter six for further anthropological detail.)

The second example is congenital adrenal hyperplasia (CAH), in which an affected genetic female will experience virilization (or masculinization) of her genitalia as a consequence of an enzyme block within the adrenal gland as previously described. Genetic females are exposed to high levels of androgen prenatally, resulting in genital ambiguity often requiring genital surgery. The timing of initial surgery is towards the end of the first year of life, which can be difficult for some parents. The nature of the surgery required depends on the degree of virilization, but usually the surgeon will at least need to reduce the size of the clitoris. This is done very carefully to preserve the delicate supply of nerves and blood vessels to the tip such that normal sexual relationships can be enjoyed in the future. The vaginal entrance may also need to be opened, and further surgery may be required after puberty to ensure adequate function. Medical treatment with replacement cortisol (hydrocortisone) will correct the low cortisol levels and stop the pituitary gland from secreting ACTH. This will usually switch off the adrenal production of male hormones (androgens), but inappropriate replacement or poor compliance may result in high post-pubertal androgens and further virilization. Extensive studies of these individuals show an increased preponderance of tomboyishness and rough-and-tumble play, and there is a preference for the games and toys of boys (literature review by Collaer & Hines, 1995). Females with CAH also may experience homosexual fantasies, and a percentage will have a homosexual orientation as an adult. However, their core identity as female is never questioned either pre- or post-pubertally.

The final example is that of complete androgen insensitivity syndrome (CAIS), a condition in which, despite the presence of adequate testosterone production in a genetic male, the external genitalia develop entirely along the female line as a result of the androgen receptors being unable to respond to testosterone (see above). Again, these patients may require surgical reconstruction for a functioning vagina in later life, and some female attributes they will never acquire as they are infertile and never menstruate. Despite high levels of androgen both pre- and postnatally, children with CAIS have play and behaviour appropriate to the female role. They have complete acceptance of a female core identity and very few have homosexual fantasies (Collaer & Hines, 1995). It is interesting to speculate that this indicates an abnormality also in the CNS androgen receptor, as prenatally they are exposed to normal male levels of circulating androgen.

In summary, in the presence of apparently normal male or female genitalia, the sex of rearing is not usually questioned by the individual even if there has been prenatal or pre-pubertal exposure to the contrary hormonal environment. Genetic males initially raised as females may switch to male typical behaviour and male gender identity at puberty, but only in the presence of functional androgen surges, significant virilization, and the appropriate environment/culture. Sexual orientation may be influenced by hormonal environment, but core identity is probably not affected by gonadal steroids. As a general rule, regardless of genetic or gonadal sex, individuals with disorders of intersex usually become heterosexual with respect to their sex of rearing provided that gender assignment is made before the age of 3 years.

A poignant quote from Ruth Bleier (1984), a neurobiologist and feminist, states: "Gender must seem a fragile and arbitrary thing if it depends on plastic surgery." This statement underlines the importance of counselling both the parents and (at an appropriate time) the child when surgery has been necessary to "correct " the genitalia to conform to the assigned gender.

* * *

Turning now to homosexuality and transsexuality, the factors influencing these states can be divided into neuroanatomical/ structural, hormonal, genetic, and environmental. The majority of biological research has centred around the first three factors, and only these are examined further here.

Homosexuality

The traditional (but not necessarily accurate) animal model upon which much human research has been based is the rat. Human sexuality and sexual orientation have been no exception to this.

Neuroanatomical/structural

The area of the hypothalamus within the rat brain shows clear areas of sexual dimorphism, particularly with respect to the size of certain hypothalamic nuclei. The sexually dimorphic nucleus of the pre-optic area (SDN-POA) is known to be twice the size in adult males as in adult females, and in the male it increases at birth under the influence of androgens. The nucleus does not, however, increase in size in the castrate male but will increase in a female exposed to androgen. In the male, the size is proportional to sexual behaviour/activity.

As in humans, the rat hypothalamus is the higher centre of control for reproduction and sexual function. The rat hypothalamus, under the control of neurotransmitters, produces gonadotrophin-releasing hormone (GnRH) which stimulates the pituitary gland to produce luteinizing hormone (LH) and follicular stimulating hormone (FSH). Unlike humans, however, LH and FSH are secreted in a sexually dimorphic pattern, being pulsatile in the male rat and continuous in the female (Figure 5.5). Early (prenatal) hormonal influences are thought to be organizational and irreversible, whereas later (adolescent/adult) hormonal manipulations are considered to be activational and the changes experienced reverse when the hormonal environment is altered (Collaer & Hines, 1995). Also, as in humans, the rat experiences a pre- and postnatal surge of LH, FSH, and hence sex hormones (oestradiol/testosterone), and, at least in the rat, sex steroids clearly continue to modify the structure of the hypothalamus until puberty by disrupting/altering the hormonal environment and influencing sexual behaviour. Mating behaviour of rats is affected by exposure to hormones before birth. Males that receive insufficient androgen display stereotypically female postures, whereas females that receive an excess of androgen engage in stereotypically male posturing (Byne, 1994). However, extrapolating such data as altered sexual orientation is fraught with difficulties. Byne in a review considered the example of a male mounting a female rat: both will be considered hetero-sexual. However, if a male mounts a male, the top male rat is considered heterosexual whereas the bottom male rat is considered homosexual. Similarly, with female mounting female, the top fe-male rat is considered homosexual and the bottom female rat het-erosexual (Byne, 1994).

Studies of hypothalamic nuclei in humans by several groups have shown sexually dimorphic groups of cells, described as the interstitial nuclei of the anterior hypothalamus (INAH). There are four distinct groups of these cells, assigned as INAH 1–4. LeVay (1991) described no sex difference between the volumes of Groups

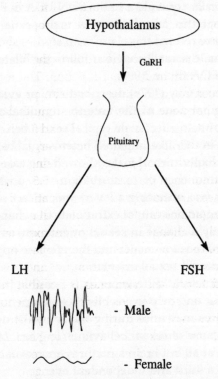

FIGURE 5.5. Pattern of secretion of LH and FSH from the rat pituitary, under hypothalamic control

1, 2, and 4 but showed INAH 3 to be larger in heterosexual men than in women and also showed the nuclei of homosexual men to have volumes comparable to those of women. Earlier studies by Swaab and Fliers (1985) and Allen, Hines, Shryne, and Gorski (1989), however, had shown results that conflicted with these, and to date there have been no studies verifying the findings of LeVay (1991). Also, as the majority of patients (both homo- and heterosexual) studied by LeVay had died of AIDS-related diseases, it is difficult to be sure of what the influence of either the effect of terminal AIDS or an altered hormonal environment may have been on the size of these nuclei. However, LeVay claims to have controlled for these factors, stating that the differences in INAH 3 volumes found by his group provide evidence for a biological substrate for sexual orientation. Another criticism of this work made by Byne (1994) is against the claim that the INAH 3 region is actually anatomically equivalent to the SDN-POA in the rat hypothalamus and that this area influences male sexual behaviour. Other workers have refuted this claim with studies showing a lack of any effect on male sexual behaviour following bilateral destruction of the SDN-POA (Byne, 1994).

Slimp, Hart, and Goy (1978) described similar evidence in the primate. The medial zone of the anterior hypothalamus (above INAH 3) was shown to affect male typical sexual behaviour in the monkey. Lesions in this area impaired heterosexual behaviour but not sexual drive. Experimental males showed decreased mounting of females, but frequency of masturbation was unchanged and access to females (via operating a lever) was in fact sought more often. However, again one cannot extrapolate this change in sexual behaviour to imply a change in sexual orientation, as these monkeys had no access to fellow males and therefore no opportunity to demonstrate an altered sexual orientation.

In terms of structural differences, it is possible that these are present in early life and help to establish sexual orientation. Alternatively, differences may arise during the course of development into adult life because of sexual behaviour/feelings, or there may be no connection at all but brain structures and sexual orientation may be linked to a third and independent event.

Hormonal

Research into human sexual dimorphism in terms of hormonal feedback mechanisms is no longer active, but in the 1970s there was great interest in the observation initially of Doerner, Rohde, Stahl, Krell, and Masius (1975) that homosexual males showed a similar positive estradiol-LH discharge to that seen in females. In adult females, ovulation occurs following a surge of LH as a consequence of positive feedback by oestradiol. Adult heterosexual males do not show an LH surge in response to oestradiol, but it was claimed that this was seen in homosexual males; it was argued that this was because their brains were inadequately masculinized (or feminized). Low levels of testosterone were also documented in homosexuals. However, subsequent research has provided conflicting results, and Gooren, van Kessel, and Harmsen-Louman (1984) finally disproved this theory by failing to confirm the previous findings in either homosexual or transsexual men or in transsexual women. It was subsequently shown that there was no sexual dimorphism of this feedback loop in either primates or humans. To take the argument further, if this system was feminized in homosexuals, then it would logically be masculinized in lesbians who would then lose the ability to menstruate or to be fertile. Clearly this has not proven to be the case.

Genetic

In 1991, Bailey provided evidence for a genetic link to male homosexuality by twin studies. In families with a homosexual proband, the concordance for homosexuality was found to be 52% in monozygotic (identical) twins, 22% in dizygotic (non-identical) twins, 9.2% in biological brothers, and 11% in adopted brothers (Bailey & Pillard, 1991). This study, however, arrives at paradoxical conclusions, as the incidence in biological brothers should equal that of non-identical twins, and it is difficult to explain why an adopted brother should have a higher incidence than a biological brother and, indeed, a higher incidence than seen in the general population (1%–5 %).

Environmental factors are very difficult to control for, and there have been very few studies on twins raised apart. Two studies looking at two pairs of identical twins found concordance for homosexuality in one pair; a larger study, looking at lesbian sisters, found no concordance in twins raised apart.

Hamer and co-workers (1993) observed a high incidence of homosexuality in maternal male relatives, suggesting an X-linked mode of inheritance, as the X chromosome has to have been inherited from the mother. Linkage analysis of the X chromosome showed a genetic marker at the end of the long arm of the X chromosome in the region of Xq28 which seemed to be shared by a higher percentage of gay brothers than would be expected by chance. The theoretical probability of two sons receiving a copy of the same Xq28 from their mother is 50%, and Hamer's group found that of 40 pairs of gay siblings, 33 instead of the expected 20 had received the same Xq28 region from the mother. However, it is important to stress that each member of the 33 concordant sibling pairs shared his Xq28 region only with his brother and not with any of the other 32 pairs. No single specific Xq28 sequence has been identified, and so far a "gay gene" has not been discovered. Initially, Hamer looked only at gay brothers but subsequently studied heterosexual brothers and lesbian sisters. In heterosexual brothers, they found a low concordance Xq28 of 22%. Linkage analysis for the Xq28 markers in lesbiansibship families was not suggestive of a link with sexual orientation, as one would predict from an X-linked study. No other group has to date been able to reproduce Hamer's data.

Perhaps the major finding of these twin studies is that despite having all of their genes in common and having prenatal and postnatal environments as close to identical as possible, approximately half the identical twins were nonetheless discordant for sexual orientation. What relevance, if any, genetic markers play is currently not known. It is possible that particular DNA sequences might somehow cause the brain to be wired specifically for homosexual orientation or perhaps a particular genetic make-up may predispose an individual to homosexuality, either in combination with a specific set of personality traits or in response to some external environmental event.

Transsexualism (gender identity disorder)

Once again, human research has taken its cue from the rodent model. Zhou and co-workers (1995) identified an area of the human hypothalamus known as the central bed nucleus of the stria terminalis (BSTc), the size of which in male-to-female transsexuals was the same as that found in females, and which was significantly larger in heterosexual men. No data are given for female-to-male transsexuals.

In the rat, the equivalent area receives fibres from the pre-optic nucleus of the hypothalamus and is sexually dimorphic. There is, again, gonadal (sex steroid) regulation of the size of these nuclei, and they contain both oestrogen and androgen receptors. Also, this nucleus has been shown to affect sexual behaviour in the rat.

In adult humans, the volume of the BSTc showed no regulation by changes in sex hormone environment, and there was no correlation with sexual orientation. Thus there is a mismatch between physical/sexual development and brain development. Zhou's group postulated further that gender identity disorder was a consequence of an altered interaction between the developing brain and sex hormones, possibly facilitated by genetic and environmental factors.

Once again, this study is arguably suspect, in that the majority of the patients had died of AIDS-related diseases and it is known that the endocrine environment in terminal AIDS is markedly abnormal. In addition, little is known of the potential effect of any contrary sex steroids and anti-androgen therapy being received by the transsexual men. As yet, no other group has reproduced these data.

Finally, one cannot consider the biological aspects of transsexualism without considering the impact on sexual function. Transsexuals, or individuals with GID, lie at the extreme ends of the sexual spectrum, and, in order to function completely in the opposite gender, they require to have the ability to have sexual intercourse. If one considers the biological male castrate with an artificial vagina, or the biological female chemically castrate with a prosthetic phallus, then clearly there are difficulties which in some individuals are almost insurmountable and which may require alternative sexual activity for gratification.

Greek mythology gives us an opinion on this rather un-discussed aspect of gender identity disorder. In Ovid's *Metamorphosis*, Teiresias the Theban was transformed into a woman for seven years for killing the female of a pair of snakes. Subsequently, the gods Hera and Zeus asked Teiresias the question as to whether a man or woman derives greater pleasure from love. Teiresias' answer caused him to be struck blind by Hera, but to be granted long life with the gift of prophecy by Zeus (whose view he had supported).

Conclusion

Thus we have accumulating data on the role of contrary hormonal influences on the developing human brain. From studies of patients with disorder of intersex, it would appear that humoral influences alone are usually insufficient to affect core-gender identity but may influence gender-determined behaviour and, rarely, sexual orientation (see chapter eleven for a discussion of the clinical issues of intersex disorders).

In cases of atypical sexual orientation and in gender identity disorder, we have tantalizing research that suggests that structural, early humoral, and genetic factors may predispose to an alteration in sexual orientation or in gender identity. It is not clear, however, whether any of the specific structural differences so far demonstrated are predisposing factors in their own right, or whether they are a result of some environmental factor or independent external event which itself is the main source of the gender identity disorder. It is likely that, as in many areas of medicine, an individual's core-gender identity and sexual orientation evolve as a consequence of many complex factors on the background of genetic predisposition and humoral conditioning. Further reproducible data from ongoing research is clearly needed before we can attempt to understand fully this fascinating conundrum.

CHAPTER SIX

The contribution of social anthropology to the understanding of atypical gender identity in childhood

Allison James

Writing about the Inuit of the Arctic, the social anthropologist Jean Briggs notes a dramatic instance of what she regards as the Inuits' response to the precariousness of their physical and social environment. Living in a land icebound and swept by bitter winds, the Inuit are ever alert to changes in the natural world and, through powerfully dangerous games, teach their children always to expect the unexpected: the Inuit world, she says, is "a place where little can be taken for granted, where answers are not fixed and nothing is ever permanently knowable" (1986, p. 2). The unpredictability of life in the Arctic circle also engenders, for the Inuit, a cultural response in which everything and everybody is regarded as possessed of shifting and multiple qualities and to represent multiple, adaptable possibilities. Nowhere is this cultural perception more apparent than in the practice of changing a child's gender. As Briggs notes:

> I was told about it on Baffin Island and saw it in the Central Arctic, but the best descriptions exist for Labrador and for east Greenland. In such cases the decision is made at birth to bring up the infant as a member of the opposite sex; boys may be

raised as girls and vice versa. Sometimes this is done in order
to reincarnate a dead child or another relative and sometimes
it is done because the parents wanted a child of the opposite
sex from the infant, often for practical reasons. If all the previous children had been girls, a new hunter would be needed; or
if the previous children had been boys the first priority might
be to have another helper in the home. Such children are
dressed and groomed as members of the opposite sex and
taught the skills of that sex. Cross-sexed upbringing sometimes ends at puberty; in other cases, individuals may retain
their cross-sexed identities for their entire lives. [p. 5]

As an account of human adaptability, these practices cannot surely
be bettered, and yet their real significance does not lie here. Rather,
the social practices of the Inuit raise important questions about the
cultural shaping of social identity and of gender socialization in
particular.

Working from within an anthropological perspective to develop this theme, this chapter sets out the contribution that a
cross-cultural approach can make to questions of atypical gender
identity. In brief, this can be summarized as follows: through its
stress on comparative ethnographic fieldwork, anthropology furnishes us with a useful cultural relativism that allows us to consider the ways in which culture shapes and is itself shaped by the
activities and understandings of people, from the most intimate of
bodily concerns to the most global of economic systems. In relation
to questions of atypical gender identity, such a comparative approach can explore the varied and different ways in which sexuality and gender are understood in other cultures and, in so doing,
can underscore the importance of disengaging concepts of sex from
those of gender. It is this sociological distinction that, it is argued,
provides a firm baseline for exploring more specifically how "gender" is enacted, rather than simply displayed, by children in specific social contexts. That is to say, it highlights the importance of
the social context in shaping our understanding of gender as something that is not given, but, rather, learnt. To foreshadow the conclusion: that in many parts of the world male and female are not
seen as the only possible gender identities and that they need not
be regarded as mutually exclusive is a valuable lesson to be drawn
from the comparative approach to the study of human behaviour

and societies offered by social anthropology. In particular, it provides a broader framework within which to understand and thereby possibly ameliorate the problems encountered by children with atypical gender identity in Western societies.

Sex, gender, and sexuality

The concept of atypical gender identity raises particular problems for social scientists, for, it could be asked, what is less open to interpretation and recasting than sexual identity? The division of humankind into male and female would, through the capacity to reproduce, appear to be the most fundamental and unalterable building blocks of human societies everywhere. Sexual dimorphism would seem to have to be a taken-for-granted. However, both historical and cross-cultural material furnishes us with examples that suggest that that is far from the case. As discussed in more detail below, some peoples recognize the possibility of a third gender, and in Western societies, until the late eighteenth century, popular and medical science assumed that there was only one. The female was regarded as but a rendering of the male. That such interpretative variations occur suggests, then, that "gender identity" may be a more important marker of personhood and self-identity than anatomical sexual identity. The implications of this are not unimportant.

However, in order to explore these issues further it is necessary, at the outset, to clarify some definitions, because it is precisely matters of classification and naming that are at the heart of the matter. In this chapter, therefore, the phrase "biological sexual identity" will be used to refer to the ways in which the body is located in terms of its being anatomically male, female, or, as explored below, a third sex which lies somewhere between these two. "Gender identity", on the other hand, will refer to the ways in which cultural ideas of how it is be a man, a woman, or indeed an "in-between" are read off people's bodies and read into what people do—how they are called, how they behave, how they think about themselves. Two important points follow on from this distinction. First, that sex does not determine gender accounts for the variation to be found in gender roles cross-culturally; for example, it explains how in some societies men may adopt more nurturing kinds of behaviour than women, while women adopt more aggressive roles. Originally explored in depth in Mead's (1935) classic cross-cultural account of sex and temperament, there is by now widespread acceptance that although a sexual division of labour may be commonly found in all societies there is no universal patterning of tasks or behaviours according to sex. Second, that sex does not determine gender can be seen in the fact that, though so common as to be regarded as inseparable, there is in fact no necessary connection or causal relationship between the two: in the case of transsexuality, for example, a man (defined anatomically as such) may nonetheless regard himself and act as if he were a woman in terms of gender role. Similarly, anatomically defined females may live and act as men.

In thus radically divorcing "sex" from "gender", the field of possibility becomes much wider than might be commonly acknowledged in Western societies, where the two are more often regarded as having an intimate, causal relationship, with any deviation being seen as aberrant and potentially stigmatizing. This was, until fairly recently, clearly the case with respect to homosexuality. In other cultures such discrepancies are far less problematic, and, while homosexuality may be frowned upon, the existence of alternative sex and gender possibilities permits so-called "deviations" from the norm to become more normalized.

The example of the hijras of India is a case in point. Hijras are a religious community of men who dress and act like women and for whom commitment to the role of hijra is signified through their impotence as men, an impotence achieved usually through the act of castration. As children, they will often have shown an interest in playing with girls, with wearing female rather than male clothing and using eye make-up; they may themselves at the age of 11 or 12 years decide to adopt the hijra role or come to it later in their teens or, as in some documented cases (Nanda, 1990), have the role of hijra suggested to them by their parents. Hijras themselves say that they were born this way, but it is clear that, while some individuals may indeed have been born with abnormal male genitals, the majority deliberately remake their bodies as "not male" in their late teens or early adulthood. However, unlike many Western transsexuals, after castration the majority do not then go on to remake these bodies as female through vaginoplasty or the use of hormonal therapy. In suggesting why this might be, Gilbert Herdt puts forward the strong case that central to the hijra identity is their very in-betweenness—their being neither man nor woman is what being a hijra is.

It is in this sense, Herdt (1996a) argues, that the hijras represent a third sex and third gender, for although hijras bear passing resemblance to the role of eunuch for example, there is a fundamental difference. Though castrated and with certain privileges denied to other men—such as the freedom to mix with women or, as in the Byzantine Empire, a deliberate choice made to enhance social status—the eunuch is still regarded as a man. This is not the case with the hijras caste. They do not see themselves as either men or women, a perception further strengthened by evidence from those minority of hijras who were literally born with ambiguous sexual characteristics. Many of these people were assigned sex as females at birth on the basis of anatomical presentation, and they were raised as females until puberty. However, following the development of male secondary sexual characteristics at puberty, or their failure to develop female ones, these individuals do not adopt a male identity. Instead, they adopt the status of hijra. Thus, as Nanda (1990) observes, "where western culture strenuously attempts to resolve sexual contradiction and ambiguities by denial or segregation, Hinduism appears content to allow opposites to confront each other without resolution" (p. 23).

As both Herdt (1996a) and Nanda (1990, 1996) describe, Hinduism as a religious philosophy is replete with images of the possibility of a third sex at the same time as it claims the complementarity of male and female roles. These are enshrined principally in the figure of Siva. In Hindu mythology, Siva incorporates both male and female characteristics but is seen in an ascetic role. However, though perceived to have renounced sex, Siva is, nonetheless, central to erotic and procreative rituals, with his most powerful symbol being the linga or phallus which is always set in the yoni, or symbol of female genitalia.

Clearly, the Indian example of the hijras cannot offer Western societies a "solution" or "model" that would be feasible or even desirable to adopt. The fact that in Indian culture there *is* the possibility of a third gender is a function of the historical, cultural role that hijras have traditionally played within Hindu mythology as well as everyday social life. They have, for example, a specific economic niche as dancers at weddings and are invited to attend to ensure the fertility of the newly married couple. The discussion here simply serves to illustrate a more fundamental point: that claims from sexology for an indisputable and essential linking of sexual and gender identity and of the necessity of sexual dimorphism are overdrawn.

Further evidence to support this claim can be drawn from Gilbert Herdt's (1996b) reinterpretation of the classic 1970s study of the hermaphrodite disorder, 5-alpha reductase deficiency syndrome (see chapter five for a discussion of this syndrome), in the Dominican Republic (see also chapter two). Briefly, normal males in rural areas were mistaken as females at birth and raised as "normal" girls until puberty, when they were said suddenly to change their gender roles and to begin acting and identifying themselves as men. The claim was made that this was evidence of "masculinized brains" which were dependent upon prenatal hormones and that this compelled them spontaneously to turn towards their "natural" sex. This was in direct contrast to the alternative earlier claim, made by Money et al. (1955, cited in Herdt, 1996b) among others, that social environment was the key to the development of unambiguous gender identity and that sex assignment needed to be made before a child was 2½ years old to avoid pathological development. Leaving aside the clinical issues in this debate, Herdt's argument is that, in the discussions that followed, the possibility of a third sex was never raised. The Dominican Republic case was simply regarded as yet another example of "mistaken" sexual identity.

Reviewing the evidence, and making comparisons with another group—the Sambia of Papua New Guinea—Herdt (1996b, based on Money, 1976) argues that although the ethnographic evidence is patchy, what has been missed in all the accounts is recognition of *guevedoche* (the local term used for these people) as a cultural system. The literal translation of this term is "eggs [meaning testicles or balls] at 12" (John Money, personal communication, 1998), and, as noted in the reports made at the time, these individuals were not only distinguished as different through this special name, but also often ridiculed by townspeople as *machihembra*—first woman, then man. Their anatomical differences had been noted within the local community, and the *guevedoche* regarded themselves as incomplete persons. In effect, argues Herdt, within local cosmology these people occupied a third sex category or classification. To support this suggestion, Herdt looks more generally at Caribbean images of gender inequality, arguing that given the emphasis on machismo, and the higher political and economic status that men have over women, it is not surprising that the majority—given the choice—swapped to a male gender role at puberty. Transformation to a male-aspiring third sex would allow these individuals on occasion to pass as men and must surely be a better option than remaining a non-fertile female. As Herdt notes: "*Guevedoche* are not so confused as to forget that by sex assignment they were not male: that is why villagers call them *guevedoche*" (1996b, p. 430).

A contrasting example is that of the Sambia of New Guinea who, though admitting the possibility of a third sex, do not, however, recognize a third gender. Classed as *turnim-man*, such individuals would, in Western terminology, be regarded as intersexed people or hermaphrodites. Sambia society is characterized by a rigid gender dimorphism, with women thought of as early maturers and naturally fertile. Men, on the other hand, are considered to mature late and to not produce semen naturally. They must be ritually inseminated (by older men in boyhood) to ensure semen production: "the ritual function of homosexual fellatio, then, is to consume sperm and thereby produce maleness" (Herdt, 1996b, p. 434). Thus those intersexed persons assigned to female at birth on the basis of a particular "reading" of their biological sexual identity and raised as females will never be properly masculinized. Already defined as female, they will not take part in such male rituals. Those who, on the other hand, are recognized as hermaphrodite at birth are assigned the status of *turnim-man* or *kwolu-aatmwol*, "turning into a man", and raised in the direction of masculinity; though a biological male sexual identity might be unclear, parents know that they will not become female and be able to bear children. However, these individuals, Herdt claims, are not regarded as fully male either; they are *turnim-man*, classed as a third sex, and rarely, if ever, undergo the full series of initiation rites that, for the Sambia, turn boys into men; that is, they are not permitted to take part in the rituals that turn anatomical males into men who are then able to perform masculine social roles. Thus, though the Sambia recognize a third sex, there is no third gender possibility comparable with that of the hijras in India.

One final set of illustrations provides yet more evidence of the importance of separating out sex from gender. Cross-cultural evidence from Native American Plains Indians, where traditionally there existed a strong sexual division of labour, nonetheless points to the existence of the acceptability of three kinds of gender crossing: (1) *berdaches*, men who took on feminine roles; (2) manly hearted women who acted like men; and (3) women chiefs who adopted a role normally only allocated to men. Among the Hua of New Guinea, on the other hand, gender assignment can vary through life. As Meigs (1990) argues, the Hua believe that the body contains a life-giving substance called *nu*, which can be both lost and gained in different ways across the life course and be passed between people. The differences between men and women are said to depend upon the amount of *nu* that a person's body has at any point in time. Gender ascription in Hua society is based, therefore, not only on anatomical distinctions but on the quantity of *nu*. Thus not only are males and females recognized, but there are two additional ritual classificatory categories of person—*figapa* and *kakora*—which represent indeterminate categories of gender. The term *figapa* is used for people whose bodies are seen to contain an excess of feminine substances: old men who have acquired *nu* through a lifetime of sexual contact with women; post-menopausal women who have not had more than three children and whose bodies therefore contain excessive amounts of *nu*, for *nu* can be dissipated through sexual activity; children of either sex who have been in close contact with women; and fertile, child-bearing women. *Kakora*, on the other hand, refers to those whose bodies contain little *nu*: for example, initiated males who have little contact with women, and post-menopausal women who have had many children. In Hua society, therefore, gender is neither fixed nor constant and need not bear any relation to anatomical differences.

Sex lessons, gendered learning

The importance of the evidence presented above lies not simply, or even, in its ethnographic curiosity, but in the lessons it provides for future practical work with children of atypical gender identity. First, it underlines the importance of developing a more liberal classification of gender categories through recognition that they are indeed *social* rather than natural classifications, arising from and through social action rather than immanent in the natural world. Second, given the social groundedness of gender, it is important to explore sociologically exactly how it is that children learn to classify their own and other children's behaviour *as* gendered. That there are lessons to be learnt from societies where more flexible sex and gender categories are recognized is noted by Herdt (1996):

> What counts is not anatomical sex as an objective fact but the cultural meaning of sex assignment in the symbolic world and its treatment of the person. The infant's anatomical ambiguity creates a horrific deficit only in a two-sex cultural category system like ours. In a three-sex system, with its more indistinct boundaries, the person's sex and identity are reckoned in relation to a more complex sexual code and social field having three alternative socialisation regimes and outcomes, each of which is known to be historically coherent: male, female and hermaphroditic. In this sense these persons are not "mistaken females" but ... third genders. The ... three-category system provides for greater fluidity in post pubertal gender-identity transition into adult roles. It is to the inherent social advantage of the hermaphrodite to "switch" from a mistaken female-defined to a male-defined hermaphrodite, once the person enters an adult career, because the power dynamics of gender roles in both [the Dominican Republic and Papua New Guinea] create such motivations. [p. 442]

With respect to Western societies, research on behalf of intersexed children or children who are homosexual should explore, then, the ways in which cultural gender boundaries are enacted during childhood, identifying those arenas of intolerance where having an ambiguous sex and/or gender identity might threaten to become problematic. Only then might any positive changes become possible.

In this respect, the social sciences have an important contribution to make. For example, in his classic study of "Agnes", an intersexed person, Garfinkel (1967) notes that Western society "prohibits wilful or random movements from one sex status to another" (p. 125), and in an earlier publication (James, 1993) I note that sexual ambiguity is recognized as problematic by children as young as 5 or 6 years: children learn to take on quite rigid gendered identities early on in their school life through the temporal and spatial structures of its social environment. Specific examples are discussed below, but what is important to note at the outset is that integral to this acquisition of a gendered identity is the recognition that there is such a thing as gendered behaviour. Central to this is the acquisition of bodily knowledge, of how to use one's body in an appropriately gendered manner.

In the earlier work cited above (James, 1993), it was argued that children who, through illness or disease, have bodies that differ may, nonetheless, dissuade other children from recognizing this difference through particular styles of social action. In essence this means achieving a fine balance in what one does between individuality and conformity: one must belong, but with flair. More recently (James, in press), these ideas have been developed in a consideration of just how this body-work is achieved, and I have suggested that children work with and on their bodies to make them look *as if* they were bodies of another kind. This is not just a matter of what Goffman (1963) terms "passing" (covering a scar, taking medication to control epileptic seizures) or more simply a pretence to avoid stigmatization. For example, a child caught out in revealing his or her ignorance will often claim, "I used to know but I've forgotten". Less obviously strategic, it is a matter of learning to embody one's body in particular ways. This practice is common to all children—not just to those with a potential stigma.

Turning to the work of the sociologist Chris Shilling (1993), it is possible to account for this body-work. Shilling has suggested that our bodies are unfinished at birth and that it is through social action that they are completed, a process most evident in, for example, the emphasis placed by different cultures and at different historical periods on women's body shape (Turner, 1992). It can also be seen in the cultural styling of ways of walking or the expression of emotion (Mauss, 1938). These provocative ideas raise the question that, if this really is the case, then it is surely in childhood that this learning is most assiduous, for the rapidity of physiological changes that the body undergoes at this time makes cultural conformity the more urgent.

Field material suggests that children learn to "finish" their body in socially appropriate ways primarily through negotiating how others read their bodies. The following example reveals how "gender" is read off the body.*

Nine-year-old "Elaine" was a tall girl with a dominant and powerful personality. The other children were cautious of her bad temper and few would dare to cross her in playground disputes. If it was her turn to be "it"—the chaser—in games of Tig, and Elaine did not want that role, she would be excused and another child would take her place. Her friendships with other girls were extremely volatile:

Helen: "Some times if you don't do it [what she wants], she blows her lid. She says: 'You don't have to be so selfish' and that. She's a bit all right, but sometimes she says, because she ain't got them [a particular pair of shoes] she says: 'Oh, they're horrible'."

And that this is an atypical female social self—bold, assertive, and dominating—was somehow thought by her friends to be reflected in an atypical female body. This is clear from her other friend Claire's description:

Claire: "Say she's got a ring on and you went like that ... [squeezes her hand] really hard, it wouldn't hurt her a bit because she's ... she comes from a tough family really, her dad was a boxer. That's where she gets her tough hands.

---

*This research was carried out in a primary school in Central England between 1988 and 1990 with children aged between 4 and 9 years, and was conducted through the use of participant observation and more formal qualitative methods.

Well, they're soft but they are really hard. She's stronger
than me. When we do weighing in Maths she has like three
kilos on her hand and does like weight lifting."

Elaine looks *as if* she has tough hands. Although her hands are
in fact soft—as soft as any other girl's hands, indeed as soft as
Claire's—the manner in which she uses her body makes them
appear *as if* they are really hard: "Well, they're soft but they are
really hard", says Claire. Thus Elaine effectively negotiates her
way past the gender stereotypes that normally would constrict her
bodily behaviour by using her body—through loud, assertive behaviour—*as if* it were the body of a boy.

Through bodily negotiation, appearances can indeed be made
deceptive, something that the girls in the example noted wryly
about the failure of some boys they knew to negotiate successfully
the limitations of their bodies. Commenting on the behaviour of
her male classmates, Christine, for example, observed that: "They
act tough. We know they are weak but they act tough. We see their
weaknesses." Such social weaknesses are literally visible upon the
surfaces of the boys' bodies: in fights and arguments their faces
redden in the same instant that they vociferously deny being hurt.
Tears well up in their eyes.

It is clear, then, that children's body-work relies upon two
kinds of seeing: first, looking at the bodies of others and interpreting the information gained to judge the status of one's own body
and, second, making one's own body look or seem *"as if"* it were
another kind of body. Thus it is that, in the classroom, children
who wish to gain favours from their teachers will straighten their
backs, fold their arms, look straight ahead, and sit still: they
present their bodies for view *"as if"* they were the bodies of those
who are orderly and well behaved. But these are the very same
bodies that in the playground must later be made to look unruly,
as if they can run fast, jump high, and fight well.

Just as they learn the broad contours of bodily style, children
also learn that bodies are gendered, and they must begin literally
to en-gender their own bodies early on in their school careers.
Field material reveals the mundane everydayness of this learning.

In the reception class, a group of four boys refused to wear
pink painting overalls, while others laughed at boys with long

and curly hair; little girls played at marriage, alternately kissing and admonishing their boy-husbands and excluding them
from the Wendy House. Long (blonde) hair was regarded by
the girls as a girl's right, and thus Susie wept when hers was
cut severely short. That it is, in part, children's culture which
sustains these stereotypes was evidenced by the fact that when
non-sexist lessons and toys were introduced at the school, it
was to the Cindy doll table that the little boys eagerly escaped.
Sanctioned by the teaching staff to step outside the masculine
role, they dressed and undressed the dolls with pleasure, while
the girls tapped out their names on the computer screen. However, by the age of 6 or 7 years traditional gendered roles are so
embedded within the school that, at playtime, it is as if an
invisible wall divides the playground: girls play skipping or
chanting games in twos or threes on the edges of the playground, while boys monopolize the central space with loud
and boisterous games of Tig. But this is not to say that boys and
girls never meet or share their games or that outside the school
context gendered roles are as strong. As Amy described to me,
she was friends with David on the way to and from school and
in the street at home, but, at the age of 7, she could never be
seen playing with him in the playground.

Such instances of prescriptive gendered behaviour—which I
have merely sketched in with these examples—are legion and have
been previously well documented in the literature (Thorne, 1993).
Of more interest is to ask how and why some children refuse these
gendered boundaries, either through a deliberate choice to flout
them or through non-recognition of their implicit and strategic
power. The "sissy" and the "tomboy" are perhaps readily identified and identifiable stereotypes of the former route, though the
negativity frequently attached to such role reversals might be seen
to counter such an argument. While a "tomboy" might perceive an
advantage in adopting a more masculine role, given the still pref-
erential male bias within Western cultures, the role of "sissy",
ridiculed by his peers, is surely not one self-ascription to which a
boy might aspire? More problematic still is to explain the seeming
"failure" of some children to heed the gendering of their child
environment at all, particularly at school. Such children find their

bodies being constantly read for clues that reveal a potential ambiguity. For boys, these might include having the wrong kinds of
shoes, wearing "girls'" pants, not being able to swear properly,
having long hair, not playing football, and running slowly. Though
clearly children may not have much choice over some of these
readings—for example, boys may have to wear clothes bought on
their behalf by adults—other body-work would seem to fall much
more under their control. Yet some children seem unable, or are
indeed perhaps unwilling, to learn from the constant critique that
they receive from their school peers. Though at present there is no
definitive answer as to how or why this should be, it is nonetheless
important that the cultural context be acknowledged in any judge-
ments being made about gender identity acquisition. One final
example underlines this point.

> Early on during fieldwork an anxious mother asked me what
> was "wrong" with her elder son: he always plays with girls,
> she told me, and now to her obvious alarm her younger son
> seemed to be following suit. Indeed this was the case: 5-year-
> old Paul was inseparable from Joy and would cry if she refused
> to play with him or left him on his own. But, by the time I
> encountered her older boy, this supposed anomalous behav-
> iour was becoming less problematic. At 9 years old, his close
> friendship with a girl was being re-read by his male peers as a
> sign of an admirable sexual precocity, rather than as, in earlier
> years, a failing masculinity. Tall and strong, though not a foot-
> ball player, Ewan was wise enough to keep close counsel and
> had managed to negotiate his way past their suspicions that he
> was not "lad enough" to belong to the company of boys. They
> left him alone, and the taunts subsided.

Conclusion

Since the late 1970s, social science research with children that ex-
plores both concepts of childhood and children's own views of the
social world have been growing rapidly (James, Jenks, & Prout,
1998). This has led to a consideration of how it is that ideas of the

child are played out for children through everyday socializing interactions and how children themselves respond to these images of who they are or should be. This in turn begs the question of "what is a child?" and underlines the socially constructed character of childhood (James & Prout, 1990; Jenks, 1982). It is quite clear, for example, that ideas about children's vulnerability and dependency, their need for protection, which in British society are understood as axiomatic conditions of childhood—indeed, these may often be framed in terms of developmental and psychological needs—are in other cultural contexts less clear. Children who make important contributions to family income, children who care-take their younger siblings, and children who are soldiers all reveal a competence and range of independent action that, in Western societies, would be seen as certainly un-childlike and may even be characterized as abusive. Acknowledgement of the importance of the social context of the family, the school, and the peer group in children's lives is crucial for our understanding of children's social, physical, and emotional development.

In relation to children of atypical gender identity, it is particularly so—for, as the brief illustrations provided above reveal, the power that children themselves have both to make their own and unmake other people's identities is not inconsiderable. The examples offer glimpses of some of the processes involved, indicating the implicit but everyday body-work that children must perform to make sure that their bodies look and act as if male or female. In Western societies, characterized as they contemporarily are by a strong sexual and gender dimorphism, that children must work to achieve either gender—but certainly not both—is the important issue. But that in childhood this gendering does require work is, I think, clear from the striking parallels to be found between Garfinkel's (1967) account of the intersexed Agnes's transition to a fully female identity and that which characterizes peer-group socialization in childhood. Garfinkel writes that, post-surgery,

> Her constant recourse to self reassessment consisted of continual comparison of anticipated and actual outcomes, of continual monitoring of expectancies and pay offs, with strong efforts to accommodate and to normalise the differences. Agnes expended a great deal of effort upon bringing ever

more areas of her life under conceptual representation and control. Expectations in areas of life that to persons better able than she to take their normal sexuality for granted would appear to be far removed from the concerns of criticism and review of "common sense knowledge" of the society were, for her, matters of active and critical deliberation. [p. 176]

As I have shown here, and elsewhere, it is precisely through similar processes of observation, monitoring, and comparison that children get to know the common-sense world, the world that they must inhabit in the future as adult men and women, for, like Agnes, they cannot take on trust that which, as yet, they know little about.

CHAPTER SEVEN

Some developmental trajectories towards homosexuality, transvestism, and transsexualism: mental health implications

A

Homosexual experience during adolescence

Fiona Tasker

Mental health implications

During their adolescent years, young persons' increasing awareness of erotic attraction, together with their increasing interpersonal sexual experience, raises profound questions concerning the formation of sexual identity. Although sexual identity may be questioned at any point in the life-course, the initial formation during adolescence sets the stage on which later revisions are undertaken. For young people who experience only heterosexual attractions, fantasies, and sexual encounters, how to assimilate these into easily accessible mainstream cultural scripts of sexual behaviour is at least clear, although this process is rarely achieved without some anguish and guilt. In contrast, positive images of lesbian and gay relationships are rarely portrayed in mainstream culture, and young people who have homosexual attractions, fantasies, and sexual encounters may find that their experiences are ignored or at worst regarded negatively. Thus, integrating same-gender sexual experience into the sexual self-image can present a significant challenge to self-esteem and mental well-being.

Certainly issues concerning homosexuality are not unusual in therapy with adolescents, although they may be made manifest in different ways. In some cases homosexuality will be raised as an issue in the referral, because the adolescent himself or herself is concerned about his or her sexual identity. Alternatively, the young person's parents or other adults may raise it as the cause of their concern. In other situations, it may become a subsequent consideration to the presenting problem. In the minority of cases, the adolescent will be certain of his or her homosexual interest and wish to develop a lesbian, gay, or bisexual identity, though his or her sexual attraction is not the result of a choice. However, in many instances the clinician is faced with a young person who is uncertain what direction his or her sexual identity will ultimately take.

It is helpful to place this uncertainty as to the destination of sexual identity within the context of our best estimates of the proportion of the general population who report homosexual relationships. Given the stigmatization of homosexual relations and the consequent need for secrecy, accurately estimating the proportion of adult women and men with lesbian and gay relationships is difficult, and figures vary considerably. In the most recent large-scale British survey (National Survey of Sexual Attitudes and Lifestyles: Wellings, Wadsworth, & Johnson, 1994), 6.1% of men and 3.4% of women aged 16 years and over reported some homosexual experience in their lifetime, but only 1.1% of men and 0.4% of women reported a gay or lesbian relationship in the preceding year. On the other hand, estimates of the proportion of the adult population in the United States identifying as lesbian, gay, or bisexual range from 4% to 17% (Gonsiorek & Weinrich, 1991). However, although many adult lesbians and gay men report having had same-gender sexual experiences in adolescence, others report that they had no homosexual physical contact until adulthood.

While they may have been attracted to others of the same gender as themselves during adolescence, they recalled only heterosexual sexual experiences in their teenage years. This pattern of an overtly heterosexual adolescence is more commonly reported by lesbians (Goggin, 1993).

Paradoxically, many adolescents who will later identify as heterosexual in adulthood have some same-gender sexual experiences while growing up. The proportions of men and women who report having had homosexual encounters during adolescence are greater than the proportions who later develop a gay, bisexual, or lesbian identity; for example, results from Kinsey's original study and more recent studies indicate that up to 30% of males remember some degree of homoerotic attraction or sexual experience (Kinsey, Pomeroy, & Martin, 1948; McConaghy, Armstrong, Birrell, & Buhrich, 1979).

The crucial decision for the adolescent, and for any clinician seeing these adolescents in therapy, is whether same-gender sexual interests will lead into a lesbian, gay, or bisexual identity, *or* whether these experiences will need to be accommodated within a future heterosexual identity. Some adolescents are clear about their homosexual orientation, although either they (or their parents) may be unhappy with it. Here the task is to facilitate a pathway to a positive lesbian, gay, or bisexual identity. Other adolescents are uncertain about the pattern of their erotic attractions and benefit from a safe therapeutic environment in which to reflect upon their sexual feelings and more gradually establish their sexual identity, be it heterosexual, lesbian, gay, or bisexual.

Mental health concerns

Research study after research study has shown that homosexuality is not of itself a factor associated with psychopathology (Gonsiorek, 1991). Nevertheless lesbian, gay, and bisexual youth have been found to be at unusual risk of mental health problems because of the stresses they encounter in their daily lives. For example, in their sample of nearly 200 lesbian, gay, and bisexual American youth under 22 years of age who were attending different lesbian and gay community centres in fourteen cities in the United States, D'Augelli and Hershberger (1993) found that 63% of the youth surveyed reported that they had been so worried or anxious at least once in the preceding year that they felt unable to function properly, while 33% reported excessive alcohol use and 23% reported illegal drug use. Common worries included: telling family, friends, and co-workers about their sexual orientation, problems in close relationships, dissatisfaction with their sex life, worries about HIV/AIDS (particularly in relation to gay/bisexual men), problems in developing friendships with other lesbians and gay men, and religious issues about sexual orientation. Data from the same study revealed that 42% of the sample reported having previously attempted suicide, and only 40% said that they had never considered suicide. Attempted suicide was associated with being more open about sexual orientation and having lost more friends because of their sexual orientation.

Rates of mental health problems are high in D'Augelli and Hershberger's sample, just as they are in other surveys of lesbian, gay, and bisexual youth. However, because there are no systematic studies comparing the mental health of a non-clinical sample of adolescents who have had homosexual experiences with that of a matched group of heterosexuals, it is difficult to disentangle the specific issues affecting the mental health of lesbian, bisexual, and gay youth from the general issues connected with adolescent mental health. We currently know very little about how previous victimization, gender non-conformity, sexual identity development, relationship difficulties, and other independent factors such as psychiatric history influence mental health difficulties of lesbian, bisexual, and gay adolescents.

The impact of homophobia
on sexual identity decisions

Decisions about sexual identity are not made in a neutral environment. Whether or not adolescents have had any same-gender sexual experiences, they will invariably become aware of homophobia. Even if they are not the direct target of these comments, the knowledge that others find their deepest thoughts unaccept-able creates tension between their private selves and their public selves. For young people who are beginning to identify as lesbian, gay, or bisexual, this anxiety may be compounded with feelings of guilt at allowing the comments to pass unchallenged because of fear of betraying their own feelings. The anxiety created by homophobia may lead young persons to withdraw and become increasingly socially isolated during adolescence.

The heterosexism of mainstream culture to which the majority of children have uncritical exposure means that adolescents' knowledge of lesbians, gay men, and bisexuals is likely to be lim-ited, and probably restricted to negative caricatures portrayed in popular prejudice. Furthermore, adolescents probably will have internalized cultural expectations of a heterosexual future for themselves at odds with their homoerotic sexual interest. Dealing with this internalized homophobia may well present a greater challenge than dealing with victimization of others. Although this point may appear at first glance to be more relevant to adolescents who are in the process of identifying as lesbian, gay, or bisexual, I would suggest that internalized homophobia is also an important factor in explaining the lack of self-acceptance of any early same-gender sexual experiences among adolescents who come to iden-tify as heterosexual.

Identifying as gay, lesbian, bisexual, or heterosexual

In considering adolescent sexual identity, it is often useful to con-sider models of the process of sexual identity formation, or the "coming-out" models that have been outlined for lesbians or gay men. To date, numerous models of the coming-out process have been detailed (e.g. Cass, 1979; Troiden, 1979; Woodman & Lenna, 1980). While these models often focus on different aspects of the coming-out process, they have many similarities in terms of the important features that they highlight. Nevertheless, the sequen-tial stages that all these models use to describe identity formation often obscure individual differences in experience and may blur other phases in the lives of many adolescents. After all, identity is a process, not a static achievement, and issues may need to be revisited at different times. The particular difficulties of identifying as bisexual are also rarely acknowledged in the models where the young person may be faced with a lack of acknowledgement of their heterosexual interest when integrating with lesbian and gay culture. Furthermore, these models are formed mostly from the retrospective accounts of lesbian and gay adults, and so they tend to presuppose that the end product of sexual identity is already in sight, thus ignoring the uncertainty of sexual destination experienced by most adolescents in therapy. Coming-out models may therefore be a useful narrative tool to aid the construction of an explanation of how the young person arrived at a particular point, but the danger exists for the young person in adopting them prescriptively and foreclosing on identity issues.

Nevertheless, coming-out models do highlight two main important decision points in sexual identity formation during adolescence: self-awareness, and coming out to others about sexual identity. In most cases, coming out to self will occur before coming out to others, but sometimes others will make an identification for the young person (generally making a negative construction of their activity).

Coming out to self

What do we know about how the process of self-awareness comes about? There is certainly a lack of research on adolescents as they are in the process of identifying as lesbian, gay, or bisexual. Knowledge in this field relies on the memories of adult lesbians, bisexuals, and gay men. A common theme highlighted in these studies is that many remember a sense of being different from their peers, a feeling that is sometimes present early on in childhood (Bell, Weinberg, & Hammersmith, 1981; Troiden, 1979).

Sometimes this inkling of difference is linked with feelings of alienation from same-gender peers and/or gender-atypical behaviour during childhood. The association between gender-atypical behaviour and later homosexual orientation for some gay men has been clearly established through prospective research (Bailey & Zucker, 1995; Zucker & Green, 1992). For example, of the feminine boys in Green's (1987) study, 75% to 80% were either bisexual or gay at the time of follow-up interview during late adolescence or early adulthood, compared to only one boy in the comparison group. Longitudinal research on girls who display masculine behaviour in childhood has not yet been reported. Nevertheless, a quantitative review of retrospective studies comparing the remembered gender-role behaviour of adult homosexuals, bisexuals, and heterosexuals has indicated that lesbians and bisexual women are less likely than heterosexual women to report feminine gender-role behaviour during childhood (Bailey & Zucker, 1995). However, the difference between the childhood-gendered behaviour of lesbian and heterosexual women is not so marked as that between gay and heterosexual men.

It is important to remember that retrospective studies have been criticized because of the possibility that recall of gender-role behaviour may be biased through the lens of social stereotypes (Ross, 1980). Furthermore, the processes that link gender identity, gender-role behaviour, and sexual orientation as yet remain unclear (see Bailey & Zucker, 1995). One of the main biological interpretations suggests that the prenatal or early postnatal effects of androgens influence both gender-typed behaviour and sexual orientation. Alternatively, it may be the case that nascent sexual orientation influences gender-role behaviour during childhood, such that young pre-homosexual boys imitate their mother's behaviour in order to gain their father's love and attention (Isay, 1989, 1990). On the other hand, gender-atypical behaviour during early childhood may lead to associating with an opposite-gender peer group who share the same interests, which in turn leads to an eroticization of same-gender peers who have not been the familiar companions of childhood. Compared with the relatively narrow definition of gender roles within heterosexual society, a greater tolerance of different gender roles exists within lesbian and gay communities and more freedom of expression is possible for cross-dressing and shifting other gender-defined boundaries. Thus, finding acceptance and a niche within the lesbian and gay communities may be an attractive solution of patterns of cross-gender behaviour in childhood. Finally, it has been suggested that some adolescents adopt cross-gender behaviour only after they have begun to identify their homoerotic interests, because they are uncertain how to express them except through the popular stereotypes of the "effeminate gay man" and "butch dyke" (Davies, 1996).

The majority of lesbians, bisexuals, and gay men, however, report gender-typical interests in childhood (Bancroft, 1989). For most homosexual adolescents, other processes not connected with cross-gender behaviour are therefore at work, leading to the realization of lesbian, gay, or bisexual interests, the most important of these processes being an increasing awareness of their own sexual desires. Other factors may well include identifying a preference for same-gender company and an awareness of similar cultural interests. Furthermore, for some women the political dimension of an affinity with feminist politics may be an important factor in identifying as lesbian (Kitzinger & Wilkinson, 1995).

When the individual labels his or her feelings as homoerotic, she or he takes the huge step of self-awareness linking personal experiences to personal knowledge of lesbian and gay culture. For some young people, this leads relatively swiftly to self-identification as a lesbian, gay, or bisexual adolescent, and prior feelings of being isolated and different from peers are explained, self-esteem is enhanced, and a new-found sense of destiny is pursued. Data from a community survey of American lesbian, gay, and bisexual youth suggest a positive association between self-esteem and coming out to self (Savin-Williams, 1995), although the direction of the association between self-esteem and self-acknowledgement of sexual identity is far from clear.

However, for many, self-awareness of homoerotic interest is frightening, and their response is to try to deal with same-gender sexual interest within a heterosexual developmental framework. Initially, this might be through repression and denial (e.g. through heterosexual promiscuity, recourse to drugs and/or alcohol, or retreat into aesthetic asexuality). Further on the road to integrating same-gender sexual interest within a heterosexual identity is to be able to acknowledge it as a transitory phase, or as a special case, thus owning same-sex experiences without splitting them off. But paradoxically this would be a defensive position for adolescents who will finally identify as lesbian, gay, or bisexual. The clinician is again faced with the conundrum of working with the young person to make sense of his or her sexual orientation.

For all adolescents, there is likely to be considerable stress related to both openness and concealment of sexual orientation. For the adolescent who is in the process of identifying as lesbian, gay, or bisexual, part of dealing with the inner conflict is likely to involve letting go of the assumptions and expectations of his or her earlier heterosexual identity, and these will need to be mourned before engaging fully with a new sexual identity. Neither the repression nor the expression of homoerotic desire is satisfactory: both are deeply conflictual to either private or public identity. The gap between the individual's private identity and her or his public heterosexual identity causes the tension of dishonesty and increases the level of social vigilance because of the anxiety around being found out. Depression may arise through the seeming irreconcilability of a gay or lesbian identity and the stigma associated with it. On the other hand, acknowledging homosexuality leads to the very real fear of victimization. More isolated lesbian, gay, and bisexual youth lack the social support to begin to break down the barriers between private and public identity to form a coherent view of self. Isolated youth also may be more vulnerable targets for homophobia.

Coming out to others

For lesbian, gay, and bisexual adolescents, coming out to others takes on great significance in terms of integrating the private and public sides of the self-concept. Coming out to others is also not a single event but a lifelong process of letting others know about sexual identity and constantly challenging the assumptions others make of universal heterosexuality. During adolescence, coming out to others occurs in three main contexts: in same-gender relationships and to other lesbians, gays, and bisexuals; to heterosexual peers and mainstream society; and to other family members.

Coming out in the context of a gay or lesbian relationship. For young gay or bisexual men, identifying homoerotic sexual interest often occurs outside the context of a gay relationship. Their first same-sex sexual encounters may be with other boys or men who identify as heterosexual. Casual sexual encounters may also be more desirable, because forming a relationship with someone of the same gender would mean facing up to one's own sexual identity. A steady relationship is also more likely to come to the notice of family and friends and so may be avoided for these reasons. There are also particular difficulties in Britain for young gay men aged under 18 years in developing sexual relationships because of the illegality of homosexual relationships as defined under the Criminal Justice Act (1994).

The same process can occur for young lesbians, although women are more likely than men to report that the process of identification occurred during their relationship with another woman (Bell, Weinberg, & Hammersmith, 1981; Kitzinger & Wilkinson, 1995). Savin-Williams (1995) suggests that forming a committed same-gender relationship may help adolescents towards greater self-acceptance of their sexual identity. However, some young people report that their first few same-gender sexual relationships were turbulent and unsatisfactory (Davies, 1996), an understandable finding given the external pressures on lesbian and gay relationships at a time when both partners may be unsure of their sexuality. An isolated and/or unsatisfactory relationship is unlikely to be enough to sustain a positive self-image (Hetrick & Martin, 1987).

Some authors have suggested that lesbian, gay, and bisexual youth can only build a healthy self-image within a positive lesbian/gay context. Although there is an increasingly accessible lesbian and gay literature and network of youth groups, it may still be difficult for the young person to get in contact with other lesbian and gay adolescents and begin to develop both sexual relationships and supportive friendships. This is particularly so for some groups of young people. Bisexual adolescents may face pressure or even hostility from within the lesbian and gay community towards someone who is seen as "not being able to make up her or his mind" and who retains opportunities of "passing" as a heterosexual in mainstream society. Adolescents from non-white ethnic groups may experience racism from within the lesbian and gay community, or feel that their ethnic identity is ignored or eroticized; however, it is likely that they will have experienced and internalized some of the prejudices of their own ethnic group towards homosexuals. Thus these adolescents may feel doubly marginalized because of both their ethnic and their sexual identity. Adolescents growing up outside the major metropolitan areas may not have access to lesbian or gay literature, feeling too embarrassed to purchase it in their local community and/or unable to access urban centres where there is a greater representation of lesbian and gay culture. Adolescents isolated in these ways may be at risk of victimization, exploitative sexual relations, and lack information about safe-sex practices.

Coming out to heterosexual peers.   Adolescents tend to disclose their homosexual interest to a close friend before they come out to their family (D'Augelli & Hershberger, 1993). Often the adolescent has chosen well and the close friend is accepting, although he or she may not be positive. The supportive acknowledgement of someone within the heterosexual community begins to bridge the gap between private and public self and may also provide some protection against victimization. If a friend is confided in she or he is often a close friend of the opposite gender. Same-gender friendships with heterosexual adolescents may be fraught with difficulties for adolescents who are beginning to identify homoerotic feelings. Difficulties of dealing with feelings of arousal may lead to homosexual or bisexual adolescents ending a friendship for fear of their feelings being exposed, or they may feel afraid to show friendship for fear of this being misunderstood as a pass (Hetrick & Martin, 1987).

Even if a close friend is supportive, the heterosexual peer-group culture as a whole is hostile. Pilkington and D'Augelli (1995) found that 80% of the lesbian, gay, and bisexual American youth in their study reported verbal abuse specifically directed at their sexual orientation (48% reporting that this had occurred on more than two occasions). Young gay men were more likely to report experiencing verbal abuse compared with young lesbians. Other authors suggest that the lesbian, gay, and bisexual youths who are most at risk of being abused are those who do not conform to cultural ideals of gender-appropriate masculine and feminine behaviours and roles (Davies, 1996). In Pilkington and D'Augelli's study, 44% of those surveyed reported that they had been threatened with physical violence, while 17% reported actual physical assault and 22% reported sexual assault. In Britain, the only evidence that we have is a recent survey by the pressure group Stonewall, in which nearly one in three men and one in four women of the over 4,000 lesbians, gay men, and bisexual women and men of all ages who were surveyed reported having experienced some form of homophobic physical assault (Mason & Palmer, 1996). Fear of victimization among young people may lie behind social anxiety, truancy from school, or employment problems, which may bring them into therapy (Davies, 1996).

Coming out to other family members. Most gay, lesbian, and bisexual adolescents grow up in heterosexual families in which no one else is known to be homosexual. Many adolescents are reluctant to discuss their sexuality with parents, who they fear will not react positively. In their community survey D'Augelli and Hershberger (1993) found that of the nearly 200 lesbian, gay, and bisexual youth (aged under 22 years) in their study, 19% said that they were closeted from all family members, 34% said that they had told a few family members but were afraid to tell others, and 48% said that they had told most or all of their immediate family and had met with a positive response. Of the adolescents who had told their parents, 20% and 28%, respectively, reported that either their mother or their father was intolerant or rejecting. In the extreme, rejection may lead to the young person leaving home. Figures from a major British housing charity indicate that 1% of the homeless 16- to 25-year-olds who have been resident in their hostels listed their sexuality as the main reason why they had left home (Centrepoint, 1996).

Young people are more likely to tell their mother about their sexuality before coming out to their father (D'Augelli & Hershberger, 1993), and so one parent may be coping with the secret alone. Parents may never have considered the possibility that their son or daughter might have gay or lesbian relationships prior to this point and may base their reactions to this news on the following homophobic misconceptions: that homosexuality is an illness, that homosexual men and women are unstable and unreliable, that homosexual men are effeminate and lesbians masculinized, that homosexuality is contagious, and that homosexual men abuse children by seduction and rape. The mother or father may also feel that she or he is in some way "to blame" for the son's or daughter's sexual orientation. These misconceptions will need to be addressed before the parent will be able to begin to re-establish a relationship with the young person (Ussher, 1991). Furthermore, each parent will need time to mourn the heterosexual future of marriage and grandchildren that they had most likely anticipated for their adolescent before they are able to adjust expectations to the possibility of family formation in the lesbian/gay life-cycle. Parents and siblings to some extent may also take on responsibility for letting the extended family know about the young person's new sexual identity. As such, they are often placed in the role of mediating between prejudice from the extended family and the young person's desire or reluctance to have his or her identity acknowledged and accepted by the wider family circle—for example, to have their partner included in family celebrations. This mediating role may be all the more difficult if the parent or sibling has unresolved prejudices or is insecure in his or her own sexuality.

Conclusions

Since Evelyn Hooker's (1957) seminal study, countless replications have confirmed that homosexuality is not indicative of mental health problems. Nevertheless, many lesbian, gay, and bisexual young people face difficulties at some point in developing a positive self-image because lesbian and gay cultures are marginalized within mainstream society. This may be even more difficult for young people who are further isolated because of their locality, ethnicity, or in other ways, and who will have less access to—or be less able to identify with—positive lesbian and gay images presented. Sexual identity issues are interwoven with other aspects of the individual's life. The widespread stigmatization of lesbian and gay sexuality leads to difficulties in finding support and making relationships, and very real fears about personal safety. It is also likely that the young person will have internalized some of the prejudices and misconceptions about homosexuality, leaving them vulnerable to low self-esteem.

Some adolescents are certain of their sexual identity relatively early on, although either they or their family may not be accepting of it. However, for many adolescents, there is the added uncertainty of sexual orientation and what to make of attractions or same-gender sexual experiences. Some young people who experience crushes and attractions or have a relationship with someone of the same gender will go on to develop a lesbian, gay, or bisexual identity, but others will need to integrate this within an emerging heterosexual identity. Sexual orientation as a major focus of identity acts as the basis of many projected hopes and expectations; thus uncertainty is of itself ridden with anxiety as to what the future holds. The clinician's awareness and acceptance of homosexual, bisexual, and heterosexual possibilities, together with the aim of not foreclosing on other potential outcomes, is important in providing a safe environment in which the young person's uncertainty can be explored and resolved.

B

Transvestism during adolescence

Susan J. Bradley

"Jeremy" was 13 years old when he was brought to the clinic by his parents because of his preoccupation with female underclothing.

The parents stated that he had had a "fetish" since the age of 4. His mother recalled that when he was small he liked to play with girls' shoes and enjoyed rubbing his hands up and down women's legs when they were wearing nylons. She also stated that at particular times during his childhood she would find a variety of things hidden throughout the house, such as her pantyhose, bras, and underwear. Mother felt that she had typically become quite angry at Jeremy on discovering that he had taken her clothes. Her husband, by contrast, was less concerned, feeling that it would go away. The event that precipitated their referral was Jeremy's breaking into their neighbour's house and taking the daughter's underwear and bras. Furthermore, mother had found sanitary pads smeared with lipstick and underwear with holes cut in them and "soiled" with faecal material.

Jeremy's mother described her pregnancy with Jeremy as difficult, primarily due to extreme nausea and vomiting for which she took Bendectin. She also required hospitalization for rehydration during the pregnancy. Feeding Jeremy was difficult for several years as he had marked regurgitation.

109

Although described as kind and loving until 8 years of age, Jeremy was also extremely hyperactive and difficult to manage. Mother acknowledged more difficulty setting limits than her husband, but also that she would become enraged with Jeremy and then later feel that she had to make up to him for what she had said. Father was working long days, and so the bulk of the responsibility for the children fell to Jeremy's mother. In addition to being difficult for his parents, from his pre-school years Jeremy presented difficulties to caretakers, requiring many changes in day-care arrangements. He was seen as having a high pain tolerance and a relative indifference to consequences, which made disciplining him quite problematic for his caretakers. Aside from the interest in nylons and shoes and a brief interest in Barbies, his play behaviour had been typically masculine.

From an early age, he began telling violent stories and threatening others who frustrated him. Hygiene was an ongoing problem, manifesting in soiling behaviour and refusal to shower. These behaviours interfered with relationships generally and he had few friends. At school, in first grade (age 6 years) he was diagnosed as hyperactive and placed on Ritalin. The parents were concerned about the possible long-term effects of this medication and took him off it. The school refused to have him unless he was on medication, resulting in a change in schools. He had then required special education placement and had failed at least two grades by the time he was seen. (In Canada, if a child is falling significantly behind his or her peers and it is felt that she or he would be disadvantaged by moving on, a year can be repeated.) As he became older, his antisocial behaviours became more problematic, with episodes of lying, stealing, slashing tyres, smashing abandoned cars, an attempt to strangle a younger student, and stealing women's clothing. He had also been engaging in "bondage" behaviours, tying up a girl while playing at her house and also tying himself up while playing on his own. At the time of assessment, he had been charged for property offences, assault, and threatening a peer and had been removed from the family home.

Relationships in the family were very conflicted, with mother wanting Jeremy home but also acknowledging that things were easier without him there. The older brother had been antagonistic to Jeremy for many years and was acutely embarrassed by his behaviour. The parents felt overwhelmed, having tried for years, with constant professional and agency involvement, to help Jeremy, but with little sense of success. His mother felt that she had failed as a parent. Her frustration with her child's refusal to comply led to irritability, arguments, and distancing in the marital relationship.

Both parents had had difficulties in their families of origin. Mother saw herself as emotional and hard on herself, and she frequently blamed herself for the family's difficulties. Father had had a stormy relationship with his own father; he had also had few friends and had dropped out of school early. He had a problem with alcoholism and was emotionally and physically abusive to his wife early on in the marriage. He joined Alcoholics Anonymous six years prior to Jeremy's birth. One year later, he suffered a stroke which left him with a mild right-sided paralysis requiring extensive physiotherapy. At the time of assessment both parents were employed, father running his own small business and mother working with a small company. There was a history of conduct problems in father's family.

Jeremy presented as somewhat short for his age. He was at times tearful in the joint interview. When seen on his own, he appeared to have difficulty expressing himself and was often vague in response to questions. He acknowledged having few friends, although he talked about previous girlfriends and about his current girlfriend with whom he had held hands and kissed. He talked about being blamed for things that his old friends had done. When asked about his mother, he initially acknowledged a lot of arguing because of his non-compliance but then went on to say that he was excited to see her when he came home from school. After a diversion to talk about his frustration with his brother, he returned to his mother, saying he "feels upset", "mad", "has hatred" at her, and swears at her. He indicated that he doesn't like it when she "ranges out" at him. He felt that they had been having trouble since he was age 12 and that he sometimes says "I want to kill her". He saw himself winning arguments with her by leaving. He could acknowledge that the difficulties are his fault because he doesn't listen and wants to do things "later". He reported that when his mother gets mad at him "it's like the person inside me leaves me and I have to take the blame". He stated that sometimes he can be really kind, but at other times he can be "bad, mad and upset". He feels shy most of the time at school and thinks that the other kids find him weird. He talked about the great difficulty he has in controlling his desire to cross-dress as though something inside of him was taking over, like "The Terminator". Despite his parents' reports that they were continuing to find bags of women's clothing in his room, he reported a declining use of cross-dressing over the six months prior to the assessment. He denied sexual arousal with the cross-dressing. He did acknowledge occasional thoughts about being a girl in the context of the sense that girls don't get yelled at and he hated being yelled at. However, he had no other wishes about being a girl. He indicated that he understood what masturbation was but denied engaging in this behaviour, the reason being that he felt that he would get someone upset. He denied any symptoms indicative of temporal lobe epilepsy, although he reported that he had been knocked unconscious at age 11 when another boy hit him on his forehead with a golf club.

Psychological testing included assessment of intelligence and achievement, parental, teacher, and youth report on standardized behaviour checklists, projective testing, and sexual orientation and gender identity questionnaires. On the Wechsler Intelligence Scale for Children (WISC–R), Jeremy's verbal IQ was 71, his performance IQ 106, with a full-scale IQ of 86. There was considerable inter-subtest scatter, Jeremy doing particularly poorly on the Comprehension subtest, on which he received a scaled score of 1. On the Wide Range Achievement Test–Revised (WRAT–R), Jeremy scored equivalent to a Grade 4 level on the spelling subtest and to a Grade 6 level on reading and arithmetic. On the Child Behaviour Checklist (CBCL), Jeremy's mother identified 66 items as characteristic of his behaviour, summing to 114, well within the clinical range. He had elevations on five of eight narrow-band scales: Anxious/ Depressed, Social Problems, Attention Problems, Delinquent Behaviour, and Aggressive Behaviour. Both the Internalizing and Externalizing T scores were elevated. Mother also endorsed possible gender dysphoria and confusion for Jeremy. Father reported a similar profile, although he also rated concerns about Thought Problems, specifically "seeing things that aren't there" like "dead bodies in ditches and the Ladies' washrooms". The Teacher Report Form (TRF) of the CBCL, filled out by several teachers, identified many problems, well within the clinical range. On the Youth Self Report, Jeremy reported clinically significant problems on Delinquent Behaviour and Social Problems and was in the borderline range on Aggressive Behaviour. When doing the Rorschach, Jeremy appeared to be overstimulated, frequently rotating the cards and needing to stop himself. His responses, however, did not indicate difficulty with reality testing. A central issue that emerged in the protocol was control of aggression, anger, and hostility. There were many percepts that involved malevolent interactions between objects, often resulting in intense destruction (e.g. "kid ... sitting on a chair reading and he got blown away", "a dragon flying down to wreck something, he's ticked off"). There was also a sense of felt deprivation in the protocol, suggesting that underneath the overt anger and aggression are strong, unmet dependency needs ("a butterfly ... going over to a flower to suck pollen"). Other responses in the protocol suggest that Jeremy felt different from others and alienated. On the Draw A Person, Jeremy drew a man first, with typical male appurtenances such as beard, pipe, and hat but hands with no fingers. His drawing of a female was more filled in, but the figure wore thick boots and had no hair and a lopsided grin. On the gender identity and sexual orientation questionnaires, Jeremy reported only heterosexual feelings, some sexual experience with girls, but no intercourse. He endorsed use of female undergarments but denied being aroused or masturbating when cross-dressed. He reported occasional wishes to be the opposite sex but denied a desire for sex reassignment and always imagined himself as a boy in fantasy.

Jeremy's story is similar to that of many of the youth seen for transvestitic behaviours in our clinic. The mental health issues are evident in his history, in our assessment, and in his responses and those of his parents and teachers on the questionnaires. I will review these to highlight the more general findings from our sample of roughly 85 adolescents seen since the late 1970s.

The history of co-morbid behavioural difficulties is common, most of these adolescents being seen as difficult and non-compliant by their parents. Comparison of CBCL scores for our transvestic fetishism (TF) adolescents with the referred and non-referred standardization samples of Achenbach shows behavioural difficulties equivalent to that of the referred standardization sample, with, on average, almost five narrow-band elevations, as well as elevated Internalizing and Externalizing Scale scores (Achenbach & Edelbrock, 1983, 1986).

The most common of the other DSM-III–R diagnoses have been Conduct Disorder, Oppositional Defiant Disorder, Attention Deficit Hyperactivity Disorder, and Overanxious Disorder. Language and learning disorders are common, as is the history of repeating a school grade. The observed verbal-performance discrepancy on the WISC–R has also been a common finding, with our sample showing a significantly lower verbal than performance IQ. Verbal Comprehension and Freedom from Distractibility were also lower than Perceptual Organization (Cohen, 1957). This is consistent with findings on adults with TF (Bowler & Collacott, 1993; Steiner, Sanders, & Langevin, 1985).

The behavioural difficulties have frequently led to placement out of the family home. Mothers who have generally been most responsible for dealing with the child and his or her oppositional behaviour have usually become very frustrated, to the point of yelling and screaming, and they also acknowledge difficulty in setting limits on their child's behaviour from an early age. In some instances, mothers of boys referred for problems with TF have left their families. This, together with the increased number of out-of-home placements, probably accounts for our finding of a disproportionate number of adolescents with TF living away from their mothers.

The ambivalence in this adolescent's relationship with his mother is illustrated by Jeremy's statement that he is excited to get home and see his mother, while at the same time he expresses marked anger and hostility at her. Frequently, the TF behaviours appear to begin in the context of a mother's lack of availability or an intensification of the conflict with her. The difficulty that these adolescents have in dealing with their anger is manifest in Jeremy's case in his frequent aggressive outbursts, fantasies of dead women's bodies being found, and the malevolent percepts on the Rorschach. His concern that he is not in control of his feelings is apparent in his statements that when his mother gets upset at him he feels "as if the person inside me leaves and he is left to take the blame", and the sense that when he has urges to cross-dress it is very difficult to resist his feelings as though something inside him "like The Terminator" were taking over. Some of our more articulate adolescents describe extreme discomfort when angry, particularly at their mothers, and are aware that the cross-dressing makes them feel calmer and more in control of their feelings. The fact that so many of these adolescents have verbal expressive difficulties has undoubtedly added to their sense of not having adequate strategies for control when they become angry.

Most of the adolescents with TF seen in our clinic have social difficulties. Jeremy is more extreme than some, but many feel alienated and "weird" as expressed by Jeremy. Often, these boys have felt unable to stand up for themselves, both with their peers and with their parents. This sense of not being able to stand up for himself with his mother seems particularly frustrating for the young male adolescent and adds to his own perception of being inadequate. These behaviours often begin around puberty, a time when most male adolescents begin to resent maternal control. For the adolescent with TF, difficulty talking about conflict or any affectively laden topic exacerbates this conflict. Although some of the mothers in our sample have appeared very intimidating in their hostility, many of these adolescents seem to have difficulty in this interaction as much due to their own sensitivity as to their mother being truly overpowering.

The history of head injury with or without evidence of temporal lobe epilepsy is common. About a quarter of our sample have histories suggestive of cerebral insult. Following a theory developed initially by Epstein (1960), postulating temporal-limbic vulnerabilities in TF, we have speculated that kindling (see Glossary) may play a role in inducing sexual arousal in the context of affect arousal (Zucker & Bradley, 1995). We have not, however, been able to detect previously undiagnosed epilepsy when more than half of our sample were routinely referred for neurological consultation.

The lack of a wish for sex reassignment distinguishes the adolescent with TF from the adolescent with gender identity disorder, as does the absence of an earlier history of cross-gender behaviour aside from the cross-dressing. Some of the adolescents with TF who have engaged in this behaviour for a long time with little interference or who have more evidence of cross-gender behaviour and interests as a child may appear more confused about their wish to be the opposite sex and may have experienced more homoerotic feelings. Typically, however, these adolescents have a heterosexual orientation, although many of them have been socially too inhibited to act on their feelings.

Our understanding of these behaviours is that they have played a self-soothing role for children or adolescents who struggle with intense feelings that threaten to overwhelm their coping strategies. The factors that lead to the choice of cross-gender apparel for self-soothing are less clear. The older psychoanalytic theory posited an ambivalent tie to their primary objects such that the use of the transitional or fetishistic object maintained closeness to allay the fear that anger would destroy their relationship. This is similar to the dynamic thinking about separation anxiety. It is possible that these objects are used initially primarily as transitional objects for separation anxiety and become incorporated into a more sexualized fantasy as the adolescent discovers the self-soothing aspects of masturbation. However these behaviours begin, they appear to become integral to the adolescent's system for affect regulation and sexual arousal and, with time, appear increasingly difficult to change.

Treatment is focused on relieving the stress that contributes to the adolescent's frustration. This means work with the adolescent and his family to establish a different balance, helping the parents find ways to manage their son's resistant and non-compliant behaviour more comfortably, while simultaneously helping the adolescent to find other, more adaptive ways of handling his anger. Medication may be helpful, although there have been no controlled trials of medication in adolescents with TF. In adults, there is some evidence that anti-anxiety agents may be useful (Fedoroff, 1988, 1992; Kerbeshian & Burd, 1991; Kruesi, Fine, Valladares, Phillips, & Rapoport, 1992; Masand, 1993; Perilstein, Lipper, & Friedman, 1991).

Conclusion

Adolescents with transvestic fetishism present the clinician with an interesting and complex situation. The co-morbid behaviour difficulty is often of more concern in terms of the adolescent's long-term adjustment than is the TF. The TF behaviour, however, is often highly troubling to their families or other caretakers and is regularly a source of great embarrassment to the adolescent. Despite the embarrassment, or perhaps because of it, these adolescents are often very reluctant to engage in formal treatment. Understanding the source of their intense anger and their feeling of being inadequate to manage such feelings may be a way to help. However, these adolescents do not readily engage in talking, especially about their feelings. This may be partially related to actual language deficits or to their marked sensitivity to affect which may interfere with their capacity to use cognitive coping strategies. The families of TF adolescents frequently have trouble understanding their adolescents' behaviour, which offends their privacy, but are also often fed up with the ongoing conflict and years of professional help which has not been useful. In this regard, intervention is similar to that for the conduct-disordered adolescent and equally challenging. Reduction of the adolescent's anxiety through anxiolytics and anger management taught using a variety of coping strategies may be a more productive approach than insight-oriented treatment. Despite the challenges, these adolescents present us with interesting insights into the development of paraphilic behaviour and the complexities inherent in our efforts at intervention.

C

Transsexualism during adolescence

Peggy Cohen-Kettenis, Stephanie H. M. van Goozen,
& Leo Cohen

T he lack of experience with transsexuals is one of the reasons that many clinicians are reluctant to treat the young ones by other means than psychotherapy. It is regrettable that this reluctance to commence the sex-reassignment procedure in postpubertal children is currently determined so much by personal views and theories rather than by empirical findings. Understandable as the caution to intervene medically in these patients may be, it is also very unfortunate. In our view, delaying medical treatment, "safe" as it may seem, is not always in the best interest of the patient. Especially in patients who are not yet completely masculinized or feminized, it may cause unnecessary iatrogenic damage, because (1) the physical postpubertal changes —such as virilization in male-to-females (MFs)—are irreversible and, when not blocked in time, create life-long traces of the sex of birth; (2) adolescents who have to await medical treatment for many years may be delayed in a variety of areas (e.g. social relationships or education), because they have to live with a self-concept that is never socially acknowledged or reinforced.

Over the last ten years, we have assessed and treated several dozens of adolescent applicants for sex-reassignment surgery at our outpatient gender identity clinic. Some of these patients were diagnosed transsexuals and have undergone sex reassignment:

that is, the total process of cross-gender living, hormonal therapy, surgery, and birth certificate change. Because early hormone treatment (between 16 and 18 years) at this moment is still in an experimental phase, we have formulated a few additional requirements in order to be considered for this, including a life-long extreme cross-gender identity and a stable social background. When the applicants or patients met these criteria in addition to a DSM diagnosis of gender identity disorder, the sex-reassignment procedure was started.

Other patients were diagnosed transsexuals who did not (yet) meet the criteria for hormonal and surgical interventions or those with less severe gender identity disorders. They received psychotherapy or family therapy or were treated in inpatient clinics for a variety of problems.

From early on, we have tried to document data systematically on patients' psychological and other areas of functioning. The purpose of this contribution is to describe an adolescent population with gender identity disorders in terms of their psychological functioning, before and after treatment.

Our group of 65 patients was divided into two subgroups. The first group consisted of 42 diagnosed transsexuals: 26 female-to-males (FMs) and 16 MFs. Many, but not all of them, proceeded with the sex-reassignment procedure. The second group consisted of 23 patients with atypical or less severe gender identity disorders (8 females, 15 males). The mean age of the total sample was 17 years ($SD = 1.85$). Both groups were of average intelligence, but the transsexuals were significantly more intelligent than the group of atypicals.

In our clinical interviews, the kind and intensity of gender dysphoria is discussed extensively and applicants fill out a gender dysphoria scale. As expected, the atypical gender dysphoric group had a rather high score on the gender dysphoria scale. However, the scores of the transsexuals were significantly higher.

In order to measure their psychological functioning, we have used two self-report questionnaires. One is the Dutch Personality Inventory, NPV (Luteyn, Kok, & van der Ploeg, 1980). The NPV measures seven personality aspects: feelings of general inadequacy, social inadequacy, rigidity, hostility, complacency, dominance, and self-esteem. The other, NVM (Luteyn, Starren, & van

Dijk, 1985), is a shortened Dutch version of the Minnesota Multiphasic Personality Inventory. The NVM measures negativism, somatization, shyness, psychopathology, and extroversion.

When we compared the mean scores with those of large non-patient normative samples (Table 7.1), it appeared that the mean score of the transsexuals was largely in the average range. Only the mean average inadequacy score was in the high range for MFs. Atypicals more often scored in the unfavourable range (more inadequacy for female atypicals, more social inadequacy for male atypicals, and less self-esteem for atypicals).

Compared with normative groups, the transsexuals scored in the high range for somatization and psychopathology and in the average range for the other subscales on the NVM (see Table 7.2). The atypicals scored significantly higher than the transsexuals in shyness and psychopathology. No group mean scores of the atypicals were in the "average" range.

Although the high psychopathology scores of the transsexual group might be alarming, two facts should be kept in mind. First, for a normal population, scores between 0 and 4 are in the "average" range. The mean score of the transsexual group was 4.3, and thus this only just fell into the "high" category. Second, the psychopathology scale seems to have a bias against transsexuals. The scale consists of thirteen items, referring to odd thoughts, perceptions, and feelings. Two items may refer to psychopathology in the general population, but probably refer to real experiences in the transsexual group. One item says: "I have had strange experiences." The other says: "People say insulting and mean things about me." If in the transsexual group only one of these two items was endorsed on the basis of their transsexualism, the mean score would have been in the "average" range, after correction. The mean psychopathology score of the atypical group was much higher (7.0). Even if all atypicals would have endorsed both items, they would, after correction, still have a psychopathology score in the "high" range.

The above results show that young transsexuals may have some psychological problems, particularly in the realm of inadequacy feelings and somatization. However, in most other areas of psychological functioning they seem to do neither better nor worse than the average (Dutch) person. This is in contrast to the appli-

TABLE 7.1
Comparison of NPV scores of transsexuals
with normative non-patient samples

Inadequacy	high(MF)/above average
Social inadequacy	average
Rigidity	average
Hostility	average
Complacency	above average
Dominance	average (MF)/high (FM)
Self-esteem	average

cants who were not diagnosed as having a severe gender identity disorder and who were not allowed to start the sex-reassignment surgery (SRS) procedure.

The self-report personality questionnaires we have selected are both very thoroughly studied. They have been shown to be reliable and valid in numerous studies and are the most widely used scales in the Netherlands for both clinical and research purposes. Yet some clinicians, such as Lothstein (1984), have criticized the use of self-report questionnaires in transsexuals. He considers transsexuals to have borderline pathology and states that the intact reality-testing of individuals with borderline pathology is only expected to become impaired in unstructured situations. Clearly, self-report questionnaires are too structured to reveal this phenomenon. In

TABLE 7.2
Comparison of NVM scores of transsexuals
with normative non-patient samples

Negativism	average
Somatization	high
Shyness	average
Psychopathology	high
Extraversion	average

addition, it is generally feared that transsexuals will try to "fake good" on self-report measures in order to be referred for SRS.

We have therefore tried to gain additional information on the psychological functioning of our patient group, based on an instrument that is less subject to influences of conscious steering in responding and is also unstructured enough to capture impaired-reality testing. The Rorschach test (the famous ink-blot test), following the procedure of the Comprehensive System (Exner, 1990), was the instrument we used.

We tested three hypotheses related to psychological functioning, as assessed by the Rorschach: perceptual accuracy, disorders of thought, and self-perception (Cohen, de Ruiter, Ringelberg, & Cohen-Kettenis, 1997).

Our first hypothesis was that transsexualism is a misperception of reality and that this misperception is based on a general tendency to misperceive or misinterpret reality. Such a tendency finds its most extreme form in psychotic patients, especially schizophrenic patients. When tested by the Rorschach, the subject is asked to say what the ink-blots might be. Most responses that individuals give are consistent with the contours of the blots. The answer of a butterfly to the first blot is a common answer. Some responses, however, do not fit the contours—for example, perceiving a dog in an area usually regarded as looking like a bat or butterfly. Patient protocols typically show a greater frequency of such responses.

Our second hypothesis was that transsexualism is associated with a disturbance in thinking, such as illogical thinking, and/or "weird" thinking. One variable of the Rorschach CS in particular—the WSUM6—is sensitive to a broad spectrum of problems in thinking. This measure is a sum score based on deviations in verbal expression, logical thinking, and conceptual combinations.

Our third hypothesis was that transsexualism may develop as a response to perceptions of oneself as being damaged, injured, or defective as male or female. One of the Rorschach variables relating to self image is the MOR code used for morbid responses, and, following our hypothesis, one might expect to see a high frequency of MOR responses if the guarded-against feelings of damage have not been resolved by the cross-gender "solution".

These hypotheses were tested in the first 29 transsexual patients (20 FMs, 9 MFs) who had been referred to our clinic and for whom a Rorschach protocol was available. Their responses were compared with protocols of 24 adolescent outpatient psychiatric patients and with a sample of 25 female (but no male) university students tested in the same period for another study.

As a group, transsexuals were found to be intermediate between psychiatric patients and non-patients with regard to perceptual inaccuracy. With regard to thinking disturbances and negative self-image, there were no significant differences. To check whether our failure to find elevated MORs in the protocols of our transsexual subjects is the result of a narcissistic defence against feelings of injury and/or low self-esteem, we inspected the transsexuals' reflection responses, but no differences were found between the transsexual and the student sample.

Besides these specific hypotheses, we also checked the protocols of the transsexuals' group for other signs of pathology (e.g. general psychopathology, high levels of aggression, or restricted object relations). We did not find any elevated scores in the transsexuals group as a whole.

From these two studies, we conclude that neither the Rorschach protocols nor the personality inventories scores of the adolescent group reflected the often expected marked degree of psychopathology.

"Johanna" applied for SRS when she was 16 years old. Her father was a computer programmer, her mother a housewife. Johanna had two sisters. An older sister was a Dutch language student at the Amsterdam University, a younger one was still in high school. Johanna has always been a quiet, "easy" child. Like her sisters, she did not favour typical girls' things as a child, so her parents were not alarmed by her behaviour. She was, however, in contrast to her sisters, fond of soccer, and she had a few very close male friends. When she went to high school, she became even quieter than usual and started to make a sad impression on her parents. Her male friends went to other schools. Unlike her sisters, she never dated and she became a loner. At school, her grades were still high, and there were no other signs that something was the matter. When, one day, her mother saw her daughter putting on a very tight T-shirt of her sister's to hide her breasts, Johanna's transsexuality became apparent. Although shocked, her parents immediately sought help. The family doctor referred her to our clinic. Johanna fulfilled all necessary criteria for an early treatment. At age 17, she started using orgametril to stop her menses, and after four months testosterone was prescribed. One year later, she had breast surgery and her uterus and ovaries were removed. At 19, her birth certificate was changed. In this period, Johanna/Jaap went to university. Three months ago he came to our clinic again. He wanted to discuss a metaidoioplasty (transformation of the hypertrophic clitoris into a micropenis), with a neoscrotum and implanted testicles. Jaap told me that he is doing well. He will soon have his Masters in psychology and wants to become a licenced clinical psychologist. He has had a girl-friend for more than four years and has lived with her for about three years. Jaap wanted to take the last surgical step in order to feel more complete as a man. Sexually, he and his girlfriend have found non-coital ways to make love.

Jaap is an example of an adolescent transsexual who would have suffered tremendously from waiting for SRS even longer than he already did. Because of such potential negative consequences of delaying SRS, we have allowed applicants like him, who did not seem to have many problems other than gender dysphoria, to start with the SRS procedure even before the legally adult age, which is 18 years.

To evaluate this decision, we did a follow-up study of our first 22 transsexual patients, on average about 2.6 years after the last operation (Cohen-Kettenis & van Goozen, 1997). The main result of this study was that sex reassignment had resolved the patients' gender identity problem and had enabled them to live in the new gender quite adequately. Socially and psychologically, these adolescents did not seem to function very differently from their non-transsexual peers. Relief of gender dysphoria, however, did not solve all the patients' life problems. Sometimes non-transsexual-ism-related problems, such as shyness, had disappeared. In other cases such changes had not occurred. The new situation had even created new problems, such as in the case of FMs living as a man without a penis. This situation created practical problems such as showering in a group after certain sports activities or emotional problems such as being frustrated because of the impossibility of having intercourse with a girlfriend. The extent to which such unfavourable factors influence post-surgical functioning may depend largely on the individual's psychological strength. We therefore used several measures to assess their post-surgical psychological functioning. After treatment, the group appeared to function quite stably psychologically. Their feelings of inadequacy and self-esteem improved significantly, and they also became more extrovert and dominant. Compared to normative groups, all scores that had been in the unfavourable range before treatment had "normalized". These results suggest that they were probably capable of handling adequately the problems that occurred.

When we compared the results from the adolescent study with results from a study among 141 adult transsexuals, it appeared that the adolescents do better psychologically (Kuiper, 1991; Kuiper & Cohen-Kettenis, 1988). They also had fewer social problems, and they received much more support from their families and friends than did the adults. Part of the adolescents' better post-surgical psychological functioning might be due to the fact that, because of their convincing appearance, they pass more easily in the desired gender role than do the adults. Another aspect of this relatively positive outcome may be attributable to the more stringent criteria for treatment eligibility.

We would certainly not plead that any adolescent with a gender identity disorder should have sex-reassignment surgery. But, in our view, the results thus far should make clinicians more aware of early hormone treatment as a reasonable and effective treatment option for adolescents with a transsexual problem, and of the potential damaging effects of delaying such interventions until adulthood.

CHAPTER EIGHT

Gender identity disorder, depression, and suicidal risk

Hartwin Sadowski & Barbara Gaffney

All the adolescents seen in the Gender Identity Development Unit of the Portman Clinic have spoken of feeling "down", despairing, and depressed at times. They have spoken of feeling lonely, different from their peers, hopeless at times, and in conflict within themselves. There is a sense of despair of ever feeling complete and potent in their identity and body. Most of these youngsters have at some time spoken of their current or past suicidal feelings or attempted suicides. Some have insisted that without immediate surgery life could not go on, that they would feel impelled to kill themselves to escape what they felt was intolerable. Others struggle on, unsure of what to do for the best for their future.

It needs to be stressed that young people with a gender identity disorder face the same risk factors for depression and suicidal behaviour that affect other youth—namely, confrontation with parents, peers, and teachers, the breakup of intimate relationships, conflict with the law, and experiences of abuse or assault (Shaffer & Piancentini, 1994). However, these general risk factors assume greater importance and have a more severe impact in youngsters who have not yet attained a stable sexual orientation or who believe that they have a gender identity that is different from their sex at birth, as they feel isolated from or in conflict with their peers, their parents, and their society's values (Gibson, 1989).

Their gender confusion, their frequently marked cross-gendered behaviour (especially effeminate behaviour in boys), and often homosexual or transsexual orientation in later life may cause direct conflicts with parental and peer-group expectations, leading to social ostracism (Green, 1987; Rekers, Bentler, Rosen, & Lovaas, 1977; Sreenivasan, 1985) and renders them vulnerable to related abuse which may cause further withdrawal, hopelessness, and possibly drug abuse (Remafedi, Farrow, & Deisher, 1991; Savin-Williams, 1994). All of these themes are common findings in studies of depression and suicidal behaviour (Brent, 1997; Shaffer & Piancentini, 1994; Tayler, Burton, & Kolvin, 1992).

Unfortunately no prospective epidemiological data of depression and suicidal risk are available for youngsters with gender identity disorder. Only a few retrospective studies have been published for homosexual youngsters and transsexual adults which did not employ standardized interview measures and were related to specially selected groups (Burns, Farrell, & Brown, 1990; Huxley, Kenna, & Brandon, 1981; Mate-Kole, Freschi, & Robin, 1988; Remafedi et al., 1991; Rotheram-Borus, Hunter, & Rosario, 1992; Schneider, Farberow, & Kruks, 1989).

These retrospective studies support the clinical experience that adult transsexuals have a high lifetime prevalence of attempted suicide and depression. Indeed, 53% of 72 transsexuals surveyed by Huxley et al. (1981) had attempted suicide in their life, and 42% of males and 27% of females reported a history of drug overdose, deliberate self-harm, or alcohol misuse in Burns et al.'s study (1990). In his review for the Report of the U.S. Secretary's Task Force on Youth Suicide (Department of Health & Human Services), Gibson (1989) referred to Harry's contribution at the Secretary's Conference on Adolescent Suicide (Harry, 1986) who felt that "transsexuals may be at higher risk than homosexuals and much higher risk than the general population" to suicidal behaviour and possibly depressive disorder.

Two important risk factors for suicidal behaviour are emerging from retrospective studies of gay adults: a feminine gender role in boys and an adolescent-loner status both in females and males. Remafedi et al. (1991) demonstrated a threefold-higher likelihood for having attempted suicide, if feminine gender role behaviour was recalled by the subject. Re-examining the retrospective data from the Kinsey Institute, Harry (1983) showed a significant association in males, between attempted suicide and recalled adolescent-loner status and also childhood cross-gender behaviour, but in females only between attempted suicide and adolescent-loner status. This compares well with the clinical finding that effeminate behaviour in gender-disordered boys is met more often with disapproval and rejection by parents, teachers, and peers than tomboy behaviour in girls. However, loneliness, social withdrawal, and isolation are common in male and female youngsters with gender identity disorder.

Therapy with gender-confused adolescents needs to provide support and a space to explore gently experiences, perceptions, and assumptions that have led to alienation from peers and parents. During the assessment and therapy, it is necessary to enquire directly about suicidal thoughts and plans, which often leads to the exploration of mixed feelings about the imagined death and the strengthening of the wish to survive. This provokes extreme anxiety in the therapist which needs to be contained with the help of an experienced team in order to keep alive a space in the therapist's mind for the adolescent at risk. The following two case vignettes try to illustrate these issues and their implication for working with gender identity-disordered adolescents who are presenting with suicidal ideation and behaviour.

"Andrew" is an adolescent living with his single mother, brothers, and sisters. His father had left the family some years ago. After watching a TV programme about transsexualism, he approached his GP who referred him to the Gender Identity Development Unit of the Portman Clinic. He had also contacted the self-help group, Mermaids.

At the initial interview, Andrew stated that he was "a male-to-female transsexual and very deeply depressed". He reported himself as not having any friends or interests beyond the family. He had felt like a girl since the age of 5 when he started school and he preferred playing with girls, and, for example, he recalled daydreaming as if he were a girl and imagining a life ahead in the role of a woman. He played with his sisters' dolls and did not mix with boys or engage in male contact-sport activities. For many years, he had been regularly bullied at school and called "sissy" or "poof". His siblings were refusing to speak with him since he had revealed his wish to be female.

Whilst his mother was pregnant with one of his brothers as he entered puberty, he longed to be pregnant himself. He tried to speak of this with his mother but felt rejected in his attempts, so he "bottled it up, falling deeper and deeper into despair". He recalled hating his body for the changes brought on by puberty, and he felt isolated. As a young adolescent he took an overdose and was admitted to hospital. When he was interviewed by a psychiatrist in hospital, he furiously resisted an exploration of links between his overdose and family difficulties. He stated that it was because of bullying by the boys at school, who saw him as gay. He walked out of the overdose assessment interview after he had felt like punching the psychiatrist; significantly, he did not reveal his secret wish to be a girl, which he felt to be the reason for his overdose.

After seeing the TV programme about transsexualism, he had felt more able to talk with his mother about his wish to be female and now felt closer to her. He no longer felt as isolated as before, and the offer of an appointment at the clinic had been a relief to him. He had found out more information about transsexualism and sex-reassignment surgery, and he thought that his identity was confirmed by this. His distress was mostly centred around impatience for surgery and his imagined need to move away to another city in order to live a female life.

Andrew was offered monthly appointments with the aim of providing a space for him to consider his anxieties, conflicts, and choices. This was alongside offering, in appointments with a paediatric endocrinologist, the opportunity for him to find out more about the reality of the process of gender reassignment.

He used the appointments to engage slowly in a therapeutic relationship considering how the private becomes public. He continued to want to act in order to solve his turmoil. Some things remained unbearable and unthinkable, and so the work was cautious. One important aim was to offer him hope through the experience of feeling understood and through offering the opportunity to explore several possibilities of change, without raising unbearable inner tensions or threatening rigid and vulnerable defences. Andrew did not pursue appointments to follow up a transsexual solution; he felt more accepting of his feelings and decided to defer choices, and he left home for an exploratory art course.

* * *

"Jo", another adolescent, was referred by her psychiatrist to the Gender Identity Development Unit after she had been seen for about six months. She had felt increasingly uncomfortable with her changing body and her gender through puberty, and she did not want to be a girl. She had become increasingly depressed and suicidal, requesting mastectomy from her GP, which led to her referral to a psychiatrist.

Jo reported disliking being female for as long as she could remember and felt that she was always seen as a tomboy in her family. She preferred climbing trees, playing football, fighting, rough-and-tumble play, and mixing with boys. As a teenager, she felt attracted to women but did not feel that she was lesbian since she imagined herself to be of male gender.

When Jo saw the psychiatrist for the assessment interview, she did not report any suicidal thoughts. However, she revealed that she had felt like taking an overdose prior to seeing her GP. The psychiatrist had noticed that she had been depressed, was sleeping erratically, and had a poor appetite. Jo was speaking about the mastectomy as a first step, with a possible view to future surgery. However, she was also wary about losing the support of her family, and she anticipated rejection.

Following the psychiatrist's referral to the Gender Identity Development Unit, Jo failed to attend several appointments. She eventually came to her first appointment after feeling suicidal again and at the insistence of her GP that she should take time to think about herself before he could make a referral for surgery. Jo described herself as living in a male role both in dress, in activities, and in the way she saw herself. She preferred to be called *he* and had shortened her name to a more male-sounding abbreviation. Jo had not told her mother of her wishes but felt that her mother probably understood since she had recently accepted that Jo was wearing male clothes. Jo described her longing for surgery that would solve some of her problems, as she felt she was living in a nightmare. She felt trapped in the wrong body and unable to talk with anyone about how she felt. For some time, she had experienced suicidal thoughts and intermittent explosive outbursts. She would redirect her aggression from people she knew against herself—for example, punching walls and injuring her knuckles. In recognizing her wish to protect others from her outbursts and her terror of what she might do to herself, she felt understood, if not unburdened, and wanted further appointments. In therapy, she found a space for her innermost distress as she did not feel that she could talk to friends, fearing that she would frighten or burden them. She attended only intermittently, with lengthy intervals between appointments. The attendance needed to be facilitated by many letters and frequent liaisons with her GP to sustain contact.

Jo attended her appointments often feeling depressed and preoccupied. An important theme was envy of all who seem to be content in themselves as women or as men. She talked about distancing herself from people for fear of being hurt or rejected by them, both in the past and in the present. Fantasizing about an intimate relationship as a male, she considered the realities of what life would be like after surgery. For example, she wondered whether intercourse would hurt after sex-reassignment surgery and whether or not she would be able to have a baby and be a father. Jo felt trapped within herself and with these concerns whilst her peers were all enjoying talking of girlfriends, boyfriends, and their futures. They were not in any way confronting her, and she realized that it was her own difficulty in not being able to speak of things with them that left her feeling isolated. Jo saw the only solution to be surgery and then moving to an environment where she would not be known.

Over time, Jo complained about being kept waiting by the professionals for surgery. She felt deprived, rejected, and not heard, perceiving surgery as the solution to a catastrophic internal state. To release her tension, she started to use alcohol and cannabis but was fearful of the side-effects for her health and the disinhibition that these drugs produced. Jo felt cut off from her friends and family even whilst sitting amongst them. This left her feeling guilty of being "too much", selfish, and fearful of being rejected by those who cared for her when she felt most in distress. Together with her therapist, Jo considered how to survive whilst working out what she most wanted for herself and enabling her to find some hope and to sustain herself.

During the occasional interviews, her suicide plan was addressed, questioning her directly: when did she feel likely to act upon it, what were the underlying feelings from which she was struggling to escape, what did she do to protect herself, what resources or support could she use, both internal and external? Jo saw suicide as a solution that she could take in the face of feeling despairing and helpless. She recognized the reality that she would no longer be there afterwards to know of this relief. She also felt concerned for those who would miss her. At times, she saw suicide as a way of protecting others from her feared outbursts of envy and aggression. At other times, suicide was imagined as an escape from a body within which Jo could not live comfortably as she hated her breasts so much. On the other hand, she was terrified of destroying herself and wanted help to protect herself. In discussion with her, it was agreed to inform her GP at times of intense crises.

Whilst information was given about the choices that Jo had available to find out about sex reassignment and the possibility of meeting with other young people in a similar situation, the aim of therapy was to offer support during an adolescent developmental crisis. Jo was encouraged to explore her preconceptions and think through her identifications in therapy whilst also trying things out in her peer relationships, rather than quickly opting for a premature foreclosure of adolescent development through changes to the body. Interviews were also offered with a paediatric endocrinologist in order to address her physical, biological concerns. Support was offered in coping with the social reality of feeling different through offering contact with her family, her school, and her wider social network. Other colleagues in the team offered this work once she had agreed to it, so enhancing a facilitating environment and preventing further damage in missing out on education and links with her family.

Both Jo and Andrew had felt different from an early age, and both had kept their gender dysphoria to themselves for a long time. While Jo was accepted as a tomboy, Andrew was bullied and rejected by his peers. For both adolescents, the physical maturation of their bodies during puberty challenged their identification with the opposite sex, fuelling their severe identity crises. Their internal experience of dissociation between their self and body was magnified, and the spurt in sexual maturation challenged the psychic mechanisms that had been employed to keep their gender dysphoria from overwhelming their fragile sense of self. These adolescents become further alienated from their own body, but also from an environment that presumes a mental unity between self and body and assigns gender-role identification according to male and female genitalia and secondary sex characteristics.

Adolescents experiencing such severe internal splits will meet additional confusion about their own identity in their environment, especially with their parents, siblings, and peers. Often this confusion will lead to rejection and elicit hostile responses or abuse. Andrew's siblings refused to speak to him, and he had been bullied at school for many years; Jo anticipated rejection by her family. Under these circumstances, the normative separation from their parents and families becomes even more difficult, and coping skills and defence mechanisms can be easily overused and over-stressed (A. Freud, 1958). Family members' hostile reactions in themselves may fuel parent–adolescent conflicts or lead to unresolved family problems, which are the most commonly reported stressful events occurring just prior to both completed or attempted suicides in youths (Wagner, 1997).

Additionally, gender identity-disordered adolescents have greater difficulties in achieving a sense of their own distinct personality during their normative adolescent crisis (Erikson, 1955). It is taxing for any adolescent to negotiate his or her developmental tasks such as attaining a stable sexual identity, developing the ability to form a long-term sexual relationship, attaining a steady job or preparing for a career, and attaining a personal-value system that respects both the needs of the self and the needs of others (Schowalter, 1995). However, the combination of an internal split in respect of primary sexual characteristics and mental identification with the other gender, together with the anticipated and experienced confusion in the close environment, can lead to a severe impairment in negotiating these developmental tasks. These adolescents find themselves in an incredible paradox. How can they experiment with their first intimate relationships if their bodily sexual characteristics are so different from those with which they identify? How can they find a partner who would tolerate such unbearable splits? How will they be able to tolerate all their envy towards what they perceive as "normal" adolescents' lives, especially when exposed to peer group rejection? How will they be able to proceed in attending school or in their careers when bullied and abused?

The "inner turmoil" as represented by feelings of misery, self-deprecation, and ideas of reference which are quite common in adolescents (Rutter, Graham, Chadwick, & Yule, 1976) may further aggravate already existing gender dysphoria leading to unbearable feelings of hopelessness and frustration, both associated with suicidal intent and suicide. Hence, Andrew and Jo perceived suicide as an escape from their intolerable situations, in view of both their mental anguish and the enormous obstacles that they faced in proceeding to an adult role (Hurry, 1977, 1978).

More attention needs to be given to gender-disordered youth as a high-risk group for suicidal behaviour in order to facilitate "detection awareness" (Blumenthal & Kupfer, 1989). Once flagged as "at risk", problems in family relationships and conflicts with others related to gender identity disturbance should be carefully addressed on a longitudinal basis by health and social professionals to prevent alienation and isolation from family and peer support. From an early stage, the parents and professionals involved will have to anticipate an increasingly disturbing identity conflict in the youngster, which will be aggravated by the sexual maturation during puberty.

There needs to be a heightened awareness of general and specific risk factors in gender-disordered youth for suicide, such as social isolation and ostracism, and substance abuse (Gibson, 1989; Remafedi et al., 1991; Savin-Williams, 1994). If hopelessness, impulsivity, or the combination of hostility and aggression arise in adolescents, the likelihood of attempted suicide is especially high (Brent, 1997); at that stage, urgent support and counselling should be provided to help to deal with crisis situations, and long-term therapeutic intervention at least considered.

Often the gender-disordered youngster only starts to admit to the experienced inner confusion and split when in therapy, which provides a safe and accepting environment. Once the adolescent does not need to defend herself or himself against perceived and experienced attacks, inner fears and fantasies can be explored, as in the cases of Andrew and Jo. On the one hand, the therapist needs to respect the adolescent's respective gender identity. On the other hand, premature fixations could be questioned in order to help the adolescent remain flexible enough to think about different possible solutions to overcoming the internal split between biological sex and mental identification. Both Andrew and Jo kept the question of sex reassignment open while their alienation from their own bodies was explored. However, the maintenance of hope in the positive resolution of the identity conflict is an important task in this phase, as suggested by Di Ceglie in chapter twelve.

Furthermore, during therapy the therapist should be aware of the adolescent's developmental tasks in order to anticipate and prevent further difficulties and possible secondary handicaps escalating the mental anguish (Hurry, 1977, 1978).

Both anticipated and experienced rejection make it extremely difficult for gender identity disordered youngsters to develop trust in others and in themselves. It is difficult enough to engage and maintain adolescents in therapy, but the specific identity confusion in gender-disordered adolescents compounds this problem, and the anxieties of the therapist can become extreme and need to be contained to avoid spilling into the sessions.

Andrew's and Jo's therapies were held in mind and thus contained, especially in crisis situations, but also at other stages during their therapies by the multidisciplinary team of the Gender Identity Development Unit at the Portman Clinic. Thus, other team members could respond at crisis points and liaise with health and other professionals locally where the youngsters could be offered emergency support when the suicidal ideation would become more irresistible. This ensured that the therapeutic relationship did not completely break down due to overwhelming fears either in the youngster or the therapist.

Finally, it is important to facilitate a constant liaison between the various professionals, which helps to maintain an awareness in the larger system of the youngsters' vulnerability and supportive needs and not only in emergency situations.

Acknowledgement

With grateful acknowledgement of the support and helpful comments of the Gender Identity Development Unit's team, Portman Clinic, London, UK.

CHAPTER NINE

Gender identity development and eating disorders

Gianna Williams & Richard Graham

In this chapter we would like to present some ideas and clinical material on the relationship between eating disorders and gender identity development. The relationship between eating disorders and sexual development has been previously reported in the psychiatric literature, most notably by Crisp (1967). The emphasis has perhaps been that of the eating disorder (anorexia nervosa) controlling or reducing the feminine aspects of a developing female adolescent. As this issue has been widely addressed elsewhere, we do not focus on it within this chapter. Similarly, we do not address the research on the incidence of eating disorders in those who are either homosexual or have problems with gender identity.

It is our intention here to address the matter from a different perspective—that is, through consideration of case material in which issues of both gender development and an eating disorder were very prominent. Our perspective is to consider the link between these two areas using psychoanalytic ideas, and our clinical material is taken from psychoanalytic psychotherapy with individuals and families. Consequently, our ideas are underpinned by the concepts developed by Sigmund Freud, and the further developments of his work by Melanie Klein. In order to assist the reader's understanding of the case material, some of the relevant psychoanalytic concepts are described briefly below.

Following his psychoanalytic work with those suffering from hysteria, as well as on the basis of self-analysis and his own observations, Freud developed ideas about psychosexual development. He described the roots of adult genital sexuality as occurring in childhood, and he also noted that difficulties at earlier stages of sexual development may be seen later as difficulties in the area of adult sexuality. The first stage of psychosexual development described by Freud is the oral stage. Present from birth, the oral stage delineates the infant's preoccupation and pleasure with its mouth. Much of emotional life at this time relates to the experiences that the infant has with its mouth, notably in its relationship to food, and also to the breasts of the mother. Freud saw such stages of psychosexual development as driven by instinct, and he was much influenced in his thinking by Darwin. As the child develops, sexual development progresses through different stages, defined by which part of the body is the major preoccupation of that stage. The stages were thus oral, anal, phallic, and in adolescence genital, with a quieter period—the latency stage—in-between. In the course of his investigations into sexual development, Freud discovered one of the core aspects of emotional life and sexual development—the Oedipus situation. The acceptance of parental sexuality, plus acknowledgement of the differences between the sexes and the generations, remains the cornerstone of all psychoanalytic work, although it has been expanded upon by others, including Melanie Klein. The experience and tolerance of all the different feelings associated with the situation—notably feelings of exclusion, jealousy, rivalry, and shame—lend a particularly poignant quality to the Oedipus situation; the manner in which a person relates to these "facts of life", including the acknowledgement of death, fundamentally colours the structure and expression of the individual's personality, whatever the inherited temperament. Freud saw the Oedipus situation arising at around 3 years of age, reaching its peak at 5 years of age. Melanie Klein, through the psychoanalysis of very young children, saw Freud's view as more of a sunset than a dawn to something that had been in existence for some time, well before the third year of life. Melanie Klein also discovered many other aspects of the Oedipus situation, and she illustrated how the stages of psychosexual development as described by Freud coloured the nature of the oedipal phantasies at that age. For example, when the oral feelings predominate, there may be phantasies that the relationship of the parents to each other is that of them feeding each other at a banquet from which the infant feels painfully excluded.

In addressing the matter of gender development and eating disorders, there is thus a framework in which the two can be brought together. In our view, the configuration of the Oedipus situation strongly influences gender identity development and many other areas of instinctual life, including, of course, the eating of food. To give some further introduction to this area, we would like to introduce two case histories from the psychoanalytic literature which illustrate some of the ideas that have been used in our work.

Freud's "little Hans"

Freud was able, in the course of his writings, to present case histories that illustrated his thinking or ideas at that time. One of his most famous cases was that of little Hans (Freud, 1909b). This case not only illustrated aspects of the psychosexual development of children, but also laid the foundation for later psychoanalytic work with children. Freud himself did not conduct the analysis of little Hans; rather, he supervised the approach of Hans's father, since Hans was having a number of difficulties, mainly of a phobic type. Although this approach may seem highly unusual nowadays, it was the first example of analytic work with children, and it has certainly informed later practice.

In the case of little Hans, as described by Freud in 1909, Freud makes clear the link between phantasies related to sexuality and gender identity and phantasies related to oral issues, although that is not his major concern. Little Hans, despite the phobic elements, was a child who revealed to us many aspects of normal development, as his phantasies about the relationship between the parents were not greatly affected by his pathology. In Freud's account, Hans clearly wishes to identify with father and to become his mother's husband. He goes to the extent of suggesting that father could marry his own mother, leaving mother free to be Hans' wife, an arrangement likely to please all concerned, at least in the mind of Hans. Little Hans is also, at times, identified with mother, or is perhaps in competition with her, as he wishes to have children and be capable of bearing babies (p. 93):

Hans   "... I should so like to have children ..."

I   "Have you always imagined that Berta and Olga and the rest were your children?"

Hans   "Yes. Franzl and Fritzl and Paul too ... and Lodi."

In no uncertain terms, Hans states that what he wants is to have babies:

Hans   "So you say that daddies don't have babies. How does it work my wanting to be a Daddy?"

Although Freud does not pay an enormous amount of attention to Hans's identification with both parents, it is clearly a very central part of Hans's development to experience wishes both to be big and strong like father and to be fertile and rich with babies like his mother. Melanie Klein repeatedly confirmed this discovery in her own work; in normal development, there is always some identification with both parents.

Hans continues:

Hans   "... I'd so much like to have children; then I'd do everything for them—take them to the W.C., clean their behinds. ..."

Clearly a somewhat restricted job description.

Freud also described clearly the oral phantasies that Hans had about his mother's body, and the riches that it contained. A striking example of this is Hans's description of the inside of mother's body as full of all sorts of attractive food. Hans and his little sister could then, in the little boy's phantasy, help themselves to this food.

Hans talks further about his sister Hanna:

"They put in bread-and-butter for her, and herring, and radishes ... and as Hanna went along she buttered her bread-and-butter and ate fifty meals."

This banquet is taking place in a box, and Hans states clearly that his sister Hannah was inside that box before she was born.

Klein's "Richard"

Following Freud, Melanie Klein developed a psychoanalytic technique for work with children, and through her technique of understanding and interpreting the play of children she built further on Freud's ideas.

In the "Narrative of a Child Analysis" (Klein, 1961), she describes a relatively brief period of analysis with a boy called Richard. Richard was 10 years old when Mrs Klein started seeing him during World War II. This case enabled Mrs Klein to extend her ideas regarding the Oedipus situation and certainly demonstrated how more primitive feelings and phantasies could colour the experience of the relationship between the parents.

At a time when the oedipal jealousy and feelings of exclusion were very rife in the relationship of Richard to Mrs Klein, Richard talked about a couple, "the cook" and "Bessie", and this was clearly related to Mrs Klein and her husband in the transference relationship. Bessie and cook are described as speaking German to one another, although the actual Bessie and cook in Richard's life did not know a word of German. Melanie Klein, of course, had a Germanic-sounding accent. At this point of the analysis, the phantasy of the sexual relationship between the parents, and its oral dimension, is clearly coloured by much greater persecutory feelings than was the case for little Hans.

> Suddenly and with determination he [Richard] said that he wanted to tell Mrs K something which was worrying him very much. He was afraid of being poisoned by cook or Bessie. They would do this because he was often horrid or cheeky to them. From time to time he had a good look at the food to find out whether it was poisoned. He looked into bottles in the kitchen to see what they contained; they might have poison in them which cook would mix with his food. Sometimes he thought that Bessie, the maid, was a German spy. He occasionally listened at the keyhole to find out whether cook and Bessie were speaking German together. [p. 128]

It is of course understandable, on the basis of these very persecutory phantasies, that a theme recurrent in Richard's play is the one of separating objects standing for the father and the mother wedging the couple apart.

Here it is possible to see that Richard's Oedipus situation is complicated by the presence of strong, primitive oral phantasies and a related hostility towards the parental couple, although it would not be surprising to find similar phantasies and feelings in other children who are reluctant to eat. For Richard to develop sexually into an adult male, he needs good parental figures in his mind with whom he can identify: physical growth at puberty alone provides only the engine of change, not its direction or destination. When there are such terrifying, poisoning figures in the mind, identification is complicated, and any identification with such figures is likely to be felt as alien to the self. Richard's hatred of the sexual relationship between his parents contaminates his experience of them as providing food and care for him. The resulting paranoid ideas affected his relationship to food and clearly brought him a great deal of distress.

* * *

Some of the ideas contained in the two case histories above can be seen in a contemporary example, that of George:

"George"

The theme of a difficulty in accepting the parents' relationship with each other, paralleled by a relatively mild feeding difficulty, is evident in the case of a little boy, George, aged 9 years. George was seen for once-weekly psychotherapy for four years, and the following material is derived from this work.

George's feeding difficulties, at the time of referral, confined him to a diet based on just a few items of food. George allowed himself such items as long as they were kept totally separate. He was prepared to eat pasta, and he was prepared to eat bread. He was prepared to eat Parmesan, but the Parmesan had to be kept totally separate both from bread and from pasta.

Any food that could reasonably be married to another had to be kept firmly wedged apart from its partner.

In the course of his therapy, George's phantasies of sexual couples emerged, and they bordered on the freakish or the grotesque. The most striking phantasy was the image of a frog supposedly—perhaps with some difficulty—mating with a goldfish. It became apparent in his treatment that the theme of keeping objects separate in the sphere of sexuality (reminiscent of Richard, described above, keeping the couple apart in his mind) and the sphere of feeding were intimately related to one another. The resolution of George's oedipal conflicts led to improvements in some of his feeding difficulties. Similarly, the nature of George's identifications with his parents, particularly his father, shifted. As the pasta and Parmesan were allowed to marry, the couple in George's mind acquired more positive attributes than those to be found in the frog and the goldfish. George moved from being a rather rigid and anxious child to being more confident, more able to relate to peers, and a keen sportsman. Changes in his diet paralleled developments in his sexuality and the inhabiting of his gender identity.

The case of George confirms many of the findings of both Freud and Melanie Klein, but it is the relatively unusual one of a boy with eating difficulties. We will now describe more detailed clinical material from work with two adolescents, both of whom suffered from severe anorexia nervosa. In these cases, the development of the eating disorder was intimately connected with both gender identity and sexual development.

"Emily"

The first case is that of a young adolescent girl, Emily, who was seen in therapy three sessions per week for a period of about two years. When Emily started treatment, she was 16 years old and was maintaining her alarmingly low weight through intensive exercise. She was a very accomplished long-distance runner and since childhood had shared sports activities with her brother, who was two years older than herself, and her father. This masculine identification was a central theme in her therapy, and what appeared to be a hindrance to the healthy development of her gender identity was the partaking in a sort of masculine trinity. This trinity involved her father, her brother, and herself, and it was experienced as only having masculine aspects. This masculine identification was very present in the therapist's perception of Emily in her first session:

"The first time I saw Emily she was standing outside the entrance of the clinic in tears and gasping for breath. She was wearing a singlet vest, running shorts, and trainers. She could easily have been mistaken for a boy, given her matchstick figure."

Emily herself went on to say in this first assessment session that she felt that she got left behind by her brother, and when she was younger she and her brother always used to play together, or rather she had always tagged along when he was with his friends. She had always thought of herself as one of the boys, and she could do any of the physical things that they did. Furthermore, she said that she could play football and cricket and swim and could even keep up with them all if they had races in the garden.

Emily then moved on to describe how her father used to join in these games and how the three of them were all good at sports. Emily's more distressed feelings returned when she described to her therapist how her brother began to change when he was 12 years old. She felt that he suddenly outgrew her as a playmate. The therapist learnt later that Emily's father also stopped taking part in games at the same time, and he had put on a great deal of weight. Emily felt very excluded by these developments.

It became clear in the therapy that, as Emily's partaking in the masculine trinity collapsed, both her eating difficulties and severe claustrophobic anxieties emerged. Her claustrophobic anxieties were so severe that she had her own table and chair outside in the garden and would do her homework outside, whatever the weather, by the light of the kitchen window. She would shelter from the rain under the shed's awning. Emily would take all of her meals outside, stealing into the kitchen to take them when no one was present. If she was inside at night, all the windows were to be kept wide open, whatever the season. Emily's claustrophobia also manifested itself in her compulsive running. She described her running as something that kept her from feeling lonely. Furthermore, her participation in the masculine trinity suggested an identification with a vigorous and active father figure. (He had been a runner in his youth.) Yet this identification appeared to be a means for managing more primitive anxieties, and her severe claustrophobic anxieties were a signal of this. The nature of these primitive anxieties and fantasies emerged more fully during the course of the therapy.

After almost six months of therapy, prior to a holiday break Emily revealed a secret aspect of her eating disorder, something that she referred to as "her night-time feeds". Emily linked this with her father's activities of bringing home take-aways, and she would speak contemptuously of this activity. Emily would then, however, lurk in the kitchen, and when her father had gone she would eat the cold left-overs. It became apparent that Emily felt rather excluded and jealous of her father's solitary activities. She described her father's take-aways as something that he would take up to his bedroom as he would take a mistress. Emily could not abide the grunts that he made whilst eating. Her oedipal phantasy configuration, at this time, thus appeared to be a phantasy of quite a confused type of sexual activity. The atrocious greedy grunts had become confused with the noises of sexual activity. Eating became *the* nocturnal activity, yet it was sexualized. Emily similarly complained that her father's snoring was so loud that her mother had moved out of the marital bedroom. However, Emily had also described before this how she held quite a jaundiced view of her parents' sexuality. She was disgusted by the thought of her enormous father lying on top of her mother. Emily then went on to describe further her own nocturnal activities. She described how "in the middle of the night she would creep downstairs, take huge chunks of crusty bread and eat them in the dark. The huge chunks of bread were something filling, something she could really get her teeth into". She described her anxieties of being caught whilst doing this but also her fear of starving to death. This anxiety loomed large in the therapy, which was especially close to the time of the first holiday break, and Emily was facing again feelings of being excluded or left by the therapist.

Further anxieties emerged later as Emily revealed worries about her appearance and in particular a birthmark on her face. As a child she had felt fat and unattractive and had wanted to be rough and tough like her brother. She described cutting and scarring her arms and legs to achieve this rough-and-tough look. The consequence of this was that others perceived her as a boy. Anxieties and phantasies about her birthmark underlay such feelings about her body. She described how ashamed she was of the birthmark on her face and how she felt that her mother had caused it by having high blood pressure during pregnancy.

As mother had been hospitalized whilst pregnant, Emily was also haunted by anxieties that she had damaged her own mother. However, feelings of having been damaged by mother led to some wish for vengeance: she attacked the body of her mother's daughter, by way of the anorexia nervosa, and thus exacted the revenge upon her mother. As the therapy progressed, Emily's envy of all things male remained more than evident, but she now shared with her therapist anxieties related to identification with a damaged, collapsed mother. She compared maturity in women and men by saying that a woman's body collapses when sexual attributes develop, whilst a man goes on getting stronger. Unconsciously, she probably felt that she had taken something away from her mother at some point, and as a consequence her mother had collapsed. The birthmark was the stigma left by this crime. Emily's hatred of her chubby cheeks when she was a young child suggested the possibility of early anxieties about stealing from or depleting her mother: what she took was taken away, concretely, from mother.

It emerged in parallel therapeutic work with the parents that Emily's experiences were linked to experiences in the family prior to and just after her birth. The death of Emily's paternal grandmother immediately preceded her birth, and she had been an important figure for both parents. Emily's mother, somewhat distant from her own family, had greatly suffered from this loss. Emily's mother was then devastated on seeing Emily and her birthmark after delivery; she had asked: "What's wrong with her?" The birthmark generated in mother feelings of guilt, which did indeed lead to some collapse or depression. There were descriptions of Emily's early life, in which she was said to be "always at the breast" and her mother very depressed. Emily's own phantasies suggested that she felt that she had caused this collapse in some way. Emily also felt that she had been punished for this and was reminded of her guilt forever more, as represented by the stigma of the birthmark. Her defence against this cluster of anxieties and feelings was found in idealization of, and identification with, all things male; her eating disorder achieved this identification and removed, along with all female attributes, the possibility of collapse.

"Sullivan family"

We would now like to present some material from the assessment of a family in which the issues of gender identity loomed large. This family had referred themselves to a clinic at the suggestion of a family friend and were requesting help for their 17-year-old daughter, "Joanne", who was suffering from severe anorexia nervosa. At the first meeting, mother, father, and Joanne attended, and most immediately striking was Joanne's very masculine appearance. She was not only thin and stripped of any overt female characteristics, but her short, lank, fair hair, T-shirt, and tie-dye trousers, plus heavy canvas boots, suggested something rather military and masculine. She was like a young adolescent male. Her parents' appearances were much more conventional.

After hearing from the mother how the problem was one of "anorexia", Joanne herself said that she thought that things were not too difficult on the "food front" (food *was* a battle-front) but that she was exercising excessively. The problem of the anorexia was reported to have started a year prior to this meeting. Joanne herself felt not only that her over-exercising was the greatest problem, but that she could walk a great deal at even lower weights than she was at that point (she weighed approximately 5 st 7 lb [about 35 kg]). She felt anxious that she got excitement from being able to do things at such a low weight. However, she was also concerned about her physical state at times and, having had a recent bone scan, was worried about the state of her bones.

In this first meeting, the therapists explored the difficulties that Joanne had with eating, and they learned that she would only eat the same amount of food as her mother and would feel guilty at having a second helping. However, she could eat extra food if it was left over from someone else's plate. Whilst the issue of her comparing herself with mother was addressed, the therapists learned that Joanne spent much of her time scanning her mother, feeling concerned if she thought that mother was doing too much. If she found mother doing the ironing or vacuum-cleaning late at night, she would come downstairs and stop her. This was centred on Joanne's concern as to how many calories would be burnt up at night or in the dark—the calories she would squander. If mother burnt up calories, they would have to be replaced.

Towards the end of this first meeting, the therapists learned that before the onset of the eating disorder Joanne had become withdrawn and had spent much time crying in her room, and that she felt very fearful of eating food because of a profound sense of guilt that was engendered by eating. This was elaborated further in the second meeting, in which the therapists explored how Joanne's tearfulness seemed related to a feeling that food was a death sentence: Joanne seemed to feel terribly anxious that she would take in something that would lead to her death. This seemed connected to the therapists' experience of the parents carrying this fear that she was dying; Joanne felt she took this back in with every meal, and consequently there was a great deal of anxiety and conflict in the parents about this situation. Later in that meeting, the family spoke of how Joanne would torment her mother with suggestions that she was about to eat something:

> Mrs Sullivan spoke of how Joanne would say things like "Look at these lovely cakes", in a tormenting way. Joanne smiled at this and then said that she had to model herself on her mother in terms of how much food she ate, as her mother was the only woman around. The male therapist asked Mr Sullivan if he had observed such behaviour, and he said that he hadn't seen it except when his wife was around. The therapist commented, referring also to some previous information, that there appeared to be something rather exciting for Joanne in not wanting her parents to catch her eating. Joanne then described

painfully how she would come and sit with her parents and watch TV, otherwise she would think about eating food and then feel compelled to exercise.

It was possible to understand the onset of Joanne's difficulties further in the third assessment meeting, as she described them in more detail. At this meeting we heard that Mr and Mrs Sullivan had come on their own with Joanne because their elder son, John, was qualifying as an accountant that day and was not able to come, and their younger son, Stephen, who is only 16 months older than Joanne, had just started a new job. Joanne looked even thinner and more ill, and the masculine aspects of her appearance dominated.

Mr and Mrs Sullivan complained that Joanne had been wanting to get attention, although Joanne's appearance in the room did not suggest that she was enjoying this. The female therapist asked how Joanne had been earlier in life, as we hadn't heard about that. She wondered what sort of baby Joanne had been and asked, for example, whether Joanne had been a demanding baby. Mrs Sullivan said that all her children had been born by caesarean section and that after Joanne was born she was not a cuddly baby. Mrs Sullivan went on to describe how she had always wanted a girl. Father then spoke of how he hadn't been able to cuddle Joanne after she had "grown up". Mother followed this by saying that Joanne had played in a rough-and-tumble manner with her older brothers but this had stopped when she developed breasts. Mrs Sullivan described how Joanne was blossoming into a woman at that time, but since developing the anorexia she had become a little girl again and seemed no longer self-conscious about cuddling. Mrs Sullivan then wondered whether the fact that her father had died the previous year had affected Joanne because it was around the time of her sixteenth birthday. She thought that Joanne may have felt that she didn't get enough attention at this time. Joanne was then asked by the female therapist whether her periods had stopped by the time of her sixteenth birthday, and Joanne said that they had. Joanne then disagreed with her mother and said that the anorexia had started when she was

13, after they had come back from a holiday in Canada. Mrs Sullivan continued by saying that there had been a difficult patch the following year, which eventually led to her undergoing an operation, a hysterectomy. The male therapist asked whether anyone was aware of the problems that she was having at this time. Mrs Sullivan said anxiously that she had talked to Mr Sullivan but hadn't told anyone else. He asked what had happened to her, and whether anyone else may have seen her difficulties. Mrs Sullivan spoke of how she had become very anaemic and looked pale, and Joanne commented that at that time, on certain days, her mother couldn't do anything. Mother spent many days just lying in bed. We then learnt that the concerns about Mrs Sullivan's health did not improve after her operation. Apparently, there were complications with the operation, possibly because of the previous caesarean sections, as mother's bladder was stuck to her uterus. In the post-operative period, she didn't pass any urine and was "swelling up". Joanne had been very concerned about her mother at this point. She had told the nursing staff to take good care of her mother and that her mother needed good pain relief because she was still in pain. The therapists both commented on how Joanne seemed to have felt that she had taken something from her mother at this time, almost as if mother's sexuality had to be depleted for her to enter into the arena of sexual life. These feelings had led to a profound sense of guilt. Subsequent to this, Joanne needed to ensure that her mother was well cared for and had a good amount of calories. This was a giving of something back to mother; as stated above, mother received the information to replace with food any calories that she may have used up through vacuum-cleaning or other activities. The female therapist further commented that perhaps Mrs Sullivan felt that her role as mother was taken away from her by Joanne, and Mrs Sullivan spoke of how Joanne is often in charge, especially in the kitchen.

At around this point, the male therapist commented that within the room there seemed to be a discussion, in which only the "ladies" were speaking together. There seemed to be a sense that the problems were associated with women and, furthermore, that they were "women's business". The therapists had learned that the male members of the family seemed to be doing well and didn't need to come. The family agreed to this and spoke of how John had done very well in his accountants' firm and was qualifying from a course. Stephen had also managed to get a job, which they were pleased about. The male therapist commented further that perhaps through the loss of weight Joanne wasn't so much becoming younger to look more like a little girl, but instead was somehow trying to become more masculine, as the difficulties described to us were associated with being a woman. Father commented, somewhat defensively, that Joanne still likes boys and had her eyes on a boy during a recent holiday. Joanne commented, "perhaps next year". The therapists then heard further about Joanne's current life and that she spent a lot of time staying in and did not go out or have contact with friends, and the male therapist commented that Joanne's current behaviour seemed reminiscent of that of her mother at the time when mother was ill. This again led the therapists to wonder whether Joanne felt that she had to be punished for having stolen something from mother.

The therapists were both left with strong feelings that Joanne's development into a sexual woman had been impeded by her experiences in early adolescence. The eating disorder became the means not only to reduce her femininity, but also to give her an entrance into the masculine world, which seemed so free of anxiety or guilt.

Conclusions

Melanie Klein discovered through her work with very small children that, from birth, we take in not only milk, but also representations of the thing that is thought to supply the milk. These representations, or internal objects, become more complex through development and may later resemble, fairly accurately, persons in the outside world. Earlier in development, they are much more fantastic or extreme, as they are coloured by the wild feelings of the small child; they may be magically powerful, terrifying, and so forth. During development, we identify with these internal objects, and our sense of identity is based on these representations that we have inside us, and our identifications with them. We see this clearly in the play of children, when they play out parental roles.

If the internal objects are, for whatever reason, of a more terrifying nature, they may feel quite alien inside and are good prospects neither for healthy identifications, nor for development. They may not be models of what someone wants to be when they grow up.

In the cases of George, Emily, and Joanne, phantasies of an oral nature intruded massively into their negotiations of the Oedipus situation, thus impairing sexual development and the sense of a healthy gender identity. George had such terrifying pictures in his mind of two parents coming together that he could not allow anything to come together and get inside him. This clearly applied to the food that he would eat, but it also affected his learning at school. As the figures in his mind became more benign through his therapy, he was able to let them come together, and he could identify with them more fruitfully. Emily and Joanne struggled with rather more difficult issues. Both were presented with a frightening picture of female maturity, and a sense that "It's a man's world". The previously held view that anorexia nervosa arrests pubertal development in those with anxieties about sexual development still holds true, but we hope that we have shown something more. These adolescents had a picture of development in their minds that was quite terrifying. To become an adult female was to collapse, to become ill, and the solution was to identify with the male figures who were perceived as so immune from such terrors. This is very much in keeping with the similar processes in some cases of gender identity disorder, as described by Di Ceglie in chapter two. Such ideas of illness or collapse also massively interfere with the usual and healthy processes of competition with mother, and development may always have been felt to be at mother's expense; Joanne could only eat the same amount as—or presumably less than—her mother. Whilst in no way could Emily or Joanne be thought of as having a core-gender identity problem, the distorted pictures of the two genders in their minds were clearly related to their own difficulties and appearances. The eating disorder certainly provided a sort of entrance to the masculine world, stripping them of all femininity, but it also illustrated again fears similar to those of George: the fear of taking something destructive inside.

CHAPTER TEN

Child sexual abuse and gender identity development: some understanding from work with girls who have been sexually abused

Judith Trowell

T his chapter presents some reflections on sexual abuse of children and then considers the issue of the emotional impact on girls who have been sexually abused and how it might affect their gender identity.

Case material is used to illustrate this, and then some thoughts are presented about the implications for our understanding of the development of gender identity in the light of the therapeutic work.

As will become apparent, on the basis of clinical experience and the limited current research, child sexual abuse is not usually a major contributor to the appearance of a full-blown gender identity disorder in girls. However, in some cases it can affect gender identity development, internal body representations, and sexual relationships in a considerable way, even if this does not amount to all the clinical features of a gender identity disorder.

In the late 1970s and early 1980s, the occurrence of childhood sexual abuse began to be widely recognized. The Cleveland Inquiry report was published in the United Kingdom in 1988, and in this Lord Elizabeth Butler-Sloss confirmed that sexual abuse did indeed occur and existed. Until then, many in society did not believe this to be so. What is important is to ask whether it matters that sexual abuse actually happens to children. We know about the oedipal conflict and the enormous power of the associated phantasies. But the actual physical enactment of the act of adult–child sexuality—masturbation, oral, anal, or vaginal intercourse, and then all the various other sexual acts some children experience—is a very different psychological trauma from the effect of phantasy. Violation of the actual body, and the accompanying threats to ensure silence and secrecy, are damaging in a way that differs from phantasies. The fear of violence and the actual violence that so frequently accompanies the abuse are also very different from the phantasy of destruction or murderous rage.

We have become much clearer about the problems and behaviour associated with childhood sexual abuse. Beitchman and colleagues have undertaken two extensive reviews. The first (Beitchman et al., 1991) looked at 42 different studies to draw out the short-term effects; the second (Beitchman et al., 1992) reviewed the long-term effects. These effects have been summarized by Cotgrove and Kolvin (1996) as four main long-term associations with child sexual abuse:

1. Psychological symptoms consisting of depression, anxiety, low self-esteem, guilt, sleep disturbance, and dissociative phenomena.

2. Problem behaviours including self-harm, drug use, prostitution, and running away.

3. Relationships and sexual problems—social withdrawal, sexual promiscuity, and re-victimization.

4. Psychiatric disorders, particularly eating disorders, sexualization, posttraumatic stress disorder, and borderline personality disorder.

In addition to this greater understanding of the problems and behaviour after abuse, we have also become increasingly aware, as the children and the adults abused as children have been able to speak about their experiences and seek help, that the therapeutic work needed is very complex and difficult. In order to understand and think about the emotional impact of this abuse and how to work therapeutically with abused girls, we have learnt that it is vital to draw on the understanding of child development and of sexuality and aggression that are central in object-relations psychoanalytic theory. Psychoanalytic theory has a significant contribution to make to the work—in particular, the understanding of transference, countertransference, and early mechanisms for trying to manage intense feelings such as splitting, denial, projection, and projective identification—because they are used so extensively by these girls and their families.

Sexual abuse is defined in the United Kingdom by the Department of Health (Schechter & Roberge, 1976) as "the involvement of dependent developmentally immature children in sexual activities that they do not truly comprehend and to which they are unable to give informed consent, and that violate the social taboos of family roles". In this chapter, what is being considered is contact sexual abuse, which means that the child has touched or been touched by the abuser. The acts have been kept secret and may involve bribery, threats, or violence, and some children may have been involved in multiple sexual abuse with groups of children and adults. The abuse may have occurred once or lasted over a period of years with variable frequency.

Some clinical examples
to illustrate the therapeutic intensity of the work

"Phillipa"

Phillipa, an early adolescent of age 14 years at secondary school, was referred by an outside psychiatrist for treatment; she was doing extremely well at school, spending hours there, and was reluctant to leave to go home. She was very small and uncared for but was very friendly with teachers; child sexual abuse was discovered when she talked to the Deputy Head, saying her father came to her room at night.

She was the eldest of three children, with a younger brother and then a sister. Since her sister's birth, when Phillipa was 5 years old, mother and father had been having problems. Mother adored her younger brother and sister. Phillipa had to help in the house, run errands, and give father his meals as her mother was busy with the other two children. Phillipa was very fond of her father; her father began to cuddle Phillipa a lot, then to visit her bedroom for cuddles, then to get into her bed. They had intercourse; at the start this was anal and was then vaginal for about the last three years.

The therapy

Phillipa was fostered by a teacher at school. She was very angry: "Why do I need to come? I only come because I'm made to. What do you know? What could you do—nothing. You haven't been abused—have you." I was totally useless, there was no point in her coming. In spite of this, I arranged to see her; the contempt, derision, sarcasm, denigration, went on and on. She knew more than I did about everything, was more intelligent than I was; she was sneering and mocking, relentlessly. Then she began to flaunt her sexual knowledge and to be quite provocative. She talked in a very erotic and sexualized way, becoming excited and seductive so that sometimes it felt as though she could masturbate me with her words. I began to dread her visits, her words, to dislike her intensely. And yet here was this small vulnerable child/woman who seemed desperately to need help. I felt ground down and useless. I learnt that the foster-mother felt that she couldn't get near her, and the foster-father was extremely uncomfortable.

The feeling of hopelessness and despair lead me to talk about her mother, and she became more and more repulsive. I felt that she resembled a poisonous snake. I began to talk about terror and fear and panic and feeling trapped. This latter produced a dramatic response. She began to talk and talk about her terror and sense of being trapped in her family, in her bed, with her father. She had coped by pulling the sheets up to her chin, putting her arms and head out of the top and not knowing what went on below. She insisted that she had completely cut off. She began to have terrifying night terrors—dreams that were a repetition of the abuse. She talked about her father coming home drunk, how he hated himself, how she was left to get him undressed and into bed, how one day she couldn't support him and he fell and injured himself—she was very upset but relieved. In the room with me, she began to weep. For several weeks she wept and wept through each session. Now, she was talking to her foster-mother, but when Phillipa wept for three weeks almost continuously I think everyone wondered what I was doing to her in the sessions.

Around this time she started to have symbolic dreams, nightmares of her father in a coffin: either he was dead and it was her fault, or he was being buried alive and only she knew it. She wept for her father, finding it hard to be in touch with any anger or rage and her wish to kill her father. They were both victims, he should not have done it; but her hatred of her mother was intense, vitriolic.

She also still woke up frequently at night, screaming, having felt something hard pressing against her and feeling terrified, convinced that it was her father beside her and his erect penis, and that she "knew" intercourse would follow. We understood these dreams as "memories", whereas the other dreams were more usual symbolic dreams which we could struggle to understand. It now felt that she had become a person, not a walking mind; but the pain and despair were very powerful, and at times she raged at me for having done this to her, put her in touch with feelings, tortured her. Finally, she was able to rage at her father as well as show her pity for him. She had some compassion for her mother, whom she realized wasn't aware of the abuse and had probably been quite depressed. We then had to work on her feelings of triumph over her mother and myself and how hard it was to be a teenage girl.

"Susan"

Susan, aged 9½ years, was at primary school and was referred by the social services department. She was one of four children. The mother had left when Susan was small. The elder two children were placed in a foster home. Susan and her youngest brother, about 18 months old, were placed in another foster home; this was a family with six foster children, where the parents were fostering full-time. A short-term foster-child, a girl, there whilst her mother was in hospital, when back at home told her own father about Mr X, the foster-father, touching her, Susan, and other girls; this child's father told social services. All the children were removed.

Mr X had begun touching Susan when she was small, soon after she arrived, initially masturbation of her, then mutual masturbation, then vaginal intercourse over the last few years.

Susan was in an ESN school and had been moved there after nursery class. No reason had been found for her quite serious learning difficulties.

Assessment showed a very flat, unresponsive child, and she had hearing problems—how much was she hearing, how much was subnormality or depression? Recurrent ear infections had left her virtually completely deaf in her right ear and partially deaf in the left. She was unable to cope in a group, unresponsive to counselling in school, and not speaking to her new foster-parents.

The therapy

Susan was offered twice-weekly treatment. There were weeks of saying very little, with apparently no response from her to anything. Then I became aware of her eyes, which were quite alert, watchful, usually hidden by her hair; she never appeared to look at me and still looked stupid. I was aware of feeling more and more depressed and said this to her, and how hopeless it all felt.

She began to talk with rage and hatred about her ex-foster-mother, the terrible food, the hours slaving away doing work in the house and garden, the terrible pain in her ears, and never being taken to the doctor.

At times she was very hostile and suspicious of me. She had further ear infections, and she told me that I was there in the night hitting her about the head, making her vomit, forcing burnt food, stale going-off food, down her, standing over her until she ate it. She had difficulty in sorting out me in her dreams and me at the clinic. It seemed I was seen as the cruel foster-mother.

Material from a session after six months' therapy

Susan came in and sat opposite me across the room—she could not sit further away. She had come to the room rather reluctantly but had not resisted. She did not show any interest in the paper or Plasticine as she had begun to do. She sat without any eye contact and without saying a word. I caught her looking around the room, and her eyes seemed to be darting this way and that. I said: "It seems to be hard today." No reply. I said: "Is it horrid here today?" Susan said nothing but nodded her head. I said: "Why horrid?" Susan looked at me for a moment. I said: "I was puzzled. Was it horrid here in the Clinic or outside, at school, in foster home, before?" After quite a long pause, Susan said: "You hit me." I felt very shaken—what had I done, when, why couldn't I remember? I asked: "When do you think I hit you?" Susan said very firmly: "You hit me." "Tell me", I said. She said: "Night time, night time, you hit me, wake me up hitting me." She was now holding her head in both hands and thrashing in her chair from side to side. "You hit me, I wake up. Why, why you hit me? Pain, hurt." She began to cry and, with her heels on the floor, pushed her chair as far away from me as possible. She was looking at me with fear and rage. I said: "Susan is very afraid and very angry with Dr Trowell. But Dr Trowell is in the Clinic, not in your house. Perhaps Susan had bad dream." "No", she shouted: "You hit me, you hit me, you bad."

I felt worried and a bit panicky. What if outside people could hear, what if her foster-parents or social worker thought I was abusing her. Had I hit her? What had I done and perhaps forgotten? I said: "Maybe Susan had a bad dream, a dream that was remembering bad things." Susan paused and then said: "She hit me, like you hit me, she hit me." I said: "And in the night it all gets muddled up." Silence. Then I said: "It must be very scary not knowing, is Mrs X there, are you back there and she is hurting you, or is it me, Dr Trowell. Maybe because you missed Dr Trowell and wanted me to be there." "No", she said, "You hit me, you bad. You make me eat bad things. Don't take me to doctor's. Need doctor make ears better. Don't take me. Bad." I said: "I think Susan gets in a muddle. It all gets muddled up. Mrs X, myself, her new foster-mum and her real mum. So much pain and hurt. Missing pain, earache pain and then all the pain with Mr and Mrs X hitting and hurting. It was very hard to sort it out." She began to sob. After a while I said: "Maybe the hardest thing could be sort of wanting to be hit, wanting the pain, because then Susan knew someone was there. Susan wasn't all by herself." She left tearful and down.

During this session I had been very thrown. I needed to check with myself and reassure myself that I hadn't hit her as far as I could remember. I also felt briefly furious with her for disconcerting me. I wanted to shake her and say, "Don't be so stupid. I never hit you. How dare you say that." Susan's conviction when she came in that I had hit her seemed fixed—or was it my anxiety that made it seem so? Certainly it was very hard indeed to hold on to the capacity to think and not know the answers, to stay with uncertainty.

Towards the end of the first year, she began to talk about her foster-father. She wept a great deal. He hadn't been cruel; she had felt bad, dirty, knew it was wrong but it was also good, being held, being touched, stroked; no-one else did, except she and her brother, but hardly ever. The inside bit was awful and all the mess and the smell. She thought everyone could smell it, knew it, everyone at school. Now he was in trouble and she felt sad, glad it had all stopped, but she sort of missed him. He had a terrible time with Mrs X; she was a right cow.

Now she was sobbing for her natural mother—where was she, why had she walked out, and, to a lesser extent, why hadn't their natural father kept them (she still saw him). At school, she began to learn, to ask questions; she started to try to write—for example, her name—and she drew. She began to read, about families and animals, and later to use small numbers and add up. Susan developed a real talent for drawing and painting and using clay, making animal models. She was a real star in the school kitchen and she loved cookery. She began to read in earnest—recipes and the instructions on the kiln at school.

We now went over and over the sexual abuse, her sexual feelings for girls and women and myself, her shame, her longing for babies. She wondered if she was normal—could she have them? Would she ever have normal relationships with men? My reactions were very powerful and at times difficult to cope with: despair, fear, guilt, anger, the seduction of being the good, idealized, abandoning mother—the ease with which I could have been the cruel, sadistic foster-mother.

"Jane"

Jane was 3½ years old when she was referred by the nursery. She lived with her single-parent mother. The nursery was concerned because Jane had almost no speech, seemed unable to play, and sat frequently masturbating or with other children on top of her or she on top of them, very excited and with rhythmic, thrusting pelvic movements involved in mutual masturbation. Her mother had had a series of transient co-habitees and liked to go out late in the evening, sleeping in late so that the co-habitees sometimes babysat and often got Jane up and took her to nursery. Jane was mixed-race—her mother was white, and her father (not clear who) had almost certainly been black as the co-habitees were frequently black.

Jane was interviewed about possible abuse; her mother knew nothing. Jane did not speak but did show sexual activity as part of demonstrating cuddles. There was physical evidence of abuse but no clarification as to which of Mum's partners had abused her. Jane mentioned no names. She was placed with foster-parents.

The therapy

Jane came weekly. She drew very simple stylized representations of her mother with a baby in her tummy and herself also with a baby in her tummy. She communicated this by nodding her head yes or no to suggestions. Most of the time she was very excited, running around the room or playing with the small plastic animals, which seemed to copulate indiscriminately. Or she was on the floor, legs apart, offering her genital area to be seen, to be entered, and making excited, rhythmic pelvic movements.

Gradually, Jane added to the drawings one of Jane angry, then Jane crying, Jane hurt. The face had tears running to a pool on the floor. Jane couldn't really explain further, and attempts to make contact were not easy. Jane seemed to have an idea of Mum, mother, but whether her distress related to missing her real mother was unclear. The talk of babies, herself as baby, her baby, Mum's baby, produced great excitement, as did comment on the copulating animals.

Any reference to small, sad Jane, terrified about all of this, and to how she somehow, sometimes, must feel rage or feel very bad, at fault, produced frantic activity and excitement or rage and attempts to hurt or destroy things.

She did occasionally use a small plastic telephone: this was to phone the police—"someone is hurt".

After six months, the placement began to break down, and Jane went to a residential therapeutic community.

It had often felt with Jane that she was somewhere else, not in the room at all, not really there. Thoughts were apparently limited and her feelings so volatile and extreme that it was difficult to see her as a human child. The difficulty in being with her, in thinking, in following her emotionally, left myself and those caring for her feeling hopeless, bewildered, mindless, and at times revolted by the sexualization. Foster-mother described her with some shame as a walking vagina, and "she is so little".

* * *

Phillipa presented as initially sexless, neuter; then she flaunted her sexuality, her sexualization. She subsequently became a terrified, vulnerable, and haunted small child.

Susan presented as mindless, unable to think or learn; then came her need for care, for nurturing, and, slowly, her struggle to see herself as a sexual being—homosexual, heterosexual, her longing for babies as something to love her, and her wish to care for them.

Jane was a distressing and distressed little, almost pre-verbal, animal, massively sexualized, longing for any physical contact, with no sense of personhood or identity.

Discussion

From these clinical examples of work with abused children and seeing and supervising a number of children in cases where there has been abuse or trauma, a number of thoughts and ideas have emerged.

There is a persistent and frequently unresolved question: has abuse occurred, is it real—reality—or is it imagination, or is it some form of phantasy, conscious or unconscious? Is it possible to understand this? The three clinical examples help to clarify this. Jane had clear evidence of vaginal penetration, although who had penetrated her was never confirmed. Susan showed no physical evidence of vaginal penetration; her story was believed and confirmed by other children but could not be proved. Phillipa showed evidence of anal scarring at one point; vaginal evidence was inconclusive. For these three children, society in the form of the courts decided, in the civil court, that on the balance of probabilities sexual abuse had occurred. But no abuser was prosecuted, and the situation remained open to question. This outcome is not unusual, and it leads on to discussions about children's memory, remembering and forgetting, and how we can understand a child's internal world.

Trying to understand childhood sexual abuse and its impact on thinking and memory, we have to consider posttraumatic stress disorder (PTSD), some features of which are applicable to child sexual abuse. In PTSD, there can be flashbacks, the person is awake, conscious, and is suddenly dramatically and vividly back, in the mind, in the very stressful situation, re-experiencing the events. Also they can have flashback dreams, in which they dream the re-experiencing, and if they awake during this "action-replay" dream their confusion and distress is even greater than with the awake re-experiencing. Susan and Phillipa both experienced these dreams. Experiencing a flashback, being able to distinguish phantasy from reality when the phantasy had, in fact, been a real experience, is very distressing. Phillipa would have had oedipal phantasies about her father; the sexualized enactment left her confused and bewildered as well as very distressed.

But there are other features of PTSD that also need to be considered and can be helpful in understanding why children function in the way they do after traumatic experiences. Part of PTSD is what is known as psychogenic amnesia—the memories are pushed out of the consciousness. This may be done so successfully that individuals are aware there are things that they cannot remember, but they do not know what those things are. Alongside this goes an inability to concentrate, a lack of emotional involvement, and a loss of liveliness sometimes described as a feeling of numbness. It is not surprising, therefore, that children appear to be confused and uncertain about what has happened to them—they may be suffering from psychogenic amnesia. It is also not surprising that their emotional reactions may be rather flat, that they do not show the level of distress or anger that might be expected, if they have coped with the abuse by pushing the thoughts away and damping down the feelings. It is easy to understand how rather flat accounts that do not have great detail in them lead to questions about whether the abuse occurred or not. Why it is so difficult to confirm or refute abuse in the absence of physical signs begins to make sense; the difficulty of staying with the uncertainty as far as the legal system is concerned is a large part of the problem. Posttraumatic stress disorder also involves avoidance and dissociation. The abuse victim appears to be somewhat vacant or blanks out, will pause and then change the subject completely during an interview. This is partly conscious avoidance but also seems to be a process occurring in the preconscious or the upper levels of the unconscious. Memories and experiences that are too painful and distressing are blanked out, and the child becomes very adept at doing this so that the interviewer may hardly notice the pauses and the switches in themes or diversions.

But PTSD does not explain why sexually abusive experiences cause so many difficulties. Psychoanalytic theory is needed to try to understand the persistent and long-term problems.

Childhood sexual abuse can be seen as the abusing adult's "madness" being forced into the mind of the child, and it penetrates deep into the unconscious: the child's mind is "raped".

The mechanisms used are splitting, denial, projection, projective identification, introjection (introjective identification), and manic flight. Experiences, thoughts, feelings are split off; they may then be projected or they may be denied. Understanding these processes and the phantasies that accompany them is crucial in the understanding of childhood sexual abuse. One of the things that seems to happen in sexual abuse is that the split-off denied experience forms a bubble, which can become encapsulated. It may be a very small bubble if it was an experience that did very little damage, or it may be a very large bubble if there was major emotional/psychic trauma. This bubble may then sink—a denied split-off fragment that, like an abscess, can give off undetected poison—and the person may be impaired in a number of ways: their learning capacities, their capacity to make relationships, or their complete hold on reality. Alternatively, the split-off experience, the encapsulated bubble, may be quite large and encompass quite an area of mental life and functioning and cause considerable impairment. The impairment may be significant in the area of learning, in developing relationships, or on the individual's hold on reality, but for all of them there is impairment, a block on their normal development.

If the girl has had good-enough early experiences and her development had been proceeding satisfactorily, then the abuse and its resulting split-off and denied aspects can be dealt with using displacement, disavowal, or dissociation; in a way, the child gets on with her life, and it is as if the abuse never happened. But the protective processes may fail at some point, and then awareness re-emerges: for example, when trying to make intimate relationships, when pregnant or giving birth, when her child is the age she was, or during the course of seeking help for something altogether different.

Where the abusive experience was extensive and early childhood experiences were not good enough, then the split-off denied abusive experiences seem almost to take over the whole person, leaving very little mental or emotional energy available for current life. Unconscious phantasies dominate and spill out in bizarre and disconcerting ways for the child and for those around her. It appears that the girl is using projection and projective identification as a means of struggling to retain some psychic equilibrium. The individual can go on to become a borderline personality or be overtly psychotic; the ability to establish relationships and the capacity to function can be very limited.

Jane was very confused and functioned mainly using manic flight and projective identification. This was not solely because of her age. Children of 3½ to 4 years are very much preoccupied with sexuality, but, although there is much part-object material—hands, mouths, willies, the bottom hole, the front hole—there is also a considerable involvement in relationships both in the here-and-now and with internal figures—mother, father, and any significant others. Jane was far beyond the normal small child's confusions about how babies are made, what do boys have, what do girls have, how do grown-ups differ from children. She seemed also unable to express any thoughts or feelings, any longings of an oedipal nature. Her whole body seemed in pain and sexualized, as was her mind and her relationships. What was real or imaginary, day-dream or night-dream, seemed lost.

Susan gradually came to life and made contact. She had very limited capacities to think but did struggle to distinguish phantasy-dreams, which were almost hallucinatory, from reality. Her oedipal thoughts and wishes were fulfilled. Mr X had indeed been her partner. Her rage and hatred at Mrs X, her foster-mother, had foundation but were complex, involving guilt and shame. Her capacity to struggle to try to understand was impressive. She did seem to be able to find a space, perhaps triangular, to play and to think (Britton, 1989).

Phillipa was caught in an enactment of her oedipal longings. Her capacity to process her experiences was limited, but most importantly seemed to be the loss of her feelings. She retained quite a sharp intellect. What was so difficult was her elimination and projection into those around her of her feelings, and then, when she began to feel again, to be in touch, the distress and longing were almost unbearable. It seemed much more difficult for her to struggle with the oedipal triangle; she appeared to be more stuck in a two-person relationship.

What has become increasingly obvious in this area of work is that the therapy must be in stages. The posttraumatic stress disorder must be recognized and treated. The children need to be helped to give words to the sensations, the experiences they have been through—the smells, sights, sounds, physical sensations—and to talk about their feelings about what has happened. But doing so leaves them with all the unconscious trauma, confusion, and distress untouched. This will need to be treated; it may be immediately, but some children may prefer to have a space and then begin the deeper psychoanalytic therapy work. Most, at some point in their lives, need the intra-psychic pain, conflicts, and confusion to be struggled with and resolved as far as possible, but in order to undertake this difficult and distressing psychoanalytic work they need to be in a family or substitute setting that can support them through the work.

Thoughts about the development of sexual identity

In undertaking this work, an issue that has emerged is the development of identity, particularly sexual identity. At the start of treatment, very often the central issue appeared to be "are they a person and are they sane". They have dreams, day-dreams, possibly hallucinations that involve terrifying fantasies (e.g. Phillipa's terror of being trapped, and my fantasy of a snake). The processes of coping take all the psychic energy, using projective identification to get rid of the unbearable, the unthinkable, and then having to manage the terror of retaliation, possible attacks, and persecution. But then, gradually, questions about sexuality and sexual identity come to the forefront and need to be thought about and understood.

Psychosexual development as understood psychoanalytically plays a very important part in this understanding (see Trowell, 1997a, 1997b). In particular, Melanie Klein's early papers (1932a, 1932b) are very helpful. She describes how baby boys and girls are aware of their bodies, their genitalia, as a source of pleasure very early on, boys with their penile erection and their wish to thrust forward, to penetrate, and girls with their sense of something precious inside. She suggests that alongside the oedipal longing for the parent of the opposite sex and the reverse oedipal longing for the parent of the same sex, there is for both small boys and girls a sense of the power and importance of "mother", the main female carer. Mother who cares and nurtures is also feared. (See Baker Miller, 1976; Freud, 1905e, 1931b; Jukes, 1993.) This is a complicated and complex situation for the child. Mother is loved and longed for but is also hated for depriving, for failing to meet needs, and for involvement with others. The child then fears mother's retaliation for this hatred. But, in addition, mother who has the source of life inside her, all the babies, all the penises, is feared because she is expected to wish to attack. The boy child expects mother in her envy to wish to take over his penis, and the girl child expects mother in her envy to attack the child's "womb" as a potential rival to her own. (See Klein, 1932a, 1932b; Heimann, 1951.) These are all normal phantasies and fears that have to be worked through, and with a loving, caring mother the envy, fear, and terror is slowly made bearable. However, in abusive situations there appear to be times when the child thinks that mother knew what was happening and wanted him or her to be damaged or, if not actually wanting damage inflicted, certainly failed to prevent it happening. This is an internal phantasy that becomes a thought and has nothing to do with the external reality of the circumstances of the abuse. During childhood and puberty, these issues are repeatedly reworked. Puberty for girls is particularly crucial, the onset of menstruation provoking considerable anxiety in the girl—"Have I been damaged inside?" The girl needs the "mother" to be particularly supportive and to take pride in the girl's emerging sexuality as she struggles with all the fantasies. Sexual abuse at this age, with the fantasy that mother's envy could not bear a rival and that she wanted her daughter to be damaged, seems to be a crucial factor in why sexual abuse can be so damaging.

Slowly, then, in treatment the sexual development, sexual identity, emerges as an issue. (See Breen, 1993; Mitchell & Rose, 1982.) Trying to understand the process is slow and difficult, but common themes have begun to emerge. Body gender seems to be the earliest to emerge; by this, one is considering physical gender based on genitalia and, later, secondary sexual characteristics such as breasts and fat distribution. This gives rise to an awareness that "I am a boy" or "I am a girl", maleness and femaleness. Phillipa and Susan knew that they were physically girls. Jane wanted anything that moved inside her—whether she knew male or female was uncertain, anyone's fingers would do or any body part or an inanimate object. Jane seemed to see others as part objects, not whole people, and, as her foster-mother said, behaved as a part-object herself—a walking vagina.

Children usually know their body gender early on, probably before speech is well developed, although what exactly is understood is not clear. What follows next is an awareness of oneself as a boy or girl in one's mind: one's self as an internal object has a gender attribution. This gives rise to a sense of masculinity or femininity, one of which predominates in most people. Thus, a person may have a male physical body but could have either a male or female gender in the mind. The internal object "self"—one's awareness of masculinity or femininity, one's mind gender—is conveyed non-verbally as well as verbally. It is not clear how this develops, but it appears that it takes place largely in the context of interactions and relationships with those around, plus intra-uterine and hormonal factors. Alongside the relationships in the external world, the internal object relationships appear to be very significant—for example, the mother and father internalized from the main carers, and their internalized carers from their childhood, all in interaction with unconscious phantasies.

Phillipa appeared neuter at the start of treatment and did not have a well-developed sense of her own identity internally, although she knew that she was a girl physically. Susan, however, had a sense of femininity, that she was both female and feminine. It seemed that Mr X had aided this development, his appreciation of her being conveyed to her by look, by touch, by general attitude, and presumably by his own internal object, perhaps his mother. Neither of Phillipa's parents could help her find her own internal gender: they seemed to have seen her as neuter, the alleged abuse being anal, and she could have been a boy or a girl for both parents.

Early on, at primary school, children are working through the oedipal phase and are preoccupied with a possible choice of a partner—homosexual, heterosexual, or bisexual—at some time in the future. The sexual orientation fluctuates, and this fluctuation returns in adolescence (Limentani, 1989). Small children do not usually experiment in reality, although this may happen in adolescence. Childhood sexual abuse may influence this developmental phase.

As shown by Susan, the idea of future possible sexual contact with a man with a penis terrified and revolted her, but she was also distressed at having her future sexual relationships with a woman. She found it very painful exploring, through the relationship with me and her new foster-parents, her possible sexual orientation. Was she always homosexual? Had Mr X known this and tried to change her? or was it because of what Mr X had done to her? or was it more related to her feelings in the room with me and at home with the new foster-parents? Susan struggled to find her way and is likely to have sexual relationships with men and women as she grows up. It is not clear what her eventual orientation will be.

Very closely linked with sexual orientation is object choice, but it is helpful for the girls (and boys) and the therapists to keep this as a separate phase. If a person decides that he or she is heterosexual, there is then a second stage, which involves the generational boundary. A man may have had as his sexual orientation female partners, but are they to be women or girls? A woman may settle on a homosexual orientation; does she then want as her sexual partners girls or women? There is often an assumption on the part of therapists, patients, and citizens that homosexuality involves the choice of children as object choice. This does not appear to be so, and it is important to keep this distinction. Susan was very troubled for a while as she reflected on her strong homosexual orientation. Did this mean that she wanted sex with girls or with women? There were the issues of guilt, of shame, of not knowing, but for Susan acknowledging the thoughts and feelings seemed to be helpful and to talk about the fear and anxiety for her about homosexuality and object choice so that they could be thought about and worked on.

If this phase can be negotiated, there is often a considerable step forward with the emerging of creativity. Phillipa discovered a capacity to be in touch with her feelings and have an active intelligence which arose from her recognition of her internal parental couple. Susan more obviously became creative in an artistic sense, and this produced real change in her sense of her self. (See Chasseguet-Smirgel, 1985.)

In the final years at primary school and on into adolescence, these creative thoughts began to link with the possibility of babies—real babies or intellectual babies, emotional babies, new ventures, new activities. These feelings can be described as maternal feelings: the conception, the gestation, the giving birth, the nurturing, and then the letting go. Maternal or paternal feelings are then followed by thoughts of actual motherhood, fatherhood, and, if there is to be a real baby, child-caring, parenting. Many sexually abused girls and women who were sexually abused as children find this whole phase very difficult. They may, in fact, by the physical act of intercourse become pregnant and have a child, but the mental work to prepare for their care for a child is missing. Phillipa was very distressed that she could not contemplate the possibility of having children of her own, and she seemed unable to have any sense of herself undertaking these activities. Intellectual ideas were a possibility, but real biological babies, a relationship with a partner and a baby, and sharing was felt to be totally outside the realms of possibility—the idea of being able to parent left her speechless.

Conclusions

In this chapter, starting from the experience of working with traumatized girls, ideas have been developed about the impact of trauma on the girls and on those trying to work with them. Post-traumatic stress disorder can follow abuse; it is partly a means of managing the unbearable thoughts and feelings but also, if there is frequent re-experiencing, seems to fixate the experience.

Understanding the intrapsychic phantasies and ways of dealing with these overwhelming experiences with current psychoanalytic ideas enables the children to be helped with psychoanalytic psychotherapy and psychoanalytically informed case management. Similarly, the girls' confusion and distress about their psychosexual development can be understood, relieved, and assisted.

Different psychoanalytic ideas have provided different concepts to try to make sense of these girls' material and to try to help them understand what has happened to them. Trying to integrate some of these ideas in order to help these girls and enable us to understand has been challenging and rewarding. It has also helped considerably in understanding what happens in all girls as they move from girl to young woman, to adult woman, to mother.

CHAPTER ELEVEN

Intersex disorder in childhood and adolescence: gender identity, gender role, sex assignment, and general mental health

Adrian Sutton & Jane Whittaker

There exists a rare group of babies whose biological sex is not immediately apparent at birth because the anatomical arrangement of their genitals is uncertain. In addition, there is another very uncommon group of children and adolescents whose sex has not been in question but who develop in an unexpected way: as they grow, they develop physical characteristics expected of the gender opposite to the one to which they were thought to belong. The collective term "intersex disorders" is used for the conditions that bring this about, although the underlying medical and surgical issues may be very different. Chapter five has described the influences in the womb and after birth which decide the sex of the person as it appears from the internal and external physical characteristics (further descriptions can be found in Garden, 1998). These can be summarized briefly under general headings:

1. *Departures from the usual pairing of sex chromosomes as either XX or XY.* There may be either an absence of a second X chromosome to complete the full female complement, or X or Y chro-

mosomes in excess of a basic pair: a solitary Y is not compatible with life. The XXY complement may result in unusual genitalia, but, in the other states, anatomy is congruent with chromosomes and sex assignment is unequivocal.

2. *Altered hormone production.* This too is a mixed group. Some individuals will have conditions in which the impact on them may have been life-threatening from birth or in which the maintenance of their general health and development requires very careful monitoring (e.g. congenital adrenal hyperplasia). In these people, the impact of the specific endocrine disorder on the sexual growth and development will be one facet of the overall concern for the person's welfare. In others, there may be no such concerns regarding their general health or survival.

3. *Altered responses of the body to the hormones that bring about sexual differentiation.* For some people, their body may not respond to the masculinizing hormones (androgen insensitivity syndrome: AIS), whilst in others the response may be incomplete (partial AIS). The impact upon the individual's external appearance at birth may be negligible or may present obvious and sometimes severe abnormalities of the urogenital anatomy which require complex surgical procedures. In other cases, the disorder may only declare itself when apparently paradoxical changes occur at puberty.

4. *Altered patterns of exposure to hormones in the womb.* The uterine environment may be altered by, for example, administration of synthetic progestogen to the mother to prevent miscarriage, with impact upon the developing baby. Again, the effects may be more or less obvious or serious in their immediate presentation.

5. *Hormonal influences and responsivity in utero may also lead to abnormalities of the male urogenital tract.* At an extreme end, major abdominal problems can occur (cloacal exstrophy). This condition requires complex surgical procedures to achieve a functional state, although the result may be abnormal anatomically and raise issues of gender assignment in the neonatal period or later. Lesser, but still significant, conditions of failure of completion of the normal processes may occur, producing hypospadias in which the urethra does not open at the end of the

penis: surgical interventions will be needed in some cases, but sexual assignment is unequivocal.

6. It should also be noted that links have been made with *children with traumatized genitalia* (Diamond, 1997).

Intersex disorders are rare. However, some striking and consistent themes have arisen in the authors' clinical work with children and adolescents in the second and third groups described above. In addition, there are issues from general child and adolescent mental health which are applicable to them and which can guide the clinician.

General aspects
of psychosexual development

Clinical work with young people and their parents in the area of intersex disorders demands a clear understanding of different aspects of psychosexual development to help parents disentangle these for and with their children. These are described elsewhere in this volume but can be briefly summarized here again:

• *Biological sex:* that which is endowed by the chromosomal complement and the ordinary unfolding expression of this in intrauterine development and after birth under the influence of hormones.

• *Sex assignment:* the social decision made at the time of birth, based on the examination of the external genitalia, to assign the newborn baby as a male or female or, very occasionally, as an intersex until a more definite decision is reached. This decision is registered on the birth certificate.

• *Gender identity:* the sense that the individual has of being either a male or a female. Manifestations of the emergence of this are evident during the second year of life. The developmental path is from recognition of oneself as a particular gender, through appreciation that this is fixed and, finally, that gender does not change.

- *Gender role:* those aspects of behaviour that are expected to occur predominantly in one gender or the other. Money and Ehrhardt (1972) provide the following differentiation: "gender identity is the private experience of gender role . . . gender role is the public expression of gender identity."

- *Sexual orientation:* the gender, in relation to the individual's own gender, of the "object"/person who brings about sexual arousal and who may be sought as a sexual partner. This is subject to developmental influences.

Gender identity development in intersex disorders

As is evident from the contributions in this book, the influences on gender identity development are manifold. The power of their effects in relation to each other are the subject of intense debate. The gender identity disorders occur in the absence of any demonstrable physical abnormality. Hence, the development of individuals *with* genital abnormality is of interest both in relation to them and for any insights into the development of ordinary children.

The classic study is that of Imperato-McGinley et al. (1979a). They reported a relatively high frequency of genetically determined partial AIS. The subjects were raised as females but at puberty became masculinized, developing male secondary sexual characteristics. The majority then assumed a male gender identity. This suggests that the effects of biological predisposition arising from the XY chromosome complement can automatically override the effects of nurture (see chapter two herein).

Reiner (1996), apparently supporting this, describes a teenager with the condition of mixed gonadal dysgenesis (MGD) who, having been brought up female, declared a gender identity of male on reaching teenage years. Medical and surgical interventions to assist with this redefining were carried out. Follow-up through a period of five years from initial contact at 14 years indicated a successful process, despite a lack of support for the course of action by the parents. Diamond (1997) also reports three cases indicating that gender identity is not necessarily fixed by the gender of rearing.

However, the first author of this chapter can similarly report a young person with MGD with multiple behavioural and emotional problems, but in whom there was no gender identity conflict. In addition, in a case described in chapter thirteen and reported elsewhere (Sutton, 1990), a teenager reared as female but presenting with masculinizing effects at puberty (partial AIS) was absolute in her wish to be female and underwent appropriate medical and surgical treatment for this. The period of contact extended over ten years without significant indications of dysphoria in relation to the sex of rearing, although the period of mid-adolescence was stormy.

Understanding the relationship between gender identity and intersex disorders is clearly complex. The state of knowledge is still limited, as evidenced by the need to present information on the basis of case studies rather than large series. Biology and psychology both have an influence on gender identity and gender role development and do not operate independently. Studies suggestive of an overriding biological determination such as that of Imperato-McGinley et al. may simultaneously indicate the significance of a cultural influence that has developed to tolerate and accept difference and change. This may make the likelihood of a youngster wanting to change their status—physically or otherwise—greater. However, it is possible to question some previous surgical practices in relation to assumptions made about the desirability of belonging to (being "assigned to") a particular gender. Diamond (1997) offers some guidelines for particular contingencies but also states that "sex-assignment protocols, where 'one set of rules applies to all' will not do" [italics added]. Discussing the issues to be faced when problems present at birth, Nelki and Sutton (1998) warn against precipitate action. There is professional agreement that issues relating to physical appearance and gender identity are complex and involve an unfolding developmental dynamic. The potential for different outcomes needs to be maintained as far as this is possible in relation to the young person's desires and the limits of medical and surgical possibilities.

Diamond (1997) states that the *intersexed* individuals "desire sexual function, even at the expense of cosmetic anatomy", contrasting this with Bentler's (1976) description of *transsexuals* who wish for "anatomy to coincide with psyche even if it means losing sexual function". Assumptions must not go unquestioned about the desirability of, for example, being apparently female rather than, in the eyes of the practitioners, an "inadequately" endowed male with limited or missing functions. The key would appear to be to avoid premature foreclosure of potential sensual, erotic experience of a *tactile* nature by ensuring that concern about the *visual* nature—what is looked at—does not inappropriately override other aspects of sensory experience and routes towards sensual gratification. People may gain sensual and sexual satisfaction and pleasure in living through different pathways and by means of adaptations in themselves and with a potential partner. Appreciation of this by professionals must guide their interventions.

Sexual orientation

The development of preference in relation to the object of sexual desire occurs through childhood but becomes a far more pressing issue at puberty and through adolescence. The pattern cannot be regarded as fixed during these times, and neither should it be considered an all-or-nothing affair. Initiators of arousal may occur towards both genders at particular times to a greater or lesser extent. Activity is not a necessary component. Laufer and Laufer (1984) advise against considering sexual orientation as being fixed before the end of adolescence, which they would time as being during the early 20s.

Intersex children are in a particularly complex situation. Similarities and differences become more acutely important during this stage of development: they will have to find ways of coping with their own feelings of both difference from and similarity to both male and female, even if relatively good results may have been achieved with surgical and medical interventions. Peer-group activities with underlying components that relate to sexuality and gender may not function in the same way for them. The psychic function of these developmental processes relies on both conscious and unconscious identificatory mechanisms that cannot be included in or subsumed under these activities (e.g. breast development, menarche, voice deepening) by adolescents with these disorders.

We, as observers, are in a complex situation in trying to find a way of conceptualizing and finding a language to describe whether the choice of partner of these young people is of same or different sex. Diamond (1997) suggests using a different terminology, "gynecophilic" or "androphilic", to define attraction towards women or men, respectively, with the term "ambiphilic" replacing bisexual. This may help us to delineate the situation as different from the more usual one of "heterosexual or homosexual", which may contain its own complexity of emotions both for the young person and for those in important positions in their lives. It may enable a continuation of openness in thinking to occur and make us more useful to the young people in their development. This will, hopefully, facilitate the youngster in negotiating this period, which is one of learning through experience, perhaps trial and error, without untoward effects arising through premature developmental foreclosure in relation to choice of sexual object or perhaps inhibition in the entire area of sexual life. Similarly, acting-out behaviour, which may have serious effects on their physical or emotional health, may be less likely or extensive if experimentation can be contained more in the psychological realm rather than the physical (e.g. avoidance of potentially abusive or traumatizing relationships). The young person described by Sutton in chapter thirteen clearly went through a process of androphilia to ambiphilia before finding herself most settled in a gynecophilic position. The process was one during which Sutton did feel concerned about the extent to which the patient engaged in activity, but in this case no ultimately serious effects resulted.

Working to maintain the position of making new thinking possible is particularly important. Clinical experience does not appear to describe more than the complexity and the importance of the differences between individuals in their passage through this period of life and the degree to which a satisfactory solution may be found by them.

Intersex disorder
and general mental health

Taylor and Eminson (1994) discuss the systematic difficulties in examining the experiences of children suffering from chronic physical illness and their families:

> The intuitive assumption is that suffering a chronic sickness would be burdensome to a child, and a source of sorrow to its family". [p. 737]

> The problem for psychological research is to capture the essence of what appears to be perceived intuitively by ordinary people, by affected families, by health practitioners, and by specialists working with chronic sickness. The problem for practitioners is to have a framework for understanding the basis on which a wide variety of associations between physical sickness and psychological disorder present clinically. [p. 738]

Intersex disorders are a heterogeneous group of conditions some of which may not present people with "illnesses" as such, whilst others may first declare themselves with a life-threatening illness and the need for permanent medication to ensure health and/or survival: some may require surgical interventions at different times and adherence to medication regimes in order to ensure that secondary sexual characteristics are maintained. For these reasons, it is reasonable to consider the issues that may be of relevance in Taylor and Eminson's descriptions in this context. What they state in relation to research also needs to be taken into account in clinical work in this arena, since rarity means that each person is effectively a research case: we have to "adopt a more inquisitive position, to try to determine in what ways distress is experienced and what coping is successful" (p. 746). Wallander and Varni's (1998) review also indicates the increased risk for problems in children with chronic physical disorders and emphasizes the extent of variation in outcome: the latter point underlines the importance of identifying factors that may promote or impair a better outcome.

In order to make themselves of use, professionals must appreciate the predicament of parents and children through the *unfolding* process of development from birth, through childhood and adolescence, into adulthood. Intersex conditions present greater complexity for the children themselves, parents, siblings and extended family members, professionals, and other key adults, from the point of initial diagnosis to treatments that may include regimes that present their own crises, pain, and suffering. There may be a profound significance in the impact of realizing the limitations that the condition places upon individuals in their aspirations—for example, for having boyfriends or girlfriends, for becoming sexually active, or for becoming parents in their turn. The potential for adverse impact upon the developing sense of self and upon the individual's self-esteem may generate emotional conflicts of a degree that makes the likelihood of significant mental health problems much greater. Within this, it is also essential that professionals appreciate the limitations of our knowledge and understanding: for example, do we really *know* whether emotional or behavioural problems are the consequence of physical or psychological aspects of the person, in their illness, in their particular family, at this particular time in their lives and development, and whether they are necessary and inevitable, or avoidable?

Management at the point of diagnosis

As already noted, in some conditions the point of recognition and diagnosis may also be a time of medical emergency. However, Nelki and Sutton (1998), discussing the management when the presentation is at birth, highlight the impact that indeterminacy of sex may have on professionals as well as on parents: "It is as if gender assignment is directly equated with matters of immediate survival" (p. 101). The process appears to contain a fundamental, but perhaps unconscious, element of the recognition of gender being indistinguishable from the recognition of existence—if gender cannot be assigned, can the baby truly be in existence? This may lead to unhelpful, precipitate action when the activity that actually needs to take place is the mental activity of tolerating uncertainty whilst time is made to make more informed and considered decisions. Fully appreciating the fact that the containment of shock, fear, and anxiety *is* an *active* management will be of fundamental importance even when the diagnosis occurs at a later stage.

The professional management of this stage has two components: (1) the response to the crisis of diagnosis and (2) the laying of the foundations for future care and treatment. The way in which this is negotiated in its physical and emotional aspects can help provide a framework in which difficult decisions can be taken without this feeling like an impossible task.

Management as time unfolds

A theme of this chapter has been the importance of appreciating that the intersex conditions present greater complexity for children, adolescents, and their families in their development and that consequently there needs to be greater flexibility in thinking. This is within the context of the particular impact upon the ability to maintain oneself in being able to think with clarity as described by Sutton in chapter thirteen. This makes greater than ordinary demands on the youngster and their family, *and* on professionals. Repeatedly, one hears from all parties that someone has said "the wrong thing". For example, an AIS teenager reported that her GP always immediately asked her if she was having problems with her periods. Similarly, the mother of an 8-year-old without uterus or vagina was told by the specialist that her daughter did not need to be seen again until her periods started.

In the ordinary course of growing up, children and adolescents need their parents in different ways, but not less. For children and adolescents with chronic conditions, there is a different emphasis within the overall movement through to becoming more autonomous. They require their parents and other adults to be more involved than might usually occur: this may bring with it more emotional conflict for them, their parents, and these other adults. The psychological processes of separation/individuation, and the move from childhood forms of dependence to adult forms of dependence and interdependence, are different by necessity. This may make for patterns of relating that superficially appear pathological and do bring upset with them but actually illustrate the nature of negotiation that must inevitably occur. Often a parent may be viewed as being "overprotective " or "intrusive" when, in fact, their child needs them to continue speaking for them—even though they may complain about the pattern of their involvement. This is an important issue for professionals to understand because the potential for unhelpful coalitions to be formed with youngster or parent against the other is great and may seriously undermine the overall management of their care. Youngsters may feel bullied or parents condemned, when in fact the struggle to adapt to and integrate the complex needs is at the core of their actions.

The situation when a fundamental aspect of the condition is the nature of the genitals is even more poignant. These are the parts of the body often referred to as the "private parts". They have a particular importance to the individual from the earliest stages of life, and through adolescence and adulthood they are accorded a particularly important significance in relation to the role they do or do not play in relationships. But, of necessity, the usual privacy cannot be accorded. Complex decisions may need to be made, and the youngsters may need the involvement of one or both parents in this at an age that would not be the norm in other situations. Parents will be confronted with needing to think of their children as potentially sexually active, or perhaps not, at stages that feel out of step with other aspects of the child's development and when other parents (or the same parents with their other children) do not. When this is occurring within an arena that is also filled with so much uncertainty about aspects of function and outcome, then the potential for adverse events is high. For these reasons, thinking about the mental life and development of emotions and relationships should be a central part of the care of such youngsters and their families. This is a role that requires specialist knowledge and skills in direct work with children and families alongside equivalent expertise in liaison with and consultation to other professionals. Even though no link between specific major psychiatric disorder and intersex states has been demonstrated, Nelki and Sutton (1998), Reiner (1996), and Diamond (1997) all recommend that mental health specialists should be a core component of the treatment team.

Conclusions

The uncommon nature of the intersex conditions means that systematic quantitative and qualitative psychiatric research evidence is not yet available to guide us in our clinical work. However, the experience of clinicians puts this area forward as being particularly complex. Meeting people with these conditions has a powerful impact. Working with them fundamentally challenges our thinking about issues relating to gender and sexuality, health and ill-health in relationships.

The experience with these youngsters is different from that of people with gender identity disorder. There is not an insistence that nature has got it wrong in the external representation of the internal sense of self; nor is there an insistence that the professional must now put it right by changing to that which is demanded. It seems possible to think more about accentuations of ordinary gender identity conflicts in adolescence, but with an added poignancy and complexity for the patient and the family. The added complexity of the developmental demands and stresses that may ensue from specific medical and surgical treatment required by the youngsters with intersex disorders means that this is a group of people more likely to suffer mental health difficulties.

The task for mental health professionals is to understand the difficulties, and sometimes dysphoria, created in themselves and other professionals in relation to identifying the gender of these youngsters. One could think of this as professionals and others potentially having a "gender identification disorder" when becoming involved in this arena. The challenge is to maintain in themselves and others the ability to continue thinking, to assist in avoiding unhelpful activity—particularly where that may have irreversible consequences—and to be available to support all parties through inevitable difficulties. Above all, the task is to remember the fundamentally human experiences of these people and their families as they negotiate life with this added complexity.

CHAPTER TWELVE

Management and therapeutic aims in working with children and adolescents with gender identity disorders, and their families

Domenico Di Ceglie

J an Morris, a well-known writer and journalist, who had a transsexual problem, wrote an article in a daily paper "on the sadness of living abroad" (1991). Referring to English people living in the south of France, she says:

> It is not just that I am sorry for the French, who are going to have to suffer the proximity of these cuckoos in the nests of the world; in a way I am sorrier for the English, who are going to turn themselves into *expatriates*.
>
> All over the world one sees them, the islanders, evading their heritage, looking for the London newspapers in the Spanish newsagents, talking about duchesses at the New England Tennis Clubs, and, above all, almost anywhere beautiful in France, visiting each other's houses, remembering old times, comparing Major with Thatcher, Gooch with Botham. How happy they always say they are! How sad they generally seem to me.

And later in the same article while talking about one of these expatriates, Morris comments:

I sensed an emptiness in his life, looking always for some-where better, finding nowhere that is, however bloody the weather, really and absolutely his.

Morris is here accurately describing the identity problem that some emigrants would have to face: their cultural and national identity, their roots, are in one place, but they have ended up living in another. She seems to be acutely aware of the dissonance of their condition. Interests, memories, histories, accents do not fit the culture and the geography of the host land. Any author writing a piece will not only offer observations about an outside reality, but will also tell us something about himself or herself. The sense of dislocation and dissonance described by Morris is what children with gender identity disorders may experience in their lives. Their interests, their play, their fantasies, their way of moving or talking, their way of relating to friends, or their way of seeing themselves do not fit the body that they have and the way that other people perceive them as a consequence of their bodily appearance. One might say that their psyche lives in a foreign body. An expatriate might have chosen to live in this condition (though there may really not have been a choice), but the development of a gender identity problem is largely beyond a child's own conscious control. The child feels driven to live in this confusing and bewildering condition. This observation leads to the first of the aims in management outlined in this chapter (see Table 12.1).

1.   Because gender identity problems are not, by and large, the result of a conscious choice, the attitudes, emotions, and behaviours of these children cannot be considered wrong or bad in themselves, as, quite often, the family or society tend to consider them. This attitude, if strongly expressed, may instigate in the child an unbearable sense of guilt; neither, on the other hand, can one say that the choice is the right choice or the behaviour good. This is the most immediate problem that professionals have to face with children, parents and extended family, or other agencies. Without the *recognition and the non-judgemental acceptance of the gender identity problem*, no exploration can start.

2.   Do these children and teenagers need help? An expatriate who found the situation unbearable might eventually decide to go back

TABLE 1
Primary therapeutic aims

1. To foster recognition and non-judgemental acceptance of the gender identity problem.

2. To ameliorate associated emotional, behavioural, and relationship difficulties (Coates & Person, 1985).

3. To break the cycle of secrecy.

4. To activate interest and curiosity by exploring the impediments to them.

5. To encourage exploration of mind–body relationship by promoting close collaboration among professionals with a different focus in their work, including a paediatric endocrinologist.

6. To allow mourning processes to occur (Bleiberg, Jackson, & Ross, 1986).

7. To enable the capacity for symbol formation and symbolic thinking (Segal, 1957).

8. To promote separation and differentiation.

9. To enable the child/adolescent and the family to tolerate uncertainty in the area of gender identity development.

10. To sustain hope.

home, though the person may be surprised to find that this is not the end of his or her problems. Sex reassignment would be the equivalent change for a gender-transposed child. However, for a child or an adolescent, this solution is not available and may not be desirable, because it is an irreversible step and gender identity problems in children vary in degrees of intensity, in evolution, and in eventual outcome. There is a long way to go before a more definitive solution can be reached. During this time, the child and then the adolescent has to face and overcome many hurdles, including living in an environment that may not understand her or her problems and actually works to exclude or deny them. Moreover, these children often present other emotional and behavioural difficulties, as studies by Coates and Person (1985), among others, show. Separation anxiety, depression, and other behavioural difficulties may not necessarily derive from the external environment, although social rejection, bullying, and ridicule in school clearly contribute to the problems. They are, in sum, troubled children. Therapeutic help is therefore necessary to *assist development and reduce the severity of these associated emotional and behavioural difficulties.*

3.   The need for therapy, however, is obscured by the secrecy that surrounds such problems. There is a great resistance in parents, carers, and professionals in general to recognizing gender identity problems early enough. This contributes to the child's attempts to conceal them and to split off this area of functioning from awareness within the family. They end up sometimes as children who appear rather remote and dreamy. I think that the secrecy is an important component of these problems, because when established it may produce a series of secondary phenomena that, in turn, affect the development of the child. The pursuit of secret interests, fantasies, and behaviours, although it isolates the child from his or her peer group, which is obviously an obstacle to development, may also be construed by the child as evidence that he or she possesses something very special that ordinary children do not have. In this way, an adverse situation is turned into an ideal one, for the purposes of survival. This separate area of identity becomes more and more detached from the rest of the personality. How much the secrecy, in the long term, contributes to further structuring of the AGIO remains an open question, and research in this area needs to be done. Nevertheless, *the breaking of a cycle of secrecy* is a precondition if understanding is to take place. This transformation might, in turn, require an understanding of the anxieties that sustain the secrecy. The breaking of a collusive attitude involving secrecy within the family, or within a social network such as school, may turn out to be a vehicle for change in itself.

4.   Another feature—linked with secrecy—that often characterizes these children and adolescents is the suppression of curiosity about the nature of the problem, leading to complex distortion of this function. Gender identity problems in children are often associated with what could be called "disorders of curiosity". These often manifest themselves in therapy by an intense sense of curios-

ity experienced by the therapist working with these children or adolescents. There is an interesting pattern that develops as the therapist finds that his or her curiosity cannot be satisfied. The persistence of the curiosity then leads to unusual attitudes equivalent to spying. I became aware of this problem during the therapy of an adolescent female-to-male transsexual, described in a paper I published in Italian, "The Request for Sex Change: The Therapist's Curiosity" (1991). During the sessions with this teenager, a clear pattern developed where she would give me incomplete information described in such a way as to make me extremely curious. I would therefore ask questions to clarify matters. However, most of the time, the answers—rather than clarifying any issue—would lead to more confusion, which in turn would make me feel not only more curious, but then also frustrated and angry. Quite often the curiosity was instigated through non-verbal communication. In one session, this patient, who would usually not make eye contact with me, put her hands in front of her eyes and looked at me through the gaps in her fingers as if she were spying from behind a barred window or through a keyhole. Drawing on the work of Wilfred Bion in his papers "Attacks on Linking" (1959) and "On Arrogance" (1957), I could make sense of these well-established patterns of communication in the following way. The experience to which I was subjected of intense curiosity and then of frustration in satisfying it was probably very similar to the experience that this adolescent had had in the past. Her way of looking at me in the session seemed to be a confirmation of this. Bion suggests that, when this pattern of communication occurs in the course of therapy, it is an indication of a severe disturbance of communication, which has its origin in the relationship between mother and baby. Communication through the normal use of projective identification had not been possible. The development of normal curiosity is impeded and the child introjects an experience of curiosity as a forbidden activity, and therefore learning—which relies on curiosity—is disrupted. I would add here that this barring may apply to certain areas and not to others. In my clinical experience with a number of children and adolescents, and from anecdotal reports from colleagues, I have found these features to occur frequently. On the other hand, these problems are by no means specific to gender identity disorders. Obviously, social taboos in the area of gender identity reinforce difficulties established in patterns of interaction in early childhood.

A baby born with pseudo-hermaphroditism was assigned female gender a few weeks after birth and received corrective surgery to adapt her body. During childhood, she had a number of operations for another malformation. At puberty, the parents contacted the clinic because she needed hormone therapy and the parents did not know how to tell her about her past. Her father, who was divorced, had observed the girl while bathing with her step-sister and thought that her genitals looked different. The girl, however, had apparently never asked any questions about her body and her sexuality. We strongly suspected that she felt that this was a taboo area, in which curiosity could not be exercised as she had done for the other operations.

Whatever the causation of the disorder of curiosity, *the activation of interest and the wish to explore in the child and in the family,* and the creation of a setting in which these could be exercised, are goals in working with these families. This could be attempted in many ways, including through psychotherapeutic interventions, but can also be done through other means such as a physical examination by a paediatrician who is willing to allow the child and the family to express doubts and ask questions about physical development. It is important to foster a climate that can facilitate a process of learning. A discussion of very concrete and simple facts can initiate a process of exploration, which can then be pursued in a psychotherapeutic setting. At other times, therapeutic work may generate interest in the child to explore his or her own body more.

5.   *Close collaboration* among different professionals such as psychiatrists, psychotherapists, social workers, psychologists, and paediatricians is always very important and this applies equally in the management of intersex disorder. It seems to me that in conditions where the relationship between mind and body is problematic, both components need to be taken concretely into consideration by the collaboration of professionals with a different focus. The following clinical example illustrates the usefulness of a

joint consultation with the paediatrician, as focusing on the body leads to the emergence of an experience of great psychological relevance.

"Laura", aged 9 years, felt that she was a boy. She had a well-established gender identity disorder and had even asked her mother if she could have a sex change. Her mother suffered from congenital adrenal hyperplasia, a condition that required continuous corticosteroid treatment, and she had continued therapy with prednisone during her pregnancy with Laura, which might have had a masculinizing effect on the brain of the foetus. A second daughter, three years younger than Laura, has a normal gender development in spite of the fact that the mother was on the same hormonal regimen during pregnancy. A son age 12 years, from a previous marriage, has a normal gender development to date. The mother, however, reports being depressed after the delivery of Laura, but her husband seemed unaware of this. The family had also had a complicated house move during the last months of the pregnancy. These factors were absent in the case of her younger sister.

During the joint assessment with the paediatrician, Laura showed with great pride the muscles in her arms, which in her view were very big, and, while flexing them, she said that, when she was older, with her big muscles she could protect her mother.

6.   Another feature that has been linked with gender disorders has been the difficulty in mourning a loss. In their paper "Gender Identity Disorder and Object Loss", Bleiberg, Jackson, and Ross (1986) conclude that "gender identity development is profoundly affected by the development of self and object relations, significant psychic events and conflicts, and the efforts of children to cope with such events and conflicts". They also suggest "that a group of children who *appear* to have the characteristics of a core gender identity disorder may, on closer examination, in a psychoanalytic process, be shown to base their behaviour on heightened narcissistic defences against early maternal loss. Thus, a subgroup of gender identity disorders in childhood may be conceptualised". The case of "William" in chapter thirteen illustrates this point.

The inability to mourn the loss of an attachment figure may lead to a concrete fusional identification with the lost object, which interferes with other identifications available in the course of development. The stuckness in this process generates a rigidity in the mind of the child which manifests itself in the assertion of the supremacy of the mind over the body at all costs. In the cases where inability to mourn a lost object becomes evident, *allowing the mourning process to occur* becomes a therapeutic aim.

7. Connected with this area is enabling the child to *develop a capacity for symbol formation and symbolic thinking.* I refer here to Hanna Segal's paper "Notes on Symbol Formation" (1957), in which she describes a particular type of mental functioning characterized by symbolic equations in the place of symbol formation. Children with gender identity disorder seem to present consistent areas in which concrete thinking prevails. This needs to be addressed in therapy through play and interpretation. I give here a brief example of concrete thinking from an assessment interview of an adolescent with gender identity disorder.

> "Margaret" had come to the session having missed the previous one. She said that she had had a cold and then added: "I always have a cold." After this statement, a long silence followed, during which I felt I could not make contact with her. I was also aware, from previous material, of this adolescent's difficulties in establishing close and warm relationships. I therefore interpreted to her that she was not only telling me about having had a physical illness, the cold, but also about her feeling cold and being unable to be in touch with warm feelings and that she also felt me to be cold and unresponsive to her. This probably made it difficult for her to come to the session. Margaret became bewildered by my interpretation and asked me to repeat it, which I did. In spite of my attempt to explain as clearly as I could, it became clear that Margaret could not take "cold" in a metaphorical way as a statement about feelings and relationships. For her, a cold was only a cold and there could be nothing more to it. She then said that she had been accepted for judo lessons and was very pleased with this. I asked her why she was so interested in judo, and she

replied that she liked it because you could be in physical contact with other people more than in any other sport. Her tutor had also told her that if she wanted to improve she had to show more "snap and aggression", which she lacked. From this material, it appears that she had some awareness of her difficulties in making contact with people and the need of a structure, like the judo lessons, that facilitated it. However, her capacity for linking different experiences was impaired, and she could not think in symbolic terms.

8.   Enabling mourning processes and the development of a capacity for symbolic activity links with *promoting separation and differentiation*. Differentiation of "me" and "not me", self and object, and overcoming resistance to this process needs to be explored in therapy.

> One transsexual adolescent in an early session seemed to be convinced that I could not understand her because I was just an ordinary man and not someone like her. So I said to her that as she did not know me, I wondered how she was so sure that I was so different from her. In a later session, she brought a newsletter of a transsexual organization and gave it to me. I asked what she wanted me to read, and she indicated an article by a doctor who ran a sex-reassignment clinic. I decided to read aloud the part of the article that she had indicated. Here the doctor spoke about a patient who had the same first name as the doctor. At the end of it, "Catherine" looked at me and said, with a feeling of surprise and satisfaction, "I did not know that Doctor X was a transsexual himself: he can express exactly what I feel". It seems here that the doctor and the patient had become fused in her mind. This also threw some light on her initial belief that I could understand her only if I were exactly like her. Separation and differentiation were felt to threaten this process.

> On another occasion, one male-to-female transsexual describing his relationship with his partner commented: "I hated her genitals, because I hated my genitals so much that only when I could differentiate from my partner, and feel that they didn't be-

long to me, could I start to like them." Fusion or merging and differentiation are not all-or-nothing phenomena, but are, in my view, ends of a continuum on which we move in the course of development. Stressful conditions may produce merging in a child or teenager who has achieved some sense of separateness and differentiation.

9.   From childhood until late adolescence, when a solution to the incongruence between the inner perception of one's own gender and the reality of the body becomes possible (see also Appendix A), the child or the adolescent will be in a painful transitional phase and the psychological exploration of the AGIO, and of its impact on the social sphere, may lead to the experience of uncertainty, which is often found unbearable. This may also be equated with the experience of inner chaos and disintegration, like people in the throws of a traumatic event. These experiences in turn can be communicated through conscious and unconscious ways to other family members or even the social network. The request for precipitate action, to put an end to this intolerable state, becomes very prevalent. *To enable the child/adolescent and the family to tolerate uncertainty in the area of gender identity development is an important therapeutic aim.*

10. Together with coping with uncertainty, it is crucial that the teenager, especially, is helped to maintain hope in the possibility that through psychological work and exploration a solution to the gender identity conflict can be found. The frustration produced by the undoing of a solution can be tolerated only if the teenager can live in hope that another solution can be found, or a new compromise achieved. Sadowski and Gaffney highlighted in chapter eight the high risk of suicidal attempts in teenagers with gender identity disorders. It is the tendency of these adolescents to experience psychological disintegration when a particular set of certainties and beliefs are threatened or lost, which makes them more prone to suicidal attempts. Therapeutic work with the adolescent and the family, together with social intervention (e.g. in the school), *should aim to sustain hope* that, in spite of difficulties and distress, progress towards a solution can be made. In my clinical work with teenagers, I have found a useful metaphor to be that of having the

experience of being in a dark tunnel with a light at the end of it. What is useful in this metaphor is that one needs to retain the idea that there is light at the end of the tunnel, but that only through the work of moving in the right direction can the light be reached.

* * *

These are some of the aims in therapy and management. No doubt others could be added. I ought also to say that these aims are not specific to children with gender identity disorders.

In this list, however, I have not included altering or changing the gender identity/role as one of the primary therapeutic aims. As the AGIO is the result of complex interactions and influences (see chapter two), exploring in therapy its nature and targeting the developmental processes may in turn, secondarily, lead to the evolution of the organization and, therefore, to the sense of gender identity. On the other hand this may remain unaltered. There is something mysterious about identity which makes it difficult simply to reduce it to the nature of the participating influences. Sarah Maitland, novelist and theologian, said in a 1991 BBC television "Heart of the Matter" interview: "There may be a sanctity about gender that we have not fully explored. This is quite a new question." She was alluding to the sense of respect and inviolability sanctioned by moral and religious principle. Assisting the development of these children may improve the quality of their lives and their relationships and prevent self-destructive actions and behaviours. These are in themselves very worthwhile aims.

In 1974, Green described in *Sexual Identity Conflicts in Children and Adults* the objectives of therapy that were prevalent at the time. These were:

(1) developing a relationship of trust and affection between a male therapist and the feminine boy;

(2) educating the child as to the impossibility of his changing sex;

(3) stressing to the child the advantages of participating in some of the activities enjoyed by other boys, and promoting greater comfort in such activity;

(4) educating the parents as to how they may be fostering sexual identity conflict in their child;

(5) advising the parents of the need for them to consistently disapprove of very feminine behaviour if they desire change in their sons; and

(6) enhancing the father's or father substitute's involvement in the feminine boy's life. [p. 246]

In the approach I have outlined, the therapeutic team does not aim to tackle the gender identity disorder directly; rather, they take a more neutral stance in relation to it. The understanding of the nature and characteristics of the atypical gender organization (see chapter two) may lead to changes in the child or adolescent, or in the attitudes of other family members and social network towards the child and his or her predicament. These changes may, in turn, influence the gender identity disorder. This emphasis on neutrality is particularly important with adolescents with gender identity disorders, where the fears of being controlled, invaded, or intruded upon are very strong.

The therapeutic context

I have outlined some therapeutic aims without defining beforehand the management structure in which to pursue this work, as I see these aims as reference points to be used, when appropriate, in different therapeutic contexts, ranging from family therapy, individual therapy, group work, even to working with professional networks of teachers, health visitors, social workers, and GPs involved with the case. In a family therapy session, for instance, the construction of a detailed family tree over a number of sessions may be an appropriate way to explore separation and losses in the family.

In the Gender Identity Development Unit, we offer an initial assessment in which we take a developmental history and a family history; items regarding gender identity/role development (such as toy and play preferences, clothing, peer-group relationships, rough-and-tumble play, fantasy life, role playing, etc.) are subsequently discussed over a number of sessions. What then follows can be therapy with the whole family, or individual therapy with the child and the parents separately, or only with the parents. A monthly group for parents of children and adolescents with a gender identity disorder has helped the pursuit of the therapeutic aims described. It has also helped to remove their sense of isolation and, sometimes, their sense of embarrassment and shame. In some cases, we will start with one therapeutic modality and then shift to a different one as more specific or individual needs become apparent. For instance, an initial number of sessions with the whole family may lead to the child's being seen for individual therapy and the parents for parental counselling. With late adolescents, we tend to see them separately from the parents initially. A multidisciplinary approach ensures that all aspects of the child's development are considered in the family and social contexts in which she or he lives.

In our team, the staff includes a child and adolescent psychiatrist, a child and adolescent psychotherapist, a clinical psychologist, a social worker, a paediatric endocrinologist, and a secretary. Regular team meetings are important to ensure that assessment and therapeutic plans are well coordinated and integrated, and also to provide a containing structure for the responses engendered in team members.

CHAPTER THIRTEEN

Case illustrations

A
"Jack" and "Jill":
two children with gender identity disorders

Leslie Ironside

Psychodynamic approaches to atypical gender development in the male tend to look to the specific role of the mother in the separation–individuation phase of development. Stoller (1968b) found that excessive mother–son skin-to-skin contact during the boy's earliest years inhibited the psychological separation of son from mother. Coates and Person (1985) advanced a specific hypothesis that separation anxiety—which is activated by uneven maternal availability—plays a pivotal role in the emergence of a gender identity disorder in boys. They suggested that severe separation anxiety precedes the feminine behaviour which emerges in order to restore a "fantasy tie" to the physically or emotionally absent mother. In imitating "Mommy", the boy confuses "being Mommy" with "having Mommy". Green (1987) also found that the father–son relationship was a prominent variable in cross-gender behaviours.

Less research has been conducted on female children with atypical gender patterns, though extensive cross-gender identity in females was seen by Stoller (1975) as resulting in part from an extremely distant mother–daughter relationship and a compensatory identification with the father.

As will become apparent in this case illustration, my experiences with "Jack" and "Jill" correspond in many ways with this research. Certainly my clinical approach is similar in terms of attempting to consider the symptom of a gender identity problem in the context of more global problems in the child's development and the family psychopathology.

Social forces also play a powerful role in the perception of gender identity problems and need to be kept constantly in mind. Jack and Jill probably both felt that they were restrained by a strait-jacket of social expectations, but I hope that the material I present here also illustrates a very debilitating frame of mind and difficult associated behaviour which were raising appropriate concerns and proving very difficult to manage. Both Jack and Jill seemed very unhappy at the point of referral, and their families and teachers were very concerned about them. As therapy progressed, matters did seem to change and some sense of lightness and well-being seemed to enter the picture.

A boy's story

Jack was 6 years old at referral and was diagnosed as having a gender identity disorder. My initial impression was of an intelligent and pleasant boy dressed in a stylish and immaculate way but a boy who also had a quality about him that echoed research into the physical attributes of cross-gendered boys. Zucker, Wild, and Bradley (1993) found that such boys were rated as more attractive, beautiful, cute, and pretty than a control group and proposed that it was therefore possible that the physically attractive features of the child triggered response patterns in parents and others, which reinforced feminine behaviour.[1]

---

[1] Stoller (1968b) in taking a multifactorial view of the factors contributing to gender identity problems proposed the possibility of a basic constitutional factor that might take the external form of this physical beauty and lead to an innate feminine tendency being reinforced during a critical period of an infant's development. In discussing the causality of gender identity problems, Di

I shall return to his history and details of the earlier part of his therapy in a moment, but first I would like to jump to a point many months into my work with him. He had become very preoccupied with comings and goings and hide-and-seek games, and he would often ask me to close my eyes and find him. Now this in itself is not unusual, but what was exceptional was that he would also anxiously demand that I should keep talking whilst my eyes were shut; if I didn't, he would get into quite a panic. When, after many sessions, he at last managed to let me know something more about this, he blurted out that if I didn't talk he got frightened as he did not then know where I was.

Now, what does this tell us about this boy's frame of mind? It is certainly an unusually clear statement of a fused and confused state. Inherent in the game of hide-and-seek is a certain anxiety that Jack seemed to find extremely difficult to bear. Imagine an everyday picture of a mother playing a peek-a-boo game with her infant by holding her hand over her eyes. Imagine the mother covering her eyes for slightly too long and the infant getting into a state of panic through fear of abandonment. In all likelihood, the mother would then immediately remove her hand and, depending upon the state of affairs, physically move towards or actually pick up the infant and soothe and comfort him, saying something like, "Oh, it's all right. I'm still here." In the normal course of events this would re-establish contact and contain the infant's anxieties. The whole matter would pass without causing much concern. The infant's anguish and the mother's response would be seen to be well within the bounds of appropriate behaviour at this stage of the infant's development. Returning to Jack, he seemed like an infant who found it difficult to tolerate even the slightest amount of psychic distress. The fact that I could not see him left him feeling very anxious and in a state of identification with a "no-seeing mother" which was very debilitating. He spoke of not knowing where I was

---

Ceglie (1996) also writes that a "biological contribution has to be postulated on the basis of recent research such as the hereditary (Bailey & Pillard 1991) and genetic factors (Hamer et al., 1993) identified for male homosexuals. . . . A difference has also been identified in 'the bed nucleus of the stria terminalis' of the brain between male to female transsexuals and non transsexual males (Zhou et al., 1995)."

even though his own eyes were still physically able to see me. My speaking maintained contact and contained and lessened his anxiety, thus allowing the game to continue.

This tendency to avoid the impact of certain emotional experiences is something that we are all prone to do at times of stress, and the process would seem to have its roots in an infantile attempt to find a solution to mental pain. Instead of becoming aware that we are anxious, sad, angry, jealous, envious, lonely, guilty, and so on, any one of us might at times regress and break out in some psychologically based symptom. An infant's psychological self is vulnerable as he or she requires the presence of an attentive and sensitive care-giver. If the care-giver, though, is incapable of responding accurately to his or her mental state, the infant, depending upon his or her constitution, is more likely to resort to a primitive defensive strategy. This is the hallmark of the insecurely attached child (Ainsworth, Blehar, Waters, & Wall, 1978).[2]

Jack was referred for therapy shortly after a very acrimonious parental separation. At my initial meeting with both his parents, the mutual aggression was so intense that, though they were both supportive of Jack having therapy, they felt that I should see them separately at any future meetings. Jack was in the prime care of his mother, and at a further meeting with her alone it became very apparent that, though the cross-dressing and Jack's apparent desire to be a girl were the main focus of her concerns, she was absolutely at the end of her tether and had very little self-esteem as

---

[2] In discussing the aetiology of gender identity disorder (GID), Coates and Wolfe (1995) succinctly write of how, in their view, "A shy, inhibited, highly reactive constitution can best be conceptualised as a predisposing factor that lowers the threshold for the derailment of the attachment system. As well, it increased the child's sensitivity to parental wishes. Chronic pathology in the parents leaves the sensitive, reactive child with an insecure, anxious attachment. When trauma or severe marital stress are added, causing maternal depression, a traumatic derailment of the mother–child attachment bond occurs inducing severe separation anxiety in the child. When the child's attempts to repair the derailed attachment involve gender content and he succeeds in revitalising the mother to some degree, all the factors necessary for the onset and development of GID are in place. Factors that then come to play a role in perpetuating the symptoms involve internal mechanisms in the attachment relationship and the experiences of the child with his peers" (p. 32).

a mother. She described how, when Jack was very young, he had gone into her cupboard and put on her shoes and some of her jewellery. This had at first been seen as funny, but now she did not know what to do about it. Should she go along with it, or curtail things? In a revealing statement, she asked which would be the least damaging: her feeling was that whatever she did would inflict some harm. This left her with an intractable problem. She spoke of her "complete lack of confidence" as a mother, and it soon became apparent how this permeated to all aspects of their relationship—from going to the park, to cleaning Jack's teeth. Jack also frequently suffered from chronic constipation.

At the time of referral, then, any sense of "positive attunement" (Stern, 1985) between this mother and her child seemed sadly lacking. Their relationship was fraught with difficulty, and, leaving aside the question of causality, the horse had bolted and both were being badly battered and bruised by the process. It was very apparent from the start that whatever work I would be doing with Jack, it had to be done in conjunction with giving his mother time to explore matters and establish some sense of confidence as a mother. It was also, of course, very important to endeavour to meet with Jack's father, who remained an important and influential part of the broad family configuration.

Turning now to the initial meetings with Jack: a certain anxiety is inherent in the process of a child beginning individual therapy, and, given a history of apparent separation difficulties, both his parents were understandably anxious as to how Jack would cope with seeing me alone. They felt that it would be useful for him to bring something of his own to the initial meetings to help him with this transition. This sounded very reasonable as the importance of the role of a transitional object in a child's development is widely recognized—but when the suggested object turned out to be a pair of ladies' shoes, matters seemed somewhat more complicated!

In his paper "Transitional Objects and Transitional Phenomena" (1971), the psychoanalyst and paediatrician Donald Winnicott describes how there may emerge in

> an infant's development something or some phenomenon— perhaps a bundle of wool or the corner of a blanket or eiderdown, or a word, or a tune, or a mannerism—that becomes vitally important to the infant for use at the time of going

to sleep, and as a defence against anxiety, especially of the depressive type. . . . In health, however, there is a gradual extension of the range of interest, and eventually the extended range is maintained, even when depressive anxiety is near. A need for a specific object or a behaviour pattern that started at a very early date may reappear at a later age when deprivation threatens. [pp. 4–5]

He further writes of how the transitional object—what he calls a child's first "not-me possession"—"stands for the breast, or the object of the first relationship", of it "antedating established reality testing", and of how it may "develop into a fetish object and so persist as a characteristic of the adult sexual life". The ladies' shoes do seem to share some of these features, but matters are more complex as Jack seems to have stepped right "into his mother's shoes" and, as such, into the more pathological arena of symbolic equations (Segal, 1957). The shoes, then, at least in part, do not so much symbolize the mother but, as Coates and Person (1985) hypothesized, also restore a "fantasy tie". Jack thereby was confusing "being Mommy" with "having Mommy".

My approach to the parents' suggestion of his bringing something with him was to endeavour to explore the matter whilst maintaining some sense of neutrality on the subject. In terms of my therapeutic contact with them, it was important to aim towards enabling them, as his parents, to find their own way of resolving the difficulties and in so doing promote their identity as effective parents. A lot of pressure was placed upon me to assume the role of some kind of figure of authority, but it was important not simply to act on this, as this could further denude their confidence.

In the event, when Jack's mother brought him, he did not bring anything; however, she did find it very difficult to then "set the scene" for them to separate. She seemed very anxious, seemingly wanting to leave without any sense of introduction or reassurance. Jack, understandably, became quite distressed, and I discussed with his mother the option of her staying and trying to address and think about these difficulties. She did stay, and in a fairly short while he was settled enough to agree to her going to the waiting-room. He spent much of the rest of the session alone with me but with the door open and with ready access to his mother. At the second meeting, he separated more easily and his mother left the building, though there were a number of occasions during the 50-minute session when his anxiety over her whereabouts had to be addressed.

This opening sequence illustrates an important theme that was to run through my work with both Jack and Jill, in that both these children had, in a very immediate way and perhaps for the first times in their lives, the real experience of a "parental couple"—myself and their mothers—working together to try to resolve the presenting problems. This was, I think, a very important facet of the therapeutic process as a whole.

At the second meeting, following an initial enquiry about what he liked, he spoke of his teddies and, in a fascinating way, how he "almost liked cars". He moved rapidly from one activity of his choice to another in a very unsettled way. For a brief period he did play with the cars, and in an interesting and creative way he also dressed a dinosaur up "to go out for the evening" and made jewellery with some pipe-cleaners. What was most striking, though, and indeed quite disturbing to witness, was a noticeable change of affect in his voice and mannerisms at certain times. At one point, for instance, as he was struggling to make a rainbow with some pipe-cleaners, he seemed to run into some difficulties. Pouting his lips in a crude caricature of what might stereotypically be described as "looking like a tart", he then said, in a very affected way: "Um, what luscious red lips!" This was accompanied by what seemed to be a complete change of mannerism. The pipe-cleaners and his relationship to them were suddenly transformed into something entirely different.[3]

Now, what sense can be made of this material? Returning to Winnicott, he describes how, on first discovering Darwin's *Origin of Species*, "I could not leave off reading it. At the time I did not know why it was important to me, but I see now that the main thing was that it showed that living things could be examined scientifically with the corollary that *gaps in knowledge and understanding need not scare me*. This idea meant a great lessening of tensions and consequently a release of energy for work and play" (quoted in Phillips, 1988).

---

[3] I would like to stress that this material would also have been distressing to witness if exhibited by a girl.

For Jack, the gap in his knowledge and understanding seemed to scare him, and his way of managing this seemed to be through an extraordinary transformation of both the object of his interest and his own attitude towards it. Given this brief description, it was not surprising that he was having immense difficulties in terms of his work at school. In the session, it did not seem possible for him to ask for help, and my offer of help was soundly rebuffed. There seemed little room within this state of mind to think in terms of a productive two-person relationship.

Jack's reaction seemed to indicate an instantaneous response to an overwhelming situation—defensively useful but, in the main, developmentally debilitating. I say in the main, because I think that it is also very important to acknowledge that, as with Winnicott and his reading of Darwin, there was also a creative element to Jack's response. In a most unconventional way this "interaction" with the pipe-cleaners also lessened tensions and released energy for work and play.

Jack's ongoing therapy was dominated by this frame of mind, and it took a great deal of time and painstaking work to begin to see the wood for the trees. Using some net curtains, Jack would often transform the room into a kind of "boudoir" in which he would "mince" around in a most affected way. He was furious that he could not have access to my cupboards, and at a much later time he did describe his fantasy that I kept all my ladies' shoes and dresses in there! He seemed to destroy any awareness that I had a "mind" or "sense of identity" that was distinct from his. Anything that I had he would describe as having at home—and often a better and more expensive model! This would run to any object that captured his attention—from the furniture in the room, to the garden fence outside. Any sense of difference or the possible consequential envious feelings that might be aroused were obliterated.

Jack was in weekly therapy for about two years, and during that time there were some noticeable developments in terms of how he functioned. He gradually seemed more able to tolerate some degree of psychic distress and to bear feelings of separation and envy. Rather than saying that he had a room that was the same as mine only bigger and better, he was able to speak of wishing that he was rich enough to own the building I was working in. Later, rather than enviously "usurping" some new blinds on the windows, he was able to speak of my being a "lucky boy" to have them. The endings of the sessions radically changed, too. It had been increasingly apparent that his behaviour became more "affected" as each session approached its end. This behaviour gradually diminished, and he would then start to leave in a rather manic and chaotic fashion before eventually becoming more coherent and able calmly to leave, saying "Goodbye, I will see you next week". He also began to "play" with the more physical American greeting of slapping his hand into mine and saying "take five". This also led to an element of pretend boxing. This development is interesting, as one of the defining characteristics associated with boys who are seen to have a gender identity disorder is that of the avoidance of rough-and-tumble play (Coates & Wolfe, 1995). Here, Jack seemed to show the beginnings of such play.

These developments indicated important shifts in terms of his functioning and ability to think symbolically, which coincided with his becoming more settled in general. He began to do better at school. There remained distinct difficulties in terms of his educational development, but what slowly developed was a sense of optimism in that he was beginning to show some signs of progress and an ability to use the extra help that was provided for him. His constipation problems also disappeared, and his mother felt that things were much better at home.

One of his mother's dilemmas as a parent had been that of wanting to always "make it alright" for Jack. She had found it very difficult to bear him being upset, and it was noticeable that as she and Jack, hand in hand as it were, became more able to bear distress, so the pressing symptoms subsided. A sense of positive attunement seemed to be developing between herself and her son. She had begun to feel more robust in her ability to parent and had begun to manage and limit his cross-dressing to certain times, and, in much the same way as a child gradually leaves its transitional objects behind, she also spoke of feeling that he was "needing to dress up" less and less.

Matters did not, of course, simply continue to progress smoothly, and, given the circumstances, it would have been naïve to have expected them to do so. To cite one example: Jack's mother had formed a new relationship and was planning to get married.

Jack was finding this very difficult to manage, and undoubtedly it set up very complicated new dynamics within the family structure. A summer holiday was also fast approaching. Jack's mother then phoned in some despair, saying: "The shoes are back! His father has bought him some more!" She then described how Jack had come back from his father's with a pair of girls' shoes.

Breaks were difficult, not only because of what they meant to Jack, but because his mother then also felt left on her own, having to cope with my pending absence and the absence of her own therapist. Again, she seemed to have lost her confidence as a mother and felt unable to manage. We had a fairly lengthy telephone call, and gradually she began to feel that the bubble had not completely burst and that she could tackle things and talk to Jack and his father. When I met with Jack for his last session before the break, he brought the shoes with him. He immediately proceeded to tell me how he had been out with his Dad and had asked for them. His father had bought them for him, but now he (Jack) wasn't sure he wanted them. He was able to think about this in the context of feelings engendered by the forthcoming summer break and the fury that he felt at the thought that his mother was marrying, but what was he to do? Matters seemed to have become quite split in his mind again. Could he bear to face his father if he no longer wanted the shoes, or could he bear to face his mother if he wanted to keep them? He then said that he had to sit and think about it. He moved his chair and for some minutes sat quietly pondering the problem before saying that he had decided to throw the shoes away. As his therapist, the matter that I found extremely pertinent here was not simply the decision that he had made but his apparent developing ability to tolerate thinking about his situation.

Jack often seemed absolutely enraged at his parents' separation, and filled with enormous concerns as regards his father no longer living in the family home. Though lack of space prevents me from dealing with this in any detail, I hope that this example also serves to illustrate another facet of Jack's gender identity problem which had to do with pronounced oedipal issues.

My sense of this whole incident was that with all the feelings engendered at this time, Jack was feeling particularly vulnerable—as were his mother and his father. This led to a regression and resumption of previous behaviour—probably within and between his parents as well as within Jack. He went out with his father and, in a demanding way, asked for the shoes. His father bought them for him. His father, too, found it very hard to say "no" to Jack, and maybe he also wanted to "get at" Jack's mother in some way. Returning to his mother's, Jack was faced with her despair and anger but was also desperate to wear the shoes. As his mother gathered her confidence back and was able to discuss and contain things for Jack, so his "need" to wear them seemed to diminish. I did not get the impression that he was just talked out of wearing the shoes, though no doubt this was one part of the equation.

I cite this incident in order to illustrate the complexity of matters and how particular aspects of behaviour are likely to resurface at certain times of stress due to external circumstances but also at points of developmental change such as the onset of adolescence. I think it also illustrates the importance of a long-term commitment to such cases.

A girl's story

Jill's story shares many features with those of Jack. She was also 6 years old at the point of referral. Her parents had separated when she was very young, and she, too, was primarily in the care of her mother. Matters had again been acrimonious between the parents, and access visits were problematic. Allegations of sexual abuse had been made but nothing proven.

Her mother spoke of protecting Jill from the worst arguments, though Jill herself has certainly spoken to me of remembering immense parental rows which, at the very least, bordered on physical aggression. From her perspective, they were felt to be enormous and very frightening, and she would physically hide away during these traumatic episodes. Apart from the actuality of these outbursts, the other issue that has immense relevance to this history—and, indeed, Jack's—is that she would certainly have experienced a mother and father who, through life's circumstances at that time, must have found it very difficult to pay "good-enough" parental attention to their children.

Jill was described by her mother as being a model baby until she was about 2½ years old, when, "overnight", she was seen to become "obsessed by her clothing", hating anything "girlie", and began saying that she was a boy. My impression of this was that matters had been becoming increasingly difficult within the family at the time that this particular symptom had suddenly become an issue. At this point, the quality of the mother–child dyad seemed to change radically, as something of immense importance was lost in terms of an understanding and containing (Bion, 1962) relationship between the mother and her daughter.[4]

As with Jack, I felt it important also to forge contact with Jill's father. It was some months later that I met with him as he was living in a different area. He was not as concerned about Jill but felt that the problem lay in the way her mother managed her—a picture soon arose of a mutually undermining rather than supportive parental partnership. He felt that the main difficulties were in terms of the abrasive access arrangements. He reported that he felt that matters had begun to calm down between them almost exactly to the day that the mother had sought help—as she felt more contained, she seemed less threatened by the father's presence.

Jill was causing immense concern to her mother. At the initial referral meeting with her mother, Jill was described as being dyslexic but, in addition, was seen to be very unhappy in herself and constantly demanding. Getting Jill up and dressed for school was described as a nightmare because of the prescribed skirts worn by all the girls at the school. Her mother went on to say how Jill seemed to "struggle with being a girl" and how even at the age of 6 she had spoken of a hatred and terror at the thought of growing breasts.

The mother also explained how Jill would spend hours in front of a mirror trying to get her appearance "just right" and how on

---

[4] Winnicott (1971) discusses the formation of the infant's self within the mother–child relationship. He describes the infant's experience of feeling merged with the mother to the extent that she is able to identify with the baby. In the normal course of events, she is able to reflect upon and respond appropriately to the infant's mental state by representing it to him through a language of gestures which the infant can understand. This stage is followed by a gradual psychological separation in which contact is maintained and mutual understanding elaborated through what he calls cross-identifications. Thus, the infant's mental experience of himself is gradually acquired through careful observation of his mother's mental state and her perception of his own feelings.

several occasions she had cut her own hair. As it was described, it seemed to be a process of getting rid of something that she perceived as "girlie" as well as trying to get a particular look. Jill seemed to prefer well-worn, almost scruffy clothes but within a perfectionist frame of mind that showed little allowance for anything that was not "exactly right". From the way in which it was presented, it seemed as though she was attempting to flee from a state of uncertainty and ambivalence, and perhaps from the normal childhood confusions as regards gender identity, to a state of certainty and knowing.

As with Jack's mother, the gender issue seemed to strike right at the core of her ability and identity as a mother. Struggling to fight back her tears, she spoke of feeling that she could manage anything else but this—"It gets right under my skin." She spoke of how she tried to cope with the situation by describing Jill as a "tomboy". This did serve to contain matters to a certain degree, but it was also felt to be a very contrived notion that seemed forced upon the situation through a desperate need. Matters were not as simple as the everyday use of that term implied. Clearly, in addition to whatever work was offered to Jill, there was once again a very important role to be played in working with this mother and with the father.

The similarities here with Jack are intriguing in that Jack's cross-gender behaviour also seemed to get under his mother's skin. The expression is a very interesting one because, like with Jack's cross-dressing, it implies a certain functionality behind the behaviour—namely, the re-creation of a state of fusion, admittedly of a persecutory nature, between the mother and child—and, as such, it might serve a useful function to both parties.

At the initial meetings with Jill, and much to her mother's surprise, she, in fact, separated in a relatively straightforward way and we seemed to strike a good rapport from the start. Jill was dressed in a well-worn track suit, and I found her to be an immediately likeable, attractive, and intelligent child. She was able to speak quite readily of her fears of seeing someone new, but she also spoke of wanting to "sort things out". She also told me that she was a "boy tomboy". Jill, too, seemed to want to make it quite clear that there was more to her usage of this term than is normally implied.

Her mother had taken immense initiative in terms of preparing Jill. This was very evident in the sessions, but Jill's fears and anxieties and the debilitating way that they affected her behaviour were also readily apparent. For instance, looking around at the things in the room, she quickly vetoed using the paper and paints and so on, saying that she couldn't draw. She did the same with the ball, saying that she couldn't catch. Eventually, she cautiously played with the dolls and, in relating them to the various members of the family, identified herself as a male doll. This was done without a flinch and is, I think, very instructive in terms of her internal fantasies.[5] She also spoke of how she hated having dyslexia—"Why can't I be just like other children?"—and in almost the same breath she spoke of hating herself.

She settled into weekly sessions, but her absolute despair and depression soon came to dominate the meetings. She was finding it increasingly difficult to go to school, and separating from her mother and coming to see me first thing in the morning was equally awful for her. There followed a few months of painful work in which I was in close contact with her mother, who felt that matters had to be resolved and felt confident in leaving her very distressed daughter with me. My role was complicated: in reality, I was acting as a supportive partner for the mother in bearing this difficult process, and with Jill I was both the hated object, in fantasy keeping her away from her mother, as well as a "container" trying to "digest" and make understandable her most primitive fears. She seemed terrified that her mother would not come back and, in floods of tears and desperation, would speak of her fear that her mother would die and never return. Furthermore—and I think that this indicates her depressed state—she spoke of just wanting to be at home and under her duvet in bed.

The psychoanalyst Wilfred Bion (1959, 1962) describes the anti-developmental effects of the absence of an object capable of containing an infant's anxiety, notably the fear of dying, and de-

---

[5] I am reminded here of another patient, a young man who had had to have his arm amputated. He described how in his flamboyant daydreams, which occupied a great deal of his time, he would see himself as a figure like that of the knight in shining armour victoriously saving the day but always with both his arms. His fantasy world seemed to obliterate his distress and insulate him from reality.

scribes the consequent difficulty of establishing a therapeutic alliance with such a patient when the patient is terrified of losing control and when suspicion has become part of the condition.

In the sessions with Jill, this suspicion and terror was all too apparent, but she was eventually able to begin to separate herself from these fears and "look at" what was happening rather than being enveloped by it. I was able to utilize the dolls to symbolize her feelings at the separation, with a large frog acting as a massive invader hanging over and then completely enveloping her at the point of separation. It was very important to acknowledge her experience not simply of a good object absent, but of a bad object present (O'Shaughnessy, 1964) that was felt to be persecuting and attacking and from which she felt that she could only find solace under the duvet. There are obvious echoes here of her early childhood experience. Gradually, matters began to settle, and her mother spoke of how things were beginning to seem different and becoming more manageable.

Jill began to talk of friendships with girls and of a new interest in horse riding, but she also spoke of how difficult it was to change because of the attention and comment that this might bring on her from her peer group. I think that this was a very real dilemma and that it was important that the uncomfortable feelings that were aroused were acknowledged.[6] In the transference I certainly experienced something of this when she first began to wear her school uniform to the sessions.[7]

---

[6] It was also very interesting to hear about the delicate balance of negotiation that developed in terms of her peer-group interaction which seemed to mirror an internal shift in her thinking. In the early stages of therapy, Jill had spoken in a rigid way of being absolutely aghast at the idea of having a baby when she reached adulthood, but she had gradually become more flexible in her thinking about this. At the same time, her mother and her teacher reported how her male friends were becoming less and less tolerant of her statements to them that she was a boy and that she was gradually presenting as, and being seen as, a "girl who liked to do the things boys liked doing". The progression of a more flexible internal pattern of thinking seemed intertwined with these external developments, which I do not feel were simply a compliance to group pressure.

[7] The whole issue of uniform is a very interesting one in terms of the tolerance of expressions of personal identity and bearing differences. Out of school, Jill continued to adopt her own very individual style of clothing.

As with Jack, it was delightful to witness how she gradually began to change and function in a more developmentally progressive way. In the room, besides managing and enjoying drawing and so forth, one of the most noticeable developments was how she played with the ball. She had always been attracted towards playing catch, and once she became more settled in the sessions she was able to risk doing so. At first, her anxiety meant that she hastily grabbed at the ball and inevitably dropped it. She slowly developed an ability to "bear the gap" and allow the ball to come to her. Returning after one holiday break, she proudly showed me how she could now catch with one hand—echoes again of Winnicott's self-reflection that "gaps in knowledge and understanding need not scare me" (1971).

Conclusion

By the age of 3 years, 80% of children correctly answer: "Are you like this doll [a girl] or this doll [a boy]?" (Levin, Balistrier, & Schukit, 1972). Generally by this time a child will have made an important transition by placing herself or himself in one of two groups of people, male or female, and in so doing will have had to acknowledge and tolerate not belonging to the other group. Furthermore, by the time of this initial establishment of some kind of gender identity, the child will also have passed through a number of other stages of development in terms of separation and individuation. In the normal course of events, the child will have become aware of a transition from a state of fusion with its mother to a recognition of a two-person relationship and, later, of a transition from two- to three-person relationships.[8]

One of the crucial determinants in terms of mental growth is how the child manages these transitions and whether the increased experience of separation is tolerated or denied. Something very crucial seemed to have gone awry in this process with Jack

---

[8] Different theoreticians conceptualize different stages. For example, the psychoanalyst Klein (1946) writes of the paranoid–schizoid and depressive positions, and the psychologist Piaget (1954) of the infant's development from a world of subjectivity to an appreciation of independent objects.

and Jill which had to do with the interrelationship between their external experiences and their own constitution.

There is probably common agreement that Jack and Jill's life experiences would leave them susceptible to the development of some kind of psychological difficulty, but why this should take the form of a gender identity problem is a very complex matter. There are many other children from similar backgrounds who are not identified in this way. The answer must lie in an intricate combination of biological, psychological, and social factors that interact during a vulnerable stage of development.

In terms of therapy for such children, different clinicians would obviously approach the subject from different perspectives. In describing my work with the children and their parents, I have focused primarily on the role of anxiety and the development of thought.

Observations of mechanisms that are used to create states of mind that provide protection from anxiety and pain led the analyst John Steiner (1993) to develop the concept of a psychic retreat—a state that is experienced spatially by the person as if it were a place where he or she could hide (see chapter two, p. 14). This is, I believe, a very useful way to conceptualize something of these children's immersion in their cross-gender world. In terms of the therapeutic process, this has important consequences because if this defensively useful, but developmentally debilitating, frame of mind is relinquished, this involves the person in a process similar to that of mourning. With this in mind, I would like to end with a brief quote from the poet W. B. Yeats: "Tread softly for you tread on my dreams."

B
"Teresa":
an adolescent girl who wants to become
a man—a psychoanalytic exploration

Mauro Morra

T he aim of this case illustration is to demonstrate that an accurate study of the psyche, such as can be performed in the classical psychoanalytic situation, can explain the way a transsexual presentation develops and how this relates, in my view, to a homosexual structure.

The case I want to present could be seen as a bit more than a case of homosexuality, and, at the same time, a bit less. A bit more, because the patient, a girl in her late adolescence, would not have been satisfied with a homosexual way of living: she wanted to become a man through a surgical operation. A bit less, because she had never had an actual homosexual experience: she was so ashamed of being a woman that she could not tolerate any intercourse that would disclose her female body. Her entire fantasy life was dominated by the homosexual choice of object. She fell in love with more than one female schoolmate, with her dentist's assistant, and even with some women who could be seen as mother figures. She often masturbated with the fantasy of being a man in sexual intercourse with a woman. Her future was seen only as being a man: having a wife and children.

At the time of beginning the treatment, Teresa was an 18-year-old schoolgirl who was preparing for her "A" level examinations, and I saw her while I was working in London. Her plan was to go to university, but she had also considered the possibility of having to work in order to pay for an operation to become a man. My first contact was on the telephone with her mother: as I was not sure who I was talking to, I asked, "Are you the mother?", and she answered, "Yes, I am the mother of Christine" (who is two years younger than my patient), but she immediately added: "Of course, I am the mother of Teresa as well." My feeling was of a mother more or less consciously rejecting her elder daughter.

I had a first meeting with both parents, who seemed to me excessively tolerant of the idea that Teresa would change sex. Her mother had also enquired about the practicality of the surgical operation. An accurate medical examination (including the intervention of a gynaecologist) had been performed and also a chromosome investigation, but everything had been defined as normal.

Her mother did not remember any particular problem in Teresa's early infancy: delivery, breast-feeding for six months. But later on, during the analysis, Teresa told me that at her birth she was put into an incubator because she was underweight. Her father mentioned that already when Teresa was 2 years old (roughly the date of her sister's birth), she refused to wear a skirt. Later on, there was a period of school refusal: Teresa did not want to go to school because her sister remained at home (this was the mother's explanation), but, on my questioning, her mother had not noticed any manifestation of jealousy.

When I first met the patient, she appeared calm, respectful, and cooperative. She was wearing trousers and a "unisex" jacket. Her way of holding herself was masculine, maybe a bit artificial and exaggerated. Her facial expression, on the contrary, was feminine, notwithstanding the short haircut. Her eyes were especially feminine, as was her voice. She had a nice smile. The interview was touching: she was moved to tears and affirmed that the reason for her unhappiness was the fact that she was a woman. The degree of her unhappiness was such that she had thought of suicide many times. My immediate suspicion was that her being a woman was the scapegoat for all her unhappiness and her depression, so that the fantasy of becoming a man was the magical solution for her.

Her motivation for the analysis seemed initially rather con-fused: her parents had mentioned a legal requirement for one year of psychological treatment before the operation, although it was unclear from where the parents had got this idea. But what the girl said was different: she wanted to see more clearly into herself, in view of the seriousness of the decision to undergo surgery. This seemed a sufficient motivation to me.

There were some moments during the interview when I won-dered if the girl was not near psychosis: it was when she expressed the fear that people might realize she was a woman—as if this were so difficult!—and also when she conveyed her impression that people she met in the street or on a bus could say of her: "She is a lesbian." Hearing the sound of the consonant "s" was sufficient to make her think that someone might have said the word "les-bian".

The analysis was held four times a week, and Teresa did not miss one session. The total of the sessions was 74. Unfortunately, the treatment was broken off, as often happens in similar cases, after little more than six months, but the clinical material for this period is sufficient, in my opinion, to reconstruct what happened in the patient's mind.

At some time during the treatment she wondered why I had taken her into analysis: the answer she gave herself was that I wanted to write a book on her. Initially she was rather suspicious of me, being scared that I would impose my will on her. Later on she became more confident. I did my best to keep a neutral atti-tude any time that she mentioned her determination to become a man: I think I succeeded when she talked about her love for girls or women, maybe a bit less when she gave details of the surgical operations that she had planned to undergo. I confess to being horrified by the idea of her adolescent body, well-developed and in good health, being cut, stitched up, and mutilated. I am sure she had some idea about my countertransference, and this might be the reason why she affirmed that I should not have any feelings, that I should be a cold scientist who just presses the buttons. In my opinion, she unconsciously hoped that I could help her to reach some detachment from the anxiety of the surgery.

Two features appeared immediately in analysis. The first was a clear inverted Oedipus complex: she used to embrace her mother, to kiss her as often as possible, even to touch her body. Teresa was very jealous when her father was in some kind of intimacy with her mother. Her father used to say that Teresa was in love with her own mother.

The second feature was the violence, mainly exercised against her sister, whom Teresa wanted to control and dominate. This violence sometimes had a near-sexual connotation, like kissing her against her will, embracing her, and so on. The relationship between the two sisters became so difficult that the younger girl preferred to change school, to avoid meeting her sister, as far as possible.

In the meantime, a strong attachment to me developed which was extremely spiritual. She stated that she came to me willingly, that she suffered because of the weekend separations, and that she was afraid that I might have a bad impression of her. Teresa expected that I respect her, did not oppress her, but instead tried to understand her. Her fear was, rather, that I would compel her to think in the same way as I did. I think that in the initial transference I might have represented an idealized parent, probably her mother.

From time to time, though not always, she appeared in close contact with the reality of her problem, as when she reported in analysis that she had watched some transsexuals interviewed on television. A woman who had become a man seemed neither woman nor man. In giving this account, she cried profusely, as if she realized the impossibility of her magical solution. If some element of heterosexuality made its weak appearance in the treatment, the defence appeared immediately. For instance, she unexpectedly said: "When I feel attracted to a man, maybe I would fancy kissing him, but afterwards in my imagination everything becomes unimportant." In another session, she brought a dream in which she was among the candidates for the "Miss United Kingdom" competition! In the dream, she had long hair and well-developed breasts and, after a while, she exercised on the parallel bars. Her gymnastics teacher observed in silence, smiling. She associated me with the teacher, but she added immediately that in her dream she could take advantage of the situation, as long as she was still a woman, in order to see the other girls' bodies. In reality, she explained, she liked to go into the girls' cloakroom during the gymnastics lesson.

In the same context, she affirmed that her relationship with her father had improved through me.

The honeymoon did not last much longer: already in the twelfth session she contended that in analysis there's too much talk—trying to understand if this or that came from her father or from her mother—while her need was to become stronger internally. Maybe I jumped in too quickly, interpreting as if she had asked me: "What use is surgery to become a man, if internally I feel weak?" I added that the real reason she came into analysis was to become stronger internally, to complete the external reinforcement achieved surgically. She confirmed this immediately, as she used to do any time I interpreted in the direction of her wanting to become a man. I think that I was under the influence of something similar expressed by her previously, because now, at some distance, I wonder if her request had not the opposite meaning—that is, of being helped to become stronger without becoming a man. I am sure it was not the only time I was unconsciously pushed by her to march in the direction of what she had consciously in mind—that is, to become a man.

In other circumstances I was pushed into the role of her opponent. Altogether she had a very strong power over me, as she certainly had over her parents. Most of the time, she left me in the state of impotent witness to her life-events and her reflections. At the end of the sessions I felt exhausted, and my mind was occupied by her for many hours. (Luckily she was the last patient of my working day.)

In one of the following sessions, she gave me the account that her father used to touch the legs of the two daughters or to spank them as a joke, saying, "I can do it now, because you are still little". When they had grown up a bit, their uncle, a dentist, used to say, "Let's look at your little breasts", and he would look inside their T-shirts. When these things happened, she felt offended and angry, but her sister did not. While saying this, she kept her right forearm lifted up, raising her fist. Asked by me what she thought of that gesture, she explained that she used to do that when she was very tense. I interpreted that she wanted to protect herself against me, as against an incestuous father, by having an erect penis herself. In the same atmosphere of almost incestuous situations, she added that an elder cousin had touched her breasts when she was bathing in the sea, and he had tried to put her hand on his penis. She finished the session by using an old cliché that "one always falls in love with one's analyst", but she was determined to avoid that. If she had been a woman, she added, it would have been different.

In one of the sessions immediately following, she expressed her fear of being a bad influence on another cousin's children (a little boy and a little girl), through a confusion of sexes and maybe making them become homosexual. I think that here for the first time she presented homosexuality as something negative. A defence immediately appeared, however, as a monotonous and repeated request for my authorization for her to change sex. (I do not know to what extent she was really convinced that this would be legally necessary: I rather think that she expected that I should collude with her.) She immediately added that I represented her mind, and so, if I was in agreement, her mind would be in agreement as well. I think that she had projected her reasoning faculty onto me, but, at the same time, she wanted to control both me and that part of her.

In the last session before the Christmas holidays, she related to me that she had visited an art exhibition, where she had seen the painting of a naked man and also a sculpture of a woman's head, which looked like a phallus, with the eyes as the testicles. She had the impression of feeling a penis inside her mouth. This prompted her to recall a childhood dream in which she was touching the penis of a little friend, but, after feeling guilty, she imagined touching her mother's breast. I said that she was showing me the existence of sexual images that were ambiguous, fragmentary, and interchangeable inside her. What I had in mind, stimulated by Teresa's communications, was the theory of part-object (Klein, 1936, p. 290). The woman's head, as she described it, seems to represent the combined parental couple in her fantasy.

Immediately after that, she expressed the image of a penis that was entering her body, near her heart, inside her soul, with blood and living flesh. There was no doubt that she had the fantasy of the male as extremely violent and bloodthirsty.

The same theme of masculine violence reappeared immediately after the Christmas break, but this time it was accompanied by more general violent fantasies, such as suicide (which was presented as something positive, in the face of existential anxiety), and a fantasy of total destruction through an atomic bomb, so that the whole of humankind would perish. I had no doubt that this extreme violence was her reaction when confronted by being abandoned by me for a fortnight and that the same violence could be projected onto the penis and onto the male.

Later on, when we elaborated this theme further, she would comment ironically: "So it seems that the only reason why I want to become a man is because I want to be able to rape women!" I think that there was some truth in this, because when, in other circumstances, she mentioned refined Chinese tortures, I had the feeling of her taking delight in the description and in her showing me a sadistic part of herself. Horror was present as well, as if she wanted to rape the female part of herself, the weak part that suffered because of the separation.

Some sessions later the atmosphere changed, as she again seemed to show some attachment to me, to the extent of making me feel that the weekly break of three days was too long for her. I interpreted that, adding that maybe after her final examinations we could consider increasing the frequency to five weekly sessions. She answered yes, but once again I later wondered if I had not been too quick, in some way "raping" her at her first advance.

The analysis went on, showing splitting and obsessional compulsion. She thought she could stop her negative thoughts of war, famine in the world, and so forth by buttoning her jacket or her shirt or tightening her watch-band. By doing this, she would shut what was bad inside her. Another deep structure was the confusion between different erogenous zones: when she was watching two people kissing on television, her mind used to go to excrement or to nasal mucus.

Once she astonished me by stating that men can only create through their thinking—that they cannot create children, something that only women can do. I was quite surprised by her pointing out what she would see as female superiority and by her acknowledging the different roles of men and women in creativity, which could also mean a complementary role in procreation and in analytic treatment.

A turning-point was reached in analysis when she remembered that, at 14, she and her schoolmates had decided that, were they able to concentrate on the thought that a teacher would fall down the staircase, the teacher would actually fall down. The same night, in bed, she was still thinking the same thing when she felt heat at her pubis. This seems to demonstrate the concurrence between her aggressive fantasies, her feeling of omnipotence, and her sexual excitement (we could say, of the phallic type).

All this makes me think of the recent debate in the British Psychoanalytic Society prompted by Dana Birkstead-Breen's paper, "Phallus, Penis and Mental Space"(1996). Picking up the distinction between the concept of phallus and the concept of penis, which had already been made by some analysts, the speaker said, "The phallus represents the state of completeness and of being without need, beyond the human condition" and, later on, "Penis as link is instrument of Eros whereas the phallus is instrument of Thanatos in so far as it aims to destroy that link . . . phallus as representative of omnipotence and completion"(pp. 650–651). John Steiner, in the same debate (1996), wondered if the phallic phase was nothing other than a psychic retreat based on destructive narcissism. My patient used the terms "phallus" and "penis" without distinction, but I am sure that what she had in mind was mainly the phallus.

The analysis seemed to work even too well: Teresa was able to mention the existence of both the sexual tendencies: as a man and as a woman. If she thought of herself as a man, the excitement was located at her pubis; if as a woman, at her vagina. This was when she was near her period (it was the first time that she had mentioned this). A male teacher was lecturing standing up and had his penis near her mouth: her fantasy was of taking his penis into her mouth.

She thought that I would not allow her to become a man, because if she did she could do bad things like killing. It seems that she was projecting the good part of her mind into me.

In another dream she reported that she was attacked by some male schoolmates who wanted to kill her. She defended herself with a big stick, but this broke. She replaced it with a longer one, but this one was less easy to handle. Again, there were variations on the theme of the male organ (with allusions to erection: a longer one), but this time the fantasy was once more that Teresa should protect herself against the destructive aspect of the male phallus by having a phallus herself.

Where does all this violence come from? Teresa talked about a serial killer who stabs women, and perhaps is a woman. "Maybe a woman like me" was her comment. She had an open fantasy of being a man who rapes a virgin. The latter initially would suffer, but later would enjoy it.

In the thirty-eighth session, for the first time she expressed the fear of losing contact with reality. So the problem of psychosis arose, and I wondered whether the analysis was jeopardizing her equilibrium, which was, perhaps, based on keeping a psychotic experience encapsulated. Glasser (1996) and Zachary (1996) have discussed the relationship between some transsexual states and psychotic experiences.

The sessions in the week preceding the session just quoted had been cancelled by me for a very serious family reason (my mother's death). This had stimulated the patient's frustration and jealousy. Teresa dreamt of touching her mother's breast, and she immediately expressed her jealousy, mainly concerning her sister. She was afraid that my leaving could mean that I had sent her away, which made her tense with a headache.

The following week, she communicated that she felt more free than before at school. She could accept that her schoolmates were aware that she was a female. She seemed more free with me also in talking about genitals and about her jealousy because of her parents' sexual relationship. But at the same time she was able to express her suffering because of the separation from me and from her mother. I think that it was because of such freedom that she brought the dream of a puzzle that should have had the shape of a little girl, but the little girl was not there. Later, in the same dream, she threw everything all over the room. My interpretation was that she had the expectation that together we could recreate the image of her as a little girl, but another part of her expressed the need to destroy that. The same splitting was present in another part of the dream: she was a man approaching a woman sexually—this woman alternately was her mother or herself. When I interpreted her showing me the existence of a male and a female part inside her, which alternated, she expressed her feeling that the female could be stronger but she was scared of it. In the same context, she had another fear: of falling in love with a French boy she was going to meet.

At this point of her analysis, the problem of breasts suddenly appeared: she had an idea halfway between a fantasy and a project—to have her breasts cut underneath and emptied. The reason was that summer was approaching, and she would have to take her jacket off and so would show the shape of her breasts. My impression was that Teresa was frightened by the developments of the analysis and so pushed back towards a way already known. I found the opportunity of interpreting that, and this seemed confirmed by what the patient communicated immediately: that she could not throw all her life away, her life which had been dominated by the need to become a man.

I do not think it is irrelevant that this theme was interwoven with the fantasy of attacking her breasts, which, in my opinion, could represent her mother's breasts (or myself, in the transference) through projective identification. The competition with me became stronger, so that I started thinking of a realistic possibility of the breakdown of the analysis. We were near the Easter holidays, and this stimulated some thoughts about death and how it would have been better not to have been born at all. She expressed these fantasies to her mother, and her mother's interpretation was that these were due to the separation from me. Teresa was in agreement, even when I showed her that her attacks were against her mother, not only against me. In a shaking voice she explained how she could attach herself to people and establish roots with them. The need to react against that was the reason, in my opinion, for attacking her mother and me.

Going on with the analysis, she felt alarmed by the change of her attitude with regard to her mother. At the moment of starting the analysis, she said, her mother was for her just her mother, but at present she felt a mixture of affection, sex, and violence towards her. So some vehemence was present when she was embracing her mother and sister. Faced by this violence, she hoped that God could restrain her. Again, I thought that the analysis was in danger, and this time because Teresa's open feeling was that I, and the analysis, could break her contact with reality and make her lose control of herself.

It was as if the psychosis could no longer remain enclosed because of the analytic work, and it tended to spread all over her mind. The fact is that in the following session she expressed manifold fears of being robbed, which could mean of being robbed of her pathological equilibrium. An extreme attempt at keeping her psychosis encapsulated was, in my opinion, the fantasy of becoming openly homosexual, without any surgical operation, which occupied her mind just for a moment. But the session ended in despair, because, should she follow this option, she was in need of coping with the feeling of being a prisoner of her female body.

In one of the following sessions, she expressed interest in the male genitals; however, she was ambiguous, and it was not clear if she felt attracted or wanted to take possession of them. This ambiguity was emphasized as well in Dana Birkstead-Breen's paper (1996). In a to-and-fro move, Teresa again felt irritated with me because of the imminent Easter break.

The first session after the interruption she reported that she had missed the sessions but did not say that she had missed me. If she felt agitated during the break, she lay down on a couch and asked her mother to listen to her, out of her own sight. In some way, the interchangeability between her mother and me became concrete.

I think that another danger for the continuity of the treatment was the feeling—which Teresa developed more and more—of her extreme dependence on me and of her vulnerability. She also started to cry when embracing her mother; she pestered her sister and her cousin's little girl, asking, "Do you love me? Do you love me?" In analysis, too, she appeared fragile and frightened. She expressed some doubts about her sexual interest in women, but at the same time she reiterated that she would be throwing all her previous life away should she reconsider her project of undergoing the surgery.

On the other hand, should she conclude that the transformation into a man was really impossible, her despair would be such that she could commit suicide. I felt that this was a concrete possibility and was extremely worried (this issue is discussed in chapter eight).

Despite the difficulties, the analysis was going on, and the patient brought in a dream in which she was sucking something sweet which she associated with a penis. In the same dream, she touched a woman's breast. In another dream, she was eating something liquid which she associated with sperm. I think that we reached a point in which the penis and not the phallus appeared: this seemed to replace the mother's breast. I think of the early stages of the Oedipus complex, as described by Melanie Klein: "The frustration experienced at the mother's breast leads both boy and girl to turn away from it and stimulates the infant's desire for oral gratification from the penis of the father. The breast and the penis are, therefore, the primary objects of the infant's oral desires" (1945, p. 408). The similarities and the differences between the penis and the breast, both structuring elements in the normal development of the child, were also discussed during the meeting of the British Society already quoted.

My hopes were that at the time of the analysis her mental life could start anew in an undistorted way. But Teresa could calm herself only by going back to the determination of suffocating anything that could lead to anything different from surgery. Even in homosexual intercourse with another woman, she said, she would have sexual sensations in her vagina, and she did not want that.

Stronger than before, the thought appeared that it was I who wanted her to become a woman. Another feature was something new: that both the male and female genitals were disgusting and that sexual life was not important. Hence the superiority of the phallus, as Birkstead-Breen (1996) described earlier.

On the other hand, she was tormented by the anxiety that she would lose all her schoolmates in a few weeks, because of the end of secondary school. I did not realize, at that time, that the patient was probably already determined to end her analysis, and so was preparing to lose me.

We were approaching her final examinations and the summer holidays. The need for a deeper concentration on preparing for her examinations was the easy pretext for asking for an interruption. I interpreted that Teresa was again trying to make me collude in some way, she herself becoming stronger and putting the frustration and the dependence onto me. Not denying that, she brought forward this obvious escape. Feeling at the end of my interpretive possibilities, I did not find a better solution than reminding her of our agreement that she should pay for all the sessions missed from that moment to the summer break. At this point, she confessed that her idea was not to resume her analysis in September.

The omnipotent overturning of our roles was confirmed by a dream in which she was masturbating and her parents got excited and had sexual intercourse. Teresa needed action, she said triumphantly, and the operation was action. She said that she did not want to think any more. But with her typical alternation she again expressed how she felt at ease in my consulting-room, in contradiction to what she had affirmed many times. She also had the fantasy of taking advantage of her breasts, as long as she still possessed them, by getting physical sensations from them.

The final theme of her analysis was the breast: she again planned to have her own emptied, as the first step of her sex-change surgical procedures, and she expressed her dislike of the big breasts of women who are either pregnant or feeding. I have no doubt that her fantasy was of attacking me, as the feeding breast, in a total way. Probably there was also some unconscious memory of her mother pregnant and feeding her younger sister.

On the other hand, in the final session, when I said that we had not learnt enough about why she had such a need to become a man, she answered that the main reason was her fear of being raped, and here she seemed to me quasi-delusional. I mentioned that she seemed scared of her sane part, the part that wanted to co-operate with me, in order to see more clearly into herself, and she accused me of playing a dirty game. She left calm and smiling, but without triumph.

* * *

I have no idea of what Teresa's future will be. I tend to think that the most superficial reason for breaking off the treatment was the competition with me and her impression that, instead of being able to convince me of the need for her to be operated on, there was the risk of becoming convinced herself of the need to reconsider her decision. This would have meant terrible failure and humiliation for her. But I think that under that stubbornness, which is so frequent in adolescence, there was terror: terror of being flooded with fragility, dependence, and violence. If she had to choose between being the victim of violence or the perpetrator of such violence, she would prefer the latter.

But where does all this violence—violence that could bring her to the verge of psychosis—come from?

It is likely that already at the age of 2 the foundations of Teresa's need to become a man were laid, if we take her father's communication seriously that at that age the little girl refused to wear a skirt. Can we speculate that Teresa could feel that, as a boy, she could differentiate herself from the newborn sister and be appreciated more by her mother? But let us try to understand more about the early foundations, with the help of the material. First of all, her hate of her mother's breasts seems paramount. This was expressed by a real hate of her own breasts, which she wanted to get rid of as the first surgical step. She communicated in her analysis that at the first sign of developing breasts, during her early adolescence, she actually tried to reduce them by squeezing her chest with bandages, to the point of physical pain. She stopped this practice only when she was told "it could cause a cancer".

I have already mentioned her communication of being disgusted by the big breasts of feeding mothers. We do not know what her mother's attitude was when Teresa was born and what Teresa's perceptions were at the time: certainly it was peculiar that the mother did not mention to me the experience of the baby being put into the incubator, as if it were something that could be easily forgotten and so denied.

A particular "fixation", to use the classical Freudian expression, seems to have existed in the passage from breast to penis as the essential part-object. This appeared in the analytic material when Teresa showed some interchangeability between breast and penis, both of which could have a nourishing faculty. But some ambivalence towards both appeared at the same time; if the hate of her mother's breasts can be inferred from the attacks against her own breasts, the hate of the penis can be seen in her quasi-delusional terror of being raped.

The consequence seems to have been that the penis became the phallus, a violent organ, powerful and fundamentally destructive, which she could not tolerate in other individuals (males), but which she was desperately in need of possessing herself. This possession could permit her (in her fantasy) to have her mother entirely for herself, to dominate her.

It is likely that the need to control her sister, even with violence, which was conscious and completely accepted in an ego-syntonic way, was also a powerful drive towards possessing the phallus. Teresa's most frequent homosexual fantasies were directed towards female schoolmates, who could easily represent her sister.

Once, during her treatment, I said that "possessing the penis was necessary for her in order to nail me as a woman". She found my expression particularly appropriate. On the other hand, in the last sessions, she admitted openly that she did not have a particular interest in sexual pleasure, but considered the male organ a fetish—an omnipotent and violent fetish, I could add, whose possession was necessary.

I do not want to rely on the easy explanation of blaming her parents for Teresa's pathology, but certainly, despite the appearance of a well-functioning couple, I had the impression that all might not have been as it seemed on the surface. As already said, her mother presented the patient's early childhood as absolutely normal, whereas I do not think it is normal for a baby to be put into an incubator. The mother did show some rejection of Teresa when, during our initial telephone conversation, she introduced herself as the mother of the younger daughter. Here, of course, we cannot be sure if such a rejection was the consequence of all the trouble given by Teresa, or if it was primary. Her mother definitely seemed to collude with Teresa in considering action more important than thought: I was shocked by her being so ready in enquiring about the surgery and all the relevant enterprises. Letting the girl decide for herself and take all the responsibility for her enquiries and actions would have meant neglecting her daughter's problems, she told me.

This makes me think of a case of female homosexuality as described by Freud (1920a): "The mother was tolerant, as though she appreciated the daughter's 'retirement' as a favour to her; the father was furious, as though he realized the deliberate revenge directed against himself" (p. 160). Previously, Freud had affirmed, talking about the girl, that "She realized how she could wound her father and take revenge on him. Henceforth she remained homo-sexual out of defiance against her father" (p. 159).

Even if Freud tends to consider paramount the oedipal (or maybe counter-oedipal) component of the case's psychodynamics, we could say that Freud had been shocked by some maternal collusion.

On the other hand, it is not the only point where the two cases present some similarity: Freud's patient also was 18 years old, and that analysis too was broken off after some months of analytic cooperation (how much of it apparent and how much real, it is difficult to say). Freud himself took the initiative to break off the analysis, when his patient's hostility against him as father seemed intolerable. He suggested the continuation of the treatment with a woman psychoanalyst.

I wondered whether Teresa's analysis would have had a better outcome with a woman analyst. But, after some consideration, I decided not, mainly because I thought about the woman teacher at her school whom Teresa had described as still quite attractive, even if no longer very young. After a temporary phase of silent love from the patient, a strong hostility arose against this teacher, whom she then described as negative from all points of view. I am inclined to think that a woman analyst would have provoked the same reactions.

If it is difficult to decide to what extent her mother's attitude could have favoured Teresa's compulsive need for the operation; it is equally difficult to quantify the influence of the disgust for heterosexual life that the micro-seduction from father and uncle, and real seduction from cousin, could have provoked.

In this case illustration, rather than giving an accurate account of the analytic treatment, I have chosen to pick out all the elements that could allow a psychodynamic reconstruction. An easy objection could be that even if the reconstruction is basically right, this could not entirely explain why Teresa developed such an obstinate compulsion towards a surgical change of sex. All the elements that are at the basis of Teresa's determination could have provoked different pathologies. However, we know that the problem of "the choice of the illness" is still one of the most obscure in our science.

C

"Phil":
helping a transsexual teenager
to engage in self-exploration

Paulina Reyes

P hil was referred by her parents to the Gender Identity Development Service when she was 15 years old because of
her extreme distress about her monthly periods and because she felt that she was a boy in a female body; also, she was
determined to have a sex-change operation as soon as she reached
the legal age. She had started menstruating before her fourteenth
birthday, and each month she would cry for hours and take some
days to get over it. Phil's parents were themselves very distressed
about her plight and her idea of having a sex change. Mother had
said that Phil could not stay at home if she went ahead with it.

Prior to their local clinic's assessment, Phil's parents had taken
her the year before, when her periods had started, for a private
assessment with a therapist. Phil had refused those two offers of
treatment but had accepted the referral to the Gender Identity
Development Service, which was proposed to her when she de-
clined the second offer of treatment.

Following some preliminary meetings, I offered to see Phil fortnightly, but she only accepted to come back in a month's time. She
never explicitly made a commitment to come on a regular basis;
instead, we negotiated each session at a time. However, the pattern
that developed was monthly sessions for the first seven or eight
months, then fortnightly, and it then reverted to monthly towards

the end. I accepted this pattern of attendance as it appeared to be the only way of engaging Phil in a therapeutic process, although this inevitably would limit the depth of our exploration.

The parents were seen in parallel by a child psychiatrist colleague in the team; when those meetings stopped, for six months they attended a monthly group for parents of children with gender identity problems.

Phil's appearance was that of a boy, tall and lean; she wore unisex or boys' clothes, which hid her figure. She walked slouched so as to hide any hint of her breasts. She was preparing to sit her exams that summer and was planning to go on to study drama. Phil was very vague about her childhood and told me on several occasions that she had no memories and that her mother was the one who remembered things, especially unpleasant things "like my appointments with you".

Phil told me that she had always felt like a boy, but she was not clear (or did not tell me) when she had first realized that she was not physically a boy and was not going to become one. She remembered hearing in the playground about "sex-change operations" and had immediately thought that she wanted one. She thought that girls were always screaming and shouting when playing games.

The parents described Phil as being very obstinate, and they gave as an example the fact that she had eaten the same bedtime snack for many years and would not consider any change. She was also described as very private and adverse to any discussion. Apparently there had been a lack of attention to boundaries in the household when the children were growing up, perhaps because father had done a lot of the physical care, and one wonders how that had fitted in with Phil's extreme need for privacy.

It is worth noting that Phil was perceived as dependent by father and independent by mother. This could be a reflection of Phil not relying on mother, even though she did for information and to remember her appointments with me.

The parents could talk freely amongst themselves about Phil, and they agreed that gender was a central issue. There was little discord between them, although father was less willing to communicate directly with Phil about her gender dysphoria or to challenge her in other ways, and he assumed that she did not wish to be called by her full name in public. Mother, on the other hand, was more open about her wish that Phil would change and accept being a woman, and she called her by her full name, Philippa.

I saw Phil for two and a half years; we stopped when she was 18 years old and started attending drama school and became beyond the brief of the clinic. By then, she was planning to refer herself to an adult gender-reassignment service.

Having outlined the background details, I now describe some aspects of the interaction between Phil and me during the various phases of the therapy.

During the *assessment phase,* at one point I asked Phil why she had now accepted to continue attending (I did not use the word "help"). She said that it was not because she was not upset, that feeling like a boy was not a problem—the problem was having to wait for the operation. At this point her eyes filled with tears. She also said that she wanted help for her parents, who were very upset—particularly her mother—and, she added, they needed help in coming to terms with "it". At one point, she told me that sometimes she cried at night but that she tried to forget about it.

I found her very distrustful. It was also difficult to have a conversation as her answers were monosyllabic, and she never referred directly to the gender issue as such. I told her that maybe she hoped that we could help her during the wait, and the fact that we were the specialist clinic perhaps reassured her that I would not try to dissuade her about her planned sex-change (see the discussion of therapeutic aims in chapter twelve). She agreed with me, and talking became somewhat easier after that. I also told her that she needed to keep her upset feelings quite cut-off from the rest of herself, so as not to feel too upset. She agreed, and it felt as if we had made some contact.

At our next session, she came accompanied by her mother, even though the parents were not having a meeting themselves that day. Phil acknowledged that it was a long journey and she had wanted her mother's company, but at the same time she played down her need for support. The fact that one of her parents always came along with her was going to be a feature of the work, and she only started coming on her own towards the end. Mother stopped being the one to bring Phil after a few times. The other feature that remained was that she always brought a book so as not to be aware of the hour-and-a-half journey, then "it didn't matter how long it took". This may be linked to the other long wait she had—the one for the sex reassignment.

During the *first phase of work* (the first seven months), Phil was silent and unfriendly each time that we met. I had to start by what felt like an "interrogation"—about school, her friends, home—and she would smile and say everything was fine. I used to feel quite redundant, that I had no role to play. I had to work very hard at putting together the present and bits of information from past sessions to try to make some sense of what was going on. Usually this brought about a change, and we managed to have some real contact. She managed to tell me about crying at night, particularly when she had her periods. Towards the end of this phase, there was an acknowledgement on her part—or, rather an acceptance of my description—of her need to be cut-off from the feelings of horror at feeling imprisoned in the wrong body.

In the *second phase of therapy* (a phase of hope), lasting sixteen months, she seemed to become more hopeful. Phil was doing much better; her parents had reported that she was not getting so troubled by menstruation, even though she was still miserable on the first day. She was showing an increased interest in sexual matters, via books and TV programmes. The home atmosphere seemed happier. Phil was allowing mother to hug her.

I must say at this point that all through the therapy mother always harboured hopes that Phil would become "feminine", while Phil herself never wavered from feeling that she was a boy. However, as Phil became more able to contain her distress, mother mistook that for a lessening of the wish to become a man. Father seemed more in touch with how Phil really felt, or perhaps was more resigned.

In the sessions with me, Phil was becoming more interested in the ideas that we discussed or in my suggestions of how she might feel; however, she tended to have a concrete understanding of them. Perhaps my interpretations were mechanistic because the material at this stage was quite concrete; the most important example that she brought on several occasions, was a toy she was designing for school.

I summarized a session of this period as follows:

"Phil looked much brighter. She had brought to show me a toy which she had designed as part of her course work. It was made of colourful wooden cubes and circles (or wheels), which could be switched around and transformed into different toys, a train engine, a lorry, and a boat. She told me it was a safe toy except for the axle for the wheels, which was long and sharp."

She had also brought her design book, in which she had drawn many other designs for everyday objects that could also be transformed into something else, always useful. I interpreted these designs and toys in relation to her thoughts about her body and the transformations that she envisaged it would have to undergo, and her hopes that it would become a useful body.

She said, half-admiringly and half-resentfully, that that was very clever of me. I acknowledged her mixed feelings about what I had said—her not wanting to know, but at the same time her awareness of the seriousness of these issues and the need to think about them. For the first time we had a proper discussion about her intended sex change (which is what Phil always called it). She said that she was planning to start living as a boy once she had left school. She then referred to my interpretations as "transformations" and was quite fascinated with the idea that her communications to me could have other meanings.

During this phase, Phil started becoming more sociable and was pleased because she had been accepted by a group of youngsters at school. By now, her classmates knew that she wanted to be a boy, but she only really talked about it with her two best male friends.

At times she found these issues very difficult and was able to tell me about her sense of injustice, particularly in relation to her brother: "He's just a boy, he doesn't have a terrible problem."

She became very interested in an older female friend and they met socially a few times; Phil became full of the zest of life, going to exhibitions and the theatre, but eventually the friendship fizzled out. Phil tried to play it down, but obviously it had been a terrible disappointment, not least because it renewed her awareness of her terrible predicament. She told me that she did not want lesbian relationships, that it felt "all wrong". As Phil's relationship finished, she also became more distant and guarded.

In the *third and final phase of the therapy*, lasting seven months, things were never the same. Phil felt more acutely that she did not fit in any category and therefore that she was forced to keep her distance. This was a feature of her social life and of her relationship with me. I had to work very hard to stop our meetings from becoming bland information-gathering.

Eventually, we managed to talk about her disappointment with the therapy, because it had not taken away her feeling of not being like everybody else. She also told me once how embarrassing her feelings felt, her shame about her wishes and thoughts.

During the last year, we worked on and discussed the ending of the therapy and the choices that she had to make. Phil sat her exams successfully and was accepted at a very prestigious drama school; however, she was leaving to me the responsibility of reminding her that she now had to decide how and when she was going to start living in the male role and of all the logistics involved. She started telling me about watching gay programmes on television and attending the Gay Pride March, which I understood as Phil finding a group she could identify with and that, even though it was not the perfect match, also gave her a sense of freedom and relief.

Phil decided to stay at home and to study in a college nearby. This could be thought of as dependency; however, she was faced with some daunting tasks at the psychological and social levels, plus some quite complicated and potentially frightening medical treatment. Luckily, by now her parents were prepared to support her in this difficult endeavour.

In the final phase of the therapy, she would only allow me to talk about the practical aspects of her future plans.

When we parted, I told her that, in spite of the work having been difficult for her, she seemed to have found in the therapy a place where she could explore who she was. Phil said that she still had a long road ahead, but she felt that I had helped her.

D

"Lesley":
the struggle of a teenager with an intersex disorder to find an identity— its impact on the "I" of the beholder

Adrian Sutton

The body in relationships

Winnicott told us there is no such thing as "a baby"— there is "a mother *and* baby". The mother—or alternative primary carer—has to have a sense in herself or himself of the baby's total needs with sufficient confidence in knowing this to be "good enough": there must also be sufficient doubt in the mother's/carer's knowledge for the possibility of learning to exist.

The baby's dependency means that the parent must have access to its body to ensure the necessary care. This care must take full account of the nature and degree of physical handling that will be comforting without being intrusive, thereby promoting the baby's sense of becoming a physically and ultimately psychologically autonomous person. Respect for the experience and significance of different parts of the body means that there are variations in expectations of the rate at which responsibility for the care is abdicated by the parents and taken over by the infant/child. In the United Kingdom, the genitals are often referred to as "the private parts", thus giving acknowledgement to the special nature of experience of these parts of the body both to the individual and in relationships.

As already described in relation to general mental health issues for children and adolescents with intersex disorders (see chapter eleven), parents and children have to negotiate this process with different emphases: involvements that in a more ordinary course of events would be viewed as unhealthy now become essential. At stages in development when withdrawal from these areas in the relationship would be the norm, the medical condition will drive the opposite. This is unlikely to be a straightforward issue for young people or their parents, and the potential for conflicts in relationships and emotions is high.

Professional engagement

On entering into work in this field, the same respect for the complexity of the predicament of all parties is required from the professional. We have to be aware of the potential pitfalls, and we must make explicit the countercurrents. For this reason, my introduction in embarking on assessment and therapeutic involvement with children and families in intersex disorder includes a statement of this. I explain that we all know we are meeting because there are particular issues about "the private parts" and that this means that it can become even more complicated than usual to know what will feel manageable and acceptable to the youngster in open conversation.

Delving into the other private parts

The concept of "the unconscious" is another aspect of "the private parts"—those parts that an individual may have hidden from herself or himself. The basis of psychoanalytic practice is that issues may be unconscious for powerful reasons in the emotional history, but this may become a cause of suffering or distortion in the emotional life or development as the residual force of these early experiences exerts itself. We find, then, a force acting towards "not-knowing"—that is, repression—and other pressures that force these to become known. Due respect is therefore required for the consequences of there being both a necessity for these private parts to be seen and a fear of this happening.

Privacy and confidentiality

In attempting to write this case illustration, I found myself more than usually anxious about that particular aspect of privacy we call confidentiality. This can partly be accounted for by the fact that, with a rare condition, it is likely to be more possible to link published clinical information with a specific person. However, as will be described in the course of this case illustration, I believe that there are reasons why these conditions make this even more complex.

Originally this was to be a case history. However, I became uncomfortable with this in this context even though the particular patient had agreed that I could publish material from her treatment. She wished to be of use to others. I will use clinical information, but I have decided to do this with a different emphasis by thinking more about the impact on the other in the treatment relationship—that is, the therapist (the countertransference). This will be extended to the potential impact on others around both this patient and some others with intersex or other genital disorders whom I have treated. The result will be the withholding of some information. This will perhaps be frustrating for both reader and writer. But what may be more disconcerting is that the demand will be to look at our own metaphorical private parts if we are to make ourselves properly available to these patients. This forms part of any psychoanalytic psychotherapy training, but self-knowledge of this kind is not usually a requirement for other professionals who work alongside us in our usual activities.

Meeting Lesley

Lesley was in her early teens when I first met her. She had been perceived as female at birth, but genital abnormality had been recognized in early childhood, although a comprehensive treatment had not occurred. When she reached her teens, her voice had started breaking and deepening, her facial features coarsened, and her phallus (I deliberately use a generic term rather than one indicating either male or female) had enlarged. The diagnosis of Incomplete Testicular Feminization (Partial Androgen Insensitivity Syndrome: see chapter five for an explanation of the syndrome) was confirmed by an endocrinologist, who referred Lesley for psychiatric assessment principally because of depressive symptoms with suicidal thoughts, but, in addition, advice was being sought about sexual orientation: Lesley had reported experiencing erotic feelings towards both boys and girls of her own age.

At psychiatric consultation, Lesley presented in a very open way; she was a very engaging person. Her condition left her feeling lonely and isolated at times, but she did also talk of her relationships and their ups and downs with a quality and intensity that felt very much like the preoccupations of most young adolescent girls. However, in looking at her—her physique, the start of coarsening of facial features—and listening to her—the cracking of her voice between high and low—one saw a young adolescent boy.

The moment in the consultation when this fully formed mental image of the girl-in-relationships came together with the visual and auditory image of a boy, I felt it as a physical experience—like a hard blow to the head, which was momentarily disorientating and shocking.

Lesley was experiencing emotional difficulties and was about to embark on further medical and surgical treatment during a developmental period that places significant demands even in the ordinary course of events. She was therefore offered psychotherapy, which she accepted. Lesley terminated the therapy prematurely, which means that only limited formulations are possible.

Getting to know Lesley

Within a few weeks, Lesley spontaneously told me that she wanted to be a girl. She had never stated this before, because her parents had said not to want to be either boy or girl lest she be disappointed. Throughout her treatment, I never found myself having doubts in this respect. My sense of her was as a female, struggling with a particularly complex constellation of developmental tasks, particularly in relation to autonomy, anatomy, and sexuality. This is very striking when considering the unique countertransference impact of that first meeting.

The psychological position that Lesley had to maintain was one of feeling a strong desire in one direction whilst also having to deal with the uncertainty of factors over which she felt she had no control. Whilst consciously this tension could be talked about and to a degree contained, there were mechanisms that came into play displaying what was happening underneath.

The experience of being wronged

As mentioned earlier, Lesley was (and is) an engaging, warm person. However, there were incidents that displayed an urge to see others' discomfiture at being confused by her and gratification in this—a more aggressive side of her in relation to others. I heard accounts from much earlier in her life as well as more recently. Sometimes these lay more within the realm of practical joking and humour; some of these were ingenious and amusing, but at other times they could be less successful in acting as a safety-valve. My way of understanding this was to draw on the concept of *projective identification*. I saw the discomfiture that became manifest in others as being a manifestation of Lesley's own discomfiture, which could only be "managed" by it not being her own but theirs. The following illustrates this:

A club to which Lesley belonged went on a trip with another club of young people of her own age. One evening, a verbal message was passed along to her. A girl at the other end of the room "really fancies that lad"—i.e. Lesley. Lesley recounted this with a laugh. She did not appear to feel any upset about it but told me of the profound embarrassment of the other girl on being told that "that lad" was a girl.

Rather than feeling wrong herself, another was left feeling in the wrong—perhaps even humiliated. Using the concept of projective identification, one can say that the sense of wrong was put into the other (see chapter twelve).

A characteristic of adolescence is that thinking may only follow action. Experimentation in relationships and in the presentation of self in manner and dress may precede the possibility of articulation of the emotional and cognitive, inside or outside of therapy. One hopes that this will not produce serious or enduring adverse effects, but it can present considerable difficulties in the management of work with adolescents. Even in the privacy of the psychotherapy room, Lesley found it hard to tolerate references to the actual nature of her body: this left me feeling particularly concerned for her potential vulnerability outside that context.

It was very difficult hearing about her relationship with a boy whom she had known over a long period of time. There were elements of antisocial activity in him and intense swings of ambivalence between them. Lesley later told me of physical sexual aspects to their relationship, but during the therapy this was only tentatively hinted at. However, the continual references to her relationship with him, in conjunction with the knowledge that I had of her, both in her physical state and her emotional state, left me with a dilemma: how directly should I be asking her about her physical body and the nature of her activity with this boy—was she "asking" me to do this, or would such questioning be experienced by her as intrusive?

Because of the degree of uncertainty that I felt, I discussed it with a senior colleague. No answer readily came to mind even then, but the suggestion was made that I should put the nature of the dilemma into words with Lesley. I did this without there being a direct response from her, but the solution did come through a less direct route.

In a session soon afterwards, Lesley was telling me about a girl at college with whom she had an intensely ambivalent relationship. This girl had angered Lesley yet again: her fury continued in the session. It was puzzling since the anger arose from this girl having asked a question that superficially appeared quite innocent: the way in which it had been asked sounded rather childlike. My puzzlement stemmed from the discrepancy between the latter qualities and the strength of feeling that it evoked in Lesley. As the psychotherapy session continued, I found a particular word from one of Freud's (1905d) earlier writings in my mind. The word was "scopophilia"—a word created in translating the work into English and criticized by Bettelheim (1982).

The insistent and irritating quality of the way in which this word was in my mind forced me to examine the reasons for this. The understanding I came to was that it was a manifestation of "communication by projective identification"—best understood as being that Lesley's unconscious was communicating something to mine and that this was being indicated to me in the word "scopophilia" which also contained the requisite information in a compressed form.

So, what is the significance of this word "scopophilia"?

Freud described various aspects of ordinary healthy early childhood development focusing around what he called infantile sexuality. Scopophilia literally means "pleasure in looking". More specifically, it is used to describe a state of sensual/sexual excitation in looking at, and of interest in, the genital and sexual aspects of others. He suggested that in the ordinary course of events the "energy" associated with this is harnessed during development in the service of learning and other intellectual or aesthetic activities. It does not remain fixed and restricted in the original (instinctual) form: this process is known as sublimation. Hence, freedom to explore the world of relationships and the world in general more widely requires sufficient health in this aspect. Restrictions in this respect can emanate from a failure to move on from this (to become fixated) or because some aspect of this process was traumatic. Freud postulated *shame* as a paired opposite with scopophilia, modulating its effect on the person's actual behaviour. Shame is about how we see ourselves at a most basic level and is not necessarily dependent in any way on how others see us. There is a degree to which its impact can be a healthily moderating influence, but a similar process can occur as with scopophilia, and trauma may lead to developmentally unhealthy or hindering fixations or restrictions.

Seeing, believing, and knowing

The eyes, and looking and being looked at, also occupy particularly important positions in human relationships. We are born with the propensity to seek or hold eye contact: the most severe forms of childhood psychiatric disturbance have gaze-aversion as a fundamental component. The conscious and unconscious seeking or withholding of eye contact has special significance in shaping interactions. As well as loving looks, there is experience of being looked at as an aggressive act—the "evil eye", "if looks could kill". We also say "I see" (in English) to indicate intellectual understanding.

When we consider enquiring into—looking at—a subject that is so fundamentally sexual in its nature, we enter into an arena which is extremely highly charged.

The material already described in Lesley's therapy, along with other material not presented here, suggested that there was a complex of difficulties arising from the earliest awareness of her own difference in a physical genital sense which had led to the need to rely on the specific unconscious defence mechanisms delineated in her therapy. The effect was to cause certain aspects of her own emotional life to be obliterated from her own conscious experience and to be manifest at certain times in her relationships through the experience of the other. The issue of knowing or not knowing in relation to gender and the physical attributes of gender were at the heart of this. This was what had come together in my own struggle to know quite what to say or what to ask about—would my comments be intrusive, aggressive, looking-into events, innocent investigations, or correct professional investigation in the service of my patient?

Maintaining an ability to think properly

The clinical information presented above illustrates the challenge that we experience in starting and continuing work in this arena. The first time I met Lesley and brought together in my mind the social and emotional experience of her with my purely visual and auditory experience, it was like a blow to the head; something so complex in terms of more usual experience and expectations that it found expression as a physical sensation. As work continued with her, progress was made, but dilemmas of a specific type developed. Returning to one of Freud's original formulations of the course of early childhood development and the understanding he had of the relationship between sexual and aggressive impulses and how these were channelled (or harnessed) into the service of wider intellectual and aesthetic development was fundamentally important.

The crux in working with patients with intersex disorders, and perhaps also those with other problems in the sexual arena, is that we must simultaneously put our competencies, which have been developed at least in part from the healthy sublimation of those original infantile sexual interests, to work on issues that were originally the objects of those interests. The freedom to explore, investigate, and learn will have been influenced by the extent to which the process has been one of a healthy harnessing of the energy and vitality of these early impulses. The converse is that splitting and denial occurs—these impulses are encapsulated in an area of the mind where they cannot be used because a threat is contained in them which has to be controlled, but at a cost to the overall functioning of the individual. Mental work has to be done to keep them in their place, and experiences that might somehow incite them, giving them more force, have to be avoided. This may lead to restrictions in the mental life either in specific areas or even more generally. The people we are, the abilities we do and do not have, are significantly affected by such processes going on inside us. There is a balance between the harnessing of our capabilities and the restrictions to our functioning arising from associations with intrusive, aggressive urges: these may be experienced more or less consciously.

When we come to working in this area, we will have to revisit stimuli that will address that balance that has been obtained within us: the dynamic between those aspects that give us freedom to explore the issues for the patient and those that might be intrusive if given expression—the risk being of unhelpful or perhaps detrimental activity, or an inhibition of proper exploration and implementation of our use to the patient.

The wider perspective

I have indicated in the course of this case illustration how I came to a particular formulation in my role as a psychoanalytic psychotherapist. This was occurring as I began to meet some more youngsters and their families with issues of genital and reproductive abnormality. Although I have not met large numbers, appreciation of this issue has been underlined by their stories.

The nature of their physical condition means that there may have been medical involvement from the earliest time in their lives, particularly if they suffer from congenital adrenal hyperplasia (see chapter five), a condition that can be life-threatening once the infant is independent of the mother's circulation via the placenta.

A recurrent issue has been that of being physically examined, specifically in relation to the genitals. Of course, reluctance in relation to this is probably not uncommon, but the quality of upset and anger is different, more intense. One girl reported with fury, "He kept *looking* [at the genitals]". Similarly, there was upset in relation to anyone else being present at the time of any examination—once this point crystallized, it was simple to arrange that only the absolute minimum of staff were in the consulting-room. The paediatric surgeon (Adrian Bianchi, personal communication) involved with a number of young people whom I have also met is acutely aware of the conflicting currents that surface. There is a need for the youngster to know that they can have the anatomical potential to use their genitals, and they need them looked at for an answer in this respect. However, the strength of feeling about being in the position of being looked at means that this can be disabling and prohibitive. For this reason, carrying out an examination under general anaesthetic may be the most tolerable route by which this can happen, even if it may superficially appear rather a drastic step to take. The analogous situation in psychiatric practice would, I believe, be to use the one-way mirror with observers behind. Because of the strength of feeling engendered, I would not see such patients in clinics where I use a one-way mirror, whether for ordinary clinical purposes or for teaching.

The other important issue is in terms of the impact that the nature of intersex disorders may have on our thinking. My account has highlighted the effect on me and the challenge that this presented. Listening to children and parents and the professionals illustrated this further. For example, the girl whose anger at being repeatedly examined was mentioned above was annoyed that her GP always seemed to assume that she was coming with complaints about premenstrual or menstrual symptoms. The doctor, when I contacted her for a general discussion, immediately told me "I *always* say the wrong thing". I was able to explain to her that I found this to be a regular, if not usual, event with these youngsters. Another example was of a girl and her mother who were told that the girl did not need to return for hospital consultation until her periods started—in fact, she had congenital absence of uterus and ovaries.

Concluding comments

Intersex disorders are complex. In a world in which gender is so important and in which the complications of a simple dichotomy present so many challenges, to conceive of a third state in which the individual is neither simply one nor the other can be overwhelming. The young people themselves struggle with both the physical aspects and the sense in themselves of a belongingness which may have powerful elements of one or both genders. A simple sense of belonging to the human race is not sufficient to set these aside.

The result may be that thinking properly becomes impossible: it may produce aberrations or blind spots in thinking or responding, or it may lead to unwittingly intrusive behaviour. The effect on "the other" can be to confront fundamental aspects of his or her psychological make-up. This applies particularly to the way in which we manage ourselves in relation to the "use" that we make of others as people whom we can explore (or not) on the basis of our own interests.

To work in the arena of human need means that we have to be able to acknowledge the potential for our thinking capacity to be impaired by that very need (our own or the other's). To work in the arena of intersex disorder takes this one step further since it may incite those impulses that want the world to be there to be aggressively explored in all its secret areas. Unmodified and unmodulated, those same impulses—which can be carefully marshalled to give their energy to a structure of socialized learning, which can be put in the service of others—could leave those in need as victims of them.

Maintaining thinking ability in the face of the strength of all these processes means that we must take great care before standing too critically in judgement of things that may have been said or done and that may now seem to be wrong. It is also why it is so important that professionals specifically trained in grappling with the impact of patients on their own and other people's psychological functioning should be available to all parties through the particular developmental tasks that these young people and their families have to negotiate.

E

"William":
working with the family about unresolved
mourning and secrecy

Domenico Di Ceglie

Williiam, aged 8 years, was referred to the Gender Identity Development Unit by his mother. In her letter she
wrote:

"William has been having problems with the boys at school.
This has been going on for some 18 months, but the seriousness
of the situation has only recently come to light. He is suffering
a lot of verbal abuse, i.e. being called a poof, sissy, pervert etc.
The headmaster did take steps to stop this, but the problems
cropped up again with a different set of boys. There has been a
great deal of discussion between myself and the teachers. They
feel that they are trying to stop this victimization by their boys
but that William's own behaviour is in part to blame. On the
last occasion, the problem was exacerbated by William wearing mascara into school. We are having other troubles with
William, for example, his school work is suffering very badly
and there are behavioural problems at home. Both my husband
and I believe the situation is deteriorating and we need professional help and advice as we feel rather out of our depth!"

Following this referral, Barbara Gaffney (senior child psychotherapist in the Clinic) and I offered the family, composed of Mr
and Mrs B and William, a joint session for assessment. William is a
good-looking boy who walked tip-toeing in the long corridor. We
heard the problems already mentioned in the letter. Then William
said that he was embarrassed to talk about his games.

He managed, however, to say that he prefers to play with girls
and that he likes to play "mum and dad". He plays with cuddly
toys and fantasizes that he is "the mother feeding them". He also
plays weddings and, with some embarrassment, mentioned that
he likes to play the role of "the bride". He said that he was afraid to
mention what he feels, because this is not what a "normal boy"
feels and he was not sure if we wanted to know. The parents
added that William has a quick temper and easily gets upset.
There were difficulties at bed times and he would at times boast
and instigate jealousy in other boys.

During this session, the parents also mentioned that William
had found it difficult to come to this hospital because his grandmother, to whom he had been very close, had died here. William
was on the verge of tears when she was mentioned. At the end of
this meeting, we suggested that it was important for William to
become able to be open about his feelings; otherwise, he would
have to carry the burden of his secrets. We agreed to meet with all
of them over a number of sessions as a family on a fortnightly
basis.

During the second session, William was able to be more open
and spoke about his loneliness at play-time when he felt that he
could join neither the games of the boys nor those of the girls.
During this week he had revealed to his parents a secret game that
he played in the shed, when he imagined himself to be in a ship.
The parents tried to reassure him that this was a boy's game, but
William felt that his friends would consider it a girlish game. He
stressed that he felt embarrassed by his games and later said that
sometimes he wished he were a girl, and at other times he wished
he could play the games that boys play, like football.

He saw himself as "an out-of-the-ordinary-child". At the end of
this session, we suggested that we might try to understand why he
feels the way he does and that this might help him. We also
planned to construct a *family tree* to explore family relationships,

and this subsequently revealed that William had a strong attachment to his paternal grandmother. He was taken to his grandmother's at the age of 3 months, as his mother worked during the day. Grandmother died when he was 5. With her, he spent his time cooking, sewing, and making cakes. William described how shocked he was when he learned of his grandmother's death from cancer. When I asked him if he had been unprepared for this, he burst into tears. His mother went to console him, and William asked to stop talking about her, although he didn't want to be rude. At home he did not want to speak of her death, and apparently they had stopped mentioning her. He described, however, how he dreamt of her as being alive and making cheesecakes with him in the house as it was before grandfather changed it. He was cross with him for altering the position of the furniture and the decorations, which he wished had remained the same. He was pleased at the thought that in his grandmother's house there was still a tin of talcum powder which grandmother used after bathing him, something that he had not told his parents about and had kept jealously secret. We suggested that William could not think about his grandmother and her death, because he could not face the feeling of missing her, and his parents perhaps didn't know how to help him with this. William responded by saying that he dreams of being with her. It seemed that he resented speaking about her as it disturbed his sense of being associated with her still being alive. We also wondered if this was a dream or a fantasy or whether at times it acquired the quality of being real. In this way, the boundary between fantasy and reality became blurred. In a later session, Mr B told us that William had tried to do things with his mother in the same way as with his grandmother—for instance, cooking with her. However, William had found that his mother was not exactly as grandmother, as she would use different ingredients. This had been disappointing for him, and he had ended up doing the cooking by himself. Mrs B looked surprised and commented: "I didn't know that. I was used as a substitute!" It seemed that rather than remembering a positive experience, William was trying to re-enact it and relive it. Mrs B said that William had told her that grandmother was better than her, and he had at times refused to eat some of his mother's food that was cooked differently from grandmother's. Mrs B had found this very rejecting. We linked up William's preference for certain activities with his intense wish to remain in the past and to maintain things as they were in the house and perhaps with his identification with his grandmother, when his attempts to recreate this blissful state had failed. In this way, the mourning process could not proceed. It is possible that the initial separation from his mother at 3 months played a part in his inability to mourn the loss of grandmother and to symbolize. The paper by Bleiberg and colleagues (1986) examines in detail the relationship between gender identity problems in childhood and object loss.

I want to mention briefly another feature that emerged in the course of the family meeting. We were exploring factors that had led to William's isolation from friends while playing at home. It appeared that he wanted to impose his own games and then run them. At other times, he would pair with only one friend, usually a girl, and exclude everyone else. There was a discussion in the family about being self-centred versus a willingness to recognize other people's interests and needs, and eventually William came to recognize that at times he was "bossy". In confronting these issues, Mrs B had taken the lead and William had become cross with his mother. Father then intervened to rescue him from getting into a heated argument with his mother, by wondering why William, on the occasion mentioned, had played mainly with one girl, excluding everybody else. After pointing out the nature of this family interaction, we wondered how they dealt with differences of view at home and how much family members could listen to one another. William said very explicitly that his views were better than his parents' most of the time, and he could not use or recognize any help from his parents in solving his problems. Mother had brought one example of William being bullied at school by a friend, Nicholas. One day, Mrs B had suggested that William hit back at him. He did, and Nicholas had apparently stopped hitting him. William could not acknowledge that perhaps his mother's suggestion in this particular case could have helped him. We ended this session wondering: "Were William's ideas better than his parents' just because they were his ideas or because they were really better at times?"

From this clinical material it seemed that *self-sufficiency and arrogance* would at times prevail and have the upper hand.

Another feature that emerged was William's tendency to be passive. For instance, we were discussing why William was unhappy about playing football. He said he did not like to play, firstly, because he was the last to be picked and, secondly, because if he made a mistake he would be teased and the other children would say he was useless. His father saw him as unwilling to practise, rather than intrinsically unable to play. William thought that the boys who played were the ones who wished to take up football as a career. Football was seen by him more as a way to stardom rather than an ordinary enjoyable game. Mr B reported that he had felt the same and called himself lazy as a boy, but had found a way to cope by putting up with it. We explored the aspect of football as a team game, involving receiving and passing the ball. William complained that the other boys didn't pass the ball to him. It also emerged that he never called for the ball. This led to a discussion about activity and passivity in other areas and how taking initiative involved risk-taking.

Another incident was described at school, where a lunch-boxes monitor always put William's lunch-box on the girls' table, and William now wished to eat with the boys. The parents encouraged him to take the risk of moving his lunch-box, so that this girl monitor would understand. In subsequent sessions, we heard how William was now playing football and enjoying it, and at lunch-time he was sitting with the boys. He explained with a sense of satisfaction that he had had to move his lunch box seven or eight times before the girl monitor got the message.

Conclusion

In this presentation, I have tried to show how developmental issues, such as problems in mourning and symbol formation, narcissistic tendencies and passivity, which are common to many other emotional difficulties, may play a role in gender identity development in particular circumstances. I believe that these factors, together with biological factors, underpin identity development and determine its rigidity or flexibility (see chapter two). The psychotherapeutic exploration of these factors with William and his family seemed to promote his healthier development and to improve his inner resources and the quality of his relationships. Perhaps his gender identity development will eventually be indirectly affected, but to what extent will remain uncertain for a long time.

F
"Harriet":
a child in a primary school

Karine George

The job of a headteacher is a varied one. No day is the same, and the emotions of children and parents play a significant part in day-to-day issues. Dealing with diversity in school—be it gender, culture, race, or religion—can raise complex and controversial issues. "Gender Identity Disorder" certainly was a term that I had never heard before, and the complex issues surrounding this condition were to prove very challenging.

A recent film, *Ma Vie en Rose*, portrays the experience of a child with a gender identity problem within the family context and in his primary school setting, and it highlights the difficulties, in the social context of the school, in accepting a child who is so different from the others and who behaves in an unusual way. The various institutions that deal with the child seem to work in isolation. The psychologist who sees the child does not link with the school, the parents and teachers cannot work together, and eventually the child is asked to leave the school. These were the very same issues that we had to face in our school while trying to meet the needs of a child whose mind and body seemed to be in contradiction with each other. We hoped that, as a result of our endeavours, a different outcome from that portrayed in the film could be achieved, and this pupil remained and was educated in our school.

From the time that Harriet joined the junior school (age range: 7 to 11 years), it was noticeable how her outward appearance—her boyish haircut and clothes (trousers), even boxer shorts instead of little girls' knickers—reflected the male gender.

The issue of Harriet's appearance was raised with her mother, who appeared to gloss over the issue, explaining that knickers left marks on her legs and it was easier in boxer shorts. Clearly, the school has no jurisdiction to insist on a child's underwear. However, the explanations were weak and gave rise to concern. Yet, Harriet's outward appearance certainly confused her peers, and discussions between children revealed this—"He can't tie her shoe-lace!"

With hindsight, it was clear that mother was finding the issue difficult to grapple with. Therefore, at this time, no attempt was made by the family to raise our awareness of Harriet's inner turmoil, which in the circumstances was understandable, particularly for a mother who has to learn to cope with her own feelings before being strong enough to deal with the emotions and prejudices of others. As a school, we had no understanding of the disorder, or the emotion that was to follow, so Harriet's biological sex, as a female, was reinforced.

The first year (age 7 to 8) passed with few outward difficulties for the school, probably because Harriet was too young to articulate her feelings, together with our lack of understanding. Her requests to wear swimming trunks were quickly quashed: "Little girls wear costumes, not trunks." Harriet turned up with a costume, and we hoped that the tomboyish phase would pass.

We felt that if the parents had been stronger, perhaps insisting on Harriet's appearance as an ordinary girl, confusion over the gender would have been eradicated. How wrong we were!

Warning signs appeared in the second year (age 8 to 9). Harriet continued to dress as a boy and wore stereotypical male clothing. She had few friends and was intent on pursuing male friendships and games. All her stories contained a male character called Harry. Perhaps this was the only way that she could act out her life in her preferred gender.

Harriet had begun to see a multidisciplinary team that specialized in these types of disorders, and regular termly meetings involving the various professionals were held in school to discuss the concerns surrounding Harriet's development. Harriet and her parents also participated. These meetings proved useful in facilitating communications, removing secrecy, and facing difficult problems together.

The marked change came, however, in Year 5, our third year (age 9 to 10 years), following an interview in the national press that Harriet had with a famous interviewer in which the problems surrounding this disorder were discussed. It was almost as if Harriet were freeing herself of the burden and inner turmoil that she faced, as she proudly brought the article into school. This appeared to be a release from the secrecy of feelings and emotions that she needed to articulate freely. Whether Harriet felt that perhaps she would gain more understanding from others, and become sociably acceptable for the gender that she feels herself to be, is unclear. Instead, it produced calls from concerned parents who had heard second-hand reports of the article. They had heard words such as "transsexual" and had become alarmed: they did not want their children discussing such issues.

The school became "Piggy in the Middle". On the one hand were Harriet's parents, who had made a decision to end the secrecy and accept their child's disorder, but on the other hand it had activated a negative curiosity in others, people who wanted to know but perhaps did not understand. Careful handling of the two parties was difficult.

Harriet's desire to be accepted as a male became stronger. Such was her emotional distress, and so intense was her desire to be perceived as a boy, that through her tears she refused "point blank" to comply with her teacher's request to wear a costume during swimming lessons. This was quite out of character.

Clearly, as a headteacher, I was out of my depth. I was deskilled, to a certain extent, and needed guidance. This I sought from the professionals at the local education authority (LEA), but no one had dealt with a case like this. Only one other known case existed, and they too were trying to feel their way through similar problems.

There were no educational guidelines, and initial meetings with LEA professionals were frustrating. It really became a matter of looking at the issues that arose and using the art of compromise to reach solutions, and this seemed to be the best way forward.

As the year progressed, Harriet began to push the issue of her gender as a male. We agreed to call her Harry, re-label books and drawers, even hold a meeting with all staff to ensure that everyone did this. However, the legal advice from the education authority was not to change her "gender" to male, as technically she was born female and would need to remain on record as this. For swimming, we allowed her to wear a T-shirt and shorts, though we could not sanction her changing in the boys' changing rooms.

Both parents had hoped that we could perhaps discuss the issue with the children in school. Having now totally accepted the condition, the parents craved the acceptance of those around who, too, had known Harriet since birth. On the surface, this would seem like a simple solution, but unwritten rules state that whilst adults would tolerate different characteristics in children, attitudes to gender disorders would cause great debate and not necessarily be of benefit to understanding Harriet. As a school, we felt that this was too sensitive an issue on which to go public, but we tried to gain some understanding of the condition.

A male teacher was elected to be a listening ear if Harry had problems. She had a "Think Book", which she could use as a form of communication to this teacher should she want to.

Separating the condition from Harry's demands for more change became the central issue. What was a normal childhood reaction? What was the condition? Harry now needed time to discuss issues, to enable her to see things from other people's points of view, not just her own.

Harry refused to use the toilets and began to force the issue by her own discomfort. So we gave her the use of the caretaker's toilet. She became upset at Sports Day, so we allowed her to take part in the boys' races.

At meetings, Harry became more articulate, clearly stating her preferences for her desire to be treated as a male. Our outdoor-pursuits trip, which Harry would have thoroughly enjoyed, she passed over because we could only accommodate her in a room with girls—such was the strength of her feelings.

Harriet would not discuss any bodily changes that were likely to occur, and mention of these, in whatever guise, would reduce her to tears.

Perhaps the hardest issue to deal with was the emotions of other children when Harry asked out a girl in her class. The girl concerned wrote one of the most sensitive letters, showing maturity beyond her years. She had grappled with Harry's condition, but found the taunting and name-calling of other children difficult. This incident left an emotional trail of turmoil and needed a great deal of discussion with those children in the class who were making unkind comments. Although discussions brought an end to the incident and support was provided for the girl who was being verbally bullied, how much understanding of Harry's condition was gained by the other children is unclear.

Supporting any child and family with gender identity disorders requires time. Time and raised awareness is needed to discuss issues as they arise. Understanding and expertise is required on the part of the teachers and school staff.

My school has had a raising of awareness. I believe that Harry will grow into adulthood as a male and have whatever operation is needed. Her need seems so strong that it makes us feel that it is unlikely to change. What is sad is the prejudice that undoubtedly will follow.

CHAPTER FOURTEEN

Children of transsexual parents

A

Research and clinical overview

Richard Green

Peer-reviewed published experience with children of trans-sexual parents remains limited to my 1978 paper on sixteen children; none of these children showed evidence of gender identity disorder (Green, 1978). This report has been widely cited, including in the 1997 case before the European Court of Human Rights regarding legal parenthood of a post-operative female transsexual (*Case of X, Y and Z v. United Kingdom*, 1977).

Since this clinical experience reported twenty years ago, I have seen more than that number again of children with a transsexual parent. Most of the transsexual parents were biological fathers becoming women; the majority of the children have been pre-teen-age. Some of the children continue to live with the transsexual parent and the transsexual's spouse as one parent gender meta-morphoses. Some live with the non-transsexual parent only; of these, some have no contact with the transsexual parent and some continue with visitation contact.

These configurations elicit clinical issues of psychosexual and psychosocial development in children. They also elicit courtroom controversy over what constitutes the best interests of children.

Children of transsexual parents are seen to be at risk for gender identity confusion. Transsexual mothers and fathers present dramatically aberrant sex-typed representations of male and female. Whatever the major theory of psychosexual development in children, boys and girls of transsexual parents could be deemed at risk.

Classic psychoanalytic theory addresses the importance of the mother, father, and child during the oedipal period of development, with the pivotal elements of castration fear in the boy and penis envy in the girl. Resolution of this conflict is required to promote identification with a same-sex parent. Where the male parent becomes a woman with surgical removal of the penis, or a female parent becomes a man with surgical creation of a phallus, the normal pattern and symbols of development are radically disrupted.

Role-modelling theory emphasizes the significance of the male and female parent in the child's earliest years as it deciphers cues of what constitutes a boy or a girl. Cognitively, the child needs to understand the normal continuity of sexual development where the boy becomes a man and the girl a woman. The child needs to understand the biological basis for sex designation as male or female, so that changing superficial features such as clothing style or hairstyle does not change sex. These normal cues are radically altered and presented in a potentially confusing mix to the child when a parent begins to dress as a person of the opposite sex and receives opposite-sex hormones to modify the appearance of the body.

Some evidence suggests genetic or physiologically innate origins of atypical gender identity. To the extent that these factors are operative, children of transsexuals could have a higher probability of atypical gender development.

Transsexual parents and their marital partners react in several ways to the transsexual parent's decision to change sex, all of which may put their children at risk.

Some transsexual parents continue to live with their children during the gender transition, or they may keep in contact but from a separate residence. When parents separate, the child may be visited for a period of time by the transitioning parent, who continues to appear, to the extent possible, in the original gender role.

With time, body changes from hormone treatment render the original gender appearance of the parent difficult to maintain. Then the child may be cut off from continuing contact with the parent.

Some marital partners of transsexuals move to terminate contact between the transsexual parent and child(ren) at the start of the gender-transition process. Children may be told that the parent has moved far away and will not be able to visit. Here, children and transsexual parents suffer immediate loss, and the children are deprived of the continuity of the dual-parenting experience.

Many transsexual parents find it impossible to inform their children about their transition to the other gender. They prefer not to expose the children to this change and believe that they are protecting them by removing themselves from their lives. This is considered abandonment by the children.

Spouses may move to stop child access to the transsexual parent through a court order, and often they are successful.

The child's relationship with the non-transsexual custodial parent can become stressed in consequence of the secrecy surrounding loss of contact with the other parent. When children later discover the truth, they may become angry with their custodial parent for depriving them of contact. They may feel betrayed by both parents.

There is concern that children of transsexual parents who are aware of the gender-transition process may manifest sexual identity confusion. They may be puzzled over whether they will develop the same condition as their parents. Have they inherited transsexualism? Will they want to change sex? Will they change sex against their will?

Social embarrassment and peer-group stigma may develop for the child when neighbour children and schoolmates learn of the parent's gender transition.

Children feel anxious about their parent's health risks from treatment. They fear that the parent might die during sex-reassignment surgery.

Children benefit from knowing that the changes happening to their parent's body are only occurring because the parent is taking a special medicine that the parent wants. Children have some understanding of genetics and inheritance of features from parents.

CHILDREN OF TRANSSEXUAL PARENTS   263

Thus black parents have black children, blue-eyed parents have blue-eyed children. Children should understand that transsexualism is not inherited. Furthermore, they should know that by the time their parent was the current age of the child, the parent was already unhappy regarding gender. Since the child is not unhappy in its gender, this will not happen later to the child.

Gender (or sexual) identity contains three elements (Green, 1974): (1) sense of self as belonging to the category male/boy/man or female/girl/woman; (2) sex-typed behaviours (culturally defined masculinity and femininity); and (3) sex of preferred erotic partners or sexual orientation. Component 1 appears to manifest initially in the second or third year. Component 2 appears during the same period and becomes increasingly dimorphic with progressive childhood years. Component 3 begins to emerge near early puberty. With young children of transsexuals, it is Component 1 that generates theoretical concern.

Relevant to this concern is the concept of gender constancy, which is a variant of object constancy, the permanence to a child of an object's characteristics. As an example, when a 3-year-old is shown a picture of a cat (which it identifies correctly) and then a face of a dog is placed covering the cat's face, the 3-year-old will say that the animal is a dog. An 8-year-old will say that it is a cat with a dog mask. What, then, does the young child understand about its own gender when it sees the gender transformation of a parent? A father may begin to change external sex-typed features that are visible to the child—for example, clothing and hair length. Especially in a family in which parental or sibling nudity in the child's presence is forbidden, the only clues to sex may be the external changeable features. A cross-dressed father may be conceptualized in the same primitive fashion by the child as the cat with the dog mask. Even with the opportunity to witness the anatomic differences between the sexes, the lack of gender constancy may still affect the young child's concept of self.

The age at which gender constancy is in place is not documented with precision. Studies using somewhat different methods see it in place somewhere around 6 years. Gender constancy for the child itself may precede that for others (Eaton & Von Bargen, 1981; Marcus & Overton, 1978). However, even if the child does not yet have the cognitive capacity of gender constancy, this does not mean that it will experience gender identity confusion. Would the child also want to change sex? Not if Component 1 of sexual or gender identity is in place. If the child shows no evidence of gender identity ambiguity, there is little reason for concern that the impression of the parent will evoke cross-gender wishes in the child.

In my clinical experience, I have never seen a child of a transsexual parent who experienced gender identity confusion or gender dysphoria or manifested the diagnostic symptoms of gender identity disorder. Nor have I seen children who experienced significant peer-group teasing. Furthermore, children with gender identity disorder do not have gender-disordered parents (Green, 1974, 1987).

Yet in the face of these clinical data, some divorcing spouses of the transsexual refuse to allow any direct contact between the transsexual parent and children, and clinicians may concur with this. The stated fear is that the child's psychosexual development will be disrupted. Furthermore, some transsexual parents, fearing loss in court or publicity, may withdraw from any contact with their children. They see the loss as a price to be paid for pursuing sex reassignment. Others believe that continuing contact will harm their children and so abdicate contact. These separations are unnecessary.

Research is needed in several areas related to children of transsexuals. Patterns in transsexual families differ with respect to gender of child and gender of transsexual. Differential influences on the child with concordance or discordance between gender of child and gender of transitioning parent should be addressed. Of interest is the age of the child when there was initial awareness of the parent's gender dysphoria. While no control groups can be generated with such research to isolate variables, families can stand as contrast patterns to others in which these variables differ.

Research should examine children with continuing contact with the transsexual parent versus those with no contact, with the focus being psychosocial and psychosexual adjustment.

Non-transsexual families should be studied where, for other reasons, contact between child and one parent has been forbidden. Again, the focus should be on psychosocial and psychosexual development.

If new data from systematic research support current clinical impressions, courts may be more sympathetic to the transsexual parent's position for continuing contact. Much of the non-transsexual parent's opposition to contact is founded in anger at the transsexual spouse's decision to divorce and undergo sex reassignment. Over and above the typical generation of anger common in divorce proceedings, the transsexual's projected course evokes augmented feelings of abandonment, rejection, and betrayal.

The non-transsexual parent's new romantic partner may contribute to the opposition against the transsexual maintaining child contact. This can represent an effort to eliminate divided loyalties by the children and secure a firmer parenting position.

Some psychiatrists see the non-transsexual parent's opposition to continuing child contact to be so substantial that requiring contact over this parent's objection is predicted to be more harmful to the children than interrupting or terminating contact. No systematically collected data support this contention. Clinical data currently available do not support interrupting or terminating transsexual parent access to children. Interrupting contact for several years "until the situation stabilizes" or the angry parent becomes reconciled essentially permanently disrupts the parent–child bond.

Finally, many courts are, simply put, biased against transsexual parents. When presented with divergent professional opinions on the effects of continuing versus terminating contact, they will sway to termination.

Systematic data collection by clinical researchers who see transsexual parents may impact on the current state. Perhaps this contentious area of family law will evolve along the path of child custody and visitation disputes involving homosexual parents. In twenty years, the latter area, educated by research, evolved from the state where most homosexual parents (usually lesbian mothers) lost custody as a consequence of posited harm to their children. Currently, those issues involving the best interests of children are played out on a more level playing-field (Green, 1992).

B

Mental health issues
and some principles of management

Domenico Di Ceglie

A story is told of a young woman who in order to follow her father who wished to live in a monastery without being parted from her, dressed in male clothes and changed her name to Marino (from her original female name of Marina).

Although the father died fairly soon Marino/a continued to live in the monastery maintaining his/her secret. Marino was well loved and was cited by others for his exemplary behaviour. He used to go to the nearby village to do the shopping for the monastery and he used to spend the night at the village inn before returning the following day to the monastery with his hand cart. One day the inn keeper's daughter, who had become pregnant, accused the young monk of having raped her. Marino did not defend himself and he was inexorably thrown out of the monastery. However, he did not leave the area and remained living near the monastery in a grotto, where the child, the fruit of his presumed sin was given to him to be brought up. [Minghelli, 1996]

Eventually, Marino was re-admitted with "his child" to the monastery because of his good behaviour. A few days later Marino died, and when the brothers undressed him to wash him they discovered that he had a woman's body. The monks were so struck by Marino's acceptance of the unjust punishment without protest, and the consistency of his life as a man, that he was eventually made a saint. He apparently lived in the fifth century in a monastery near Tripoli. Historians do not tell us what the child was told about Marino and whether his or her secret was ever revealed to the child. We do not know for certain whether Marino was a transsexual; however, this story shows how the problems discussed in this chapter are not new. Our society's approach to these issues is changing as our understanding of gender identity problems develops and the negative psychological consequences of secrecy within the family become more recognized.

At present, a substantial number of people seeking sex reassignment have a family with children. A rough estimate indicates that one-third of transsexuals attending a gender identity clinic for adults in England have children. A proportion of transsexual parents are involved in court disputes to maintain or regain access to their children.

There are only a few case studies describing in some detail the problems that children have to face when confronted with changes of gender identity in one parent.

There is little research in this area (as Green discussed earlier in this chapter), and our clinical experience to date is too limited to be able to draw firm conclusions on the emotional effect on children. However, I do not think that we will find that there is a specific developmental pattern in the children of transsexuals, but, rather, that there is great variability in how children react and adapt to changes in the family brought about by the presence of a gender identity disorder in one parent.

The way in which the process of reassignment is managed by the parent, the way in which the marital relationship is affected, the attitudes of the family network and the level of support offered, the way the social environment (such as the school, the peer group) regards gender identity problems, as well as each child's vulnerability or capacity to cope with major family changes and to make sense of them, are all variables that will affect the psychological development of the children. The developmental stage of a child when the gender change takes place may also have a bearing on the effects on the child.

One aspect that all these children have in common is *facing a similar unusual situation*. The child will probably be the only one in the school with this particular issue. This characteristic may make the social environment ill-prepared to understand the particular needs of these children, and quite often a lack of familiarity with gender identity problems leads to fears, prejudices, and myths. It is in this context that a specialist service for the children of parents with a gender identity disorder can play an important role in helping them.

Two features in a service for these children are important in my view:

1.   The team should be multidisciplinary and have general experience in working with children and adolescents within a developmental perspective. It needs to be a *child-oriented service*.
2.   The team needs experience and understanding of gender identity disorders in children and adults.

Management principles

The Children Act 1989 states that "the child's welfare should be the Court's paramount consideration". Therefore, in line with current legislation, the first principle in management will be that:

•   *The developmental needs of the child shall be of paramount importance*

This has important implications in management, as the primary allegiance of the professional is to the child, and this should be made clear to the family members and the other professionals involved. Steps will need to be taken to establish a trusting relationship with the child within which wishes, anxieties, and preoccupations can be explored. Mary Lightfoot's case illustration (later in this chapter) shows how this can be achieved.

- *Openness about the gender identity issue in the parent should be aimed at and appropriate conditions for open communication created*

Family secrets or, worse, lies can have long-term detrimental effects on psychological development and lead to psychopathology (Imber-Black, 1993; Pincus & Dare, 1978). Adults who were deprived of the knowledge about a transsexual parent often complain of being kept in the dark concerning it and maintain that they should have been told earlier. Pursuing openness may require, whenever possible, joint preparatory work with both parents, and sometimes with other relatives, as information needs to be conveyed to the child in a sensitive and consistent way and a child's enquiries addressed in a similar fashion. The timing of the information is also an important aspect. This preparatory work can, in some cases, take a long time. At times, misconceptions about the capacity to understand need to be addressed. Some people believe that pre-pubertal children do not have a sense of gender identity and therefore cannot understand gender identity problems. Golombok and Fivush (1994) summarize current research findings in their book *Gender Development* as follows:

> Children begin to consistently label themselves and others as male or female sometime around the age of 2 years, and very soon after this, they begin to associate particular behaviours and traits with one gender or the other. Even more interesting, young children between the age of 3 and 6 years of age, are even more strongly stereotyped than adults. [p. 27]

In some cases involving the court, where a transsexual parent had lost contact with a child of 4 or 5 years and wished to re-establish it, other family members had wanted to delay the knowledge and the contact with the transsexual parent until the child had reached adolescence. Unless there were other factors involved, this timing is quite inappropriate. Usually the latency period (see Glossary) presents itself as a phase where conflicts around identity—including the gender identity—and sexuality are attenuated and emotional experiences are less intense in comparison with adolescence. These features make the latency period a time when the child can be prepared to deal with an unusual situation without having the burden of coping with the changes brought about by puberty and adolescence. On the other hand, if the child is not told earlier, it is likely that significant questions about the trans-sexual parent's identity will surface during adolescence, thus add-ing to the turmoil and struggle in establishing his or her own sense of identity. This may also lead, as mentioned, to recriminations about not having been told the truth earlier. The assumption here, of course, is that the secrecy surrounding the transsexual parent is not disturbed by the child acquiring the knowledge in unplanned and traumatic circumstances. In one of my cases, another child had said at school: "Your Mum used to be a man"—causing great distress to the child.

- *The child's exercise of curiosity about the parent's gender identity issue should be allowed and not suppressed*

Simple and truthful explanations should be offered. These may correct distorted perceptions or fantasies. The child's communica-tion verbally, or through play, of concerns and fears is important as it allows, if properly received by the counsellor or therapist, containment and mental digestion. It may prevent the develop-ment of psychopathology such as nightmares, as in the case discussed by Mary Lightfoot later in this chapter.

- *Gender identity disorders are not the result of a conscious choice*

This understanding of the disorder needs to be clearly conveyed to the child and to other family members; otherwise, the whole pro-cess of sex reassignment of the parent may end up being viewed by the family as a self-centred and uncaring decision in relation-ship to other family members' needs.

- *The sense of separateness and differentiation needs to be encouraged in the child*

This is an important developmental task for every child. However, more specifically, children of a parent with a gender identity disor-der may become worried—witnessing the changes occurring in the parent—that similar changes might one day happen to them. This fear becomes a threat to their developing identity. Richard Green's research (1978) shows clearly that children of transsexual parents

FIGURE 14.1

do not have major identity problems. This knowledge should be conveyed to the family, and the child's sense of uniqueness encouraged.

In other cases, the child may become trapped in the parents' marital conflict and out of guilt feel compelled to try to keep them together or to look after them by taking a parental role. This overriding preoccupation becomes an impediment to the child achieving independence and autonomy. In such cases, it is important to enable the child to separate himself or herself from the parents and leave to them the responsibility of overcoming their conflict.

During an assessment interview a child of a transsexual parent while drawing his family put himself in-between his parents, holding their hands. The other children were placed separately, playing happily together. This picture (see Figure 14.1) shows how, among the children in the family, he felt that he had to keep the parents together, and this mission set him apart from the rest of the peer group. In this case, individual sessions for the child were considered important in the management plan to provide him with a space where, through therapeutic work, he would be able to move away psychologically from this anti-developmental position.

• *Clarification of new roles in reconstituted families and what to call the parent after sex reassignment*

This task might involve the mourning of the loss of certain aspects of the previous relationship with the parent and can be a painful transition. The construction of a family tree can be used as a tool to address these issues by exploring the family history and relationships. In a child who is old enough to have developed a strong relationship with the transsexual parent, the knowledge of the change of sexual identity can produce a response akin to a mourning process, with the three typical phases of denial/protest, sadness and anger, and, eventually, acceptance of the changes. Some children and teenagers can become stuck in a particular phase of the "mourning" process, and considerable therapeutic input and patience is needed to overcome the impasse. It is also important that the transsexual parent is supported and enabled to tolerate the expression of feelings, particularly hostility and anger, directed towards him or her by their children. If this process takes a favourable course, it may lead to a new relationship developing between the children and the transsexual parent. The acceptance of the parent's new gender role leads to an agreed way of addressing the transsexual parent. It is also important, whatever term is used to address the transsexual parent, that this should not deny the previous reality of the relationship (see Mary Lightfoot's case illustration).

• *Collaboration between the parents and other family members needs to be encouraged in the best interests of the child in trying to achieve these aims*

Sometimes this cooperation is very difficult or impossible to reach, as the parents are absorbed with other overriding preoccupations or by recriminations. Transsexual parents may go through phases in which the preoccupation with their body becomes overriding. Here, I see the role of individual counselling for the parent, aimed at reducing the intensity of this preoccupation and to extending the interest and the concern to other areas of life and in particular to the care of the child. In some cases, the spouses of transsexual parents may need help in overcoming recriminations and the wish to punish their partners for the distress that they are experiencing. Counselling offered by a service that is not directly involved with the sex reassignment is more likely to be accepted.

- *Peer-group relationships and social support for the child should be facilitated*

Peer-group relationships can be difficult, as the children or teenagers may find it embarrassing and feel too ashamed to talk to friends about their family. Their sense of shame can, in turn, affect their self-esteem and confidence and possibly lead to social isolation. Issues of this kind will need to be addressed openly in counselling sessions. In dealing with peers, the children need to be helped to differentiate between privacy and secrecy; this differentiation, with parental support, will enable the children to deal appropriately with questions when they come from friends and not to expose themselves unnecessarily in social situations. Professional-network meetings of people involved with the child (e.g. teachers, social workers, GPs) can be helpful in this task.

Therapeutic setting

The above list of management principles highlights some of the aims of a programme for children of transsexual parents. In our experience at the Gender Identity Development Service at the Portman Clinic, we believe that the therapeutic context in which to achieve these tasks has to be flexible. A plan of intervention needs to adjust to the needs of each individual case and to the reality of what it is possible to achieve at that particular stage of family life. In our service, we do not have a rigid routine but arrange family meetings or individual meetings with the child or children concerned and the parents, who can be seen jointly or separately. A careful consideration of information available at the time of the referral directs the initial approach. Sometimes, family meetings lead to individual sessions; at other times, individual sessions may lead to family meetings later. One or two interviews may be all that is needed in some cases, long-term work in others.

Conclusion

From the experience to date, we have become convinced that the involvement of children and other family members at the beginning of the process of sex reassignment should be attempted. This might prevent further difficulties and long-term negative effects on the children; in some cases, it may also avoid lengthy and complex disputes in court.

We also think that the gender identity services for adults and the gender identity services for children and adolescents (a child-oriented service) should collaborate, as it is important that the two different focuses of work are recognized and conflicts of needs faced and possibly resolved—through the understanding of the conscious and unconscious dynamics involved.

C

Issues facing the child of a transsexual parent

Mary Lightfoot

L ittle is known about the effect on children of parents going through treatment for sex reassignment. In his review on this subject, Richard Green (see earlier in this chapter) confirms this view, and in his 1978 study he found that the 16 children in his sample reported childhood toy, game, clothing, and peer-group preferences that are typical for their sex; and, of the 13 older children, erotic fantasies or overt sexual behaviour were all heterosexually oriented. Four of the girls in this study "had seen their biological mother emerge through androgen treatment and sex reassignment surgery to become their 'legal father' and then marry their 'stepmother'. All of these girls (were) feminine and heterosexually oriented" (p. 693).

The feeling of lack of fit between mind and body is distressing and tends to be a central preoccupation for the person concerned. It is also distressing for those attached to that person. Although there may not be any great risk to a child's gender identity or sexual orientation, there may be other effects of the parent's condition.

A paper by Joanna Sales (1995) describes work with the children of a transsexual father who were living with their mother. Sales highlights two broad issues, the first being the children's difficulty in relating to their father following his taking on the role of a woman, and the second being the issues around marital breakdown and living in a reconstituted family.

When relatives become aware that a family member has a gender identity disorder and is transsexual, there may be a shocked
reaction and rejection, so that relationships are broken and normal
family support is removed. The condition can be embarrassing to
talk about and may call forth ridicule from others and unsympathetic curiosity. The concern about trying to resolve the lack of fit
between mind and body can be all-consuming and cause emotional lability and depression with sometimes self-destructive
feelings. Changes attendant on sex reassignment are also stressful
and may make the transsexual parent very self-absorbed and anxious about body image, more moody, and therefore less available
to children.

The following account describes the experience of "Frances",
who is the child of a female-to-male transsexual. Individual work
with her raised a number of issues. Caution is needed in generaliz-
ing too freely from this child's experience as the issues raised are
based on her particular experience and reactions: other children
might react differently.

Issues

Five main issues were raised during the contact with Frances.

- *Separation and loss*

There tends to be family breakdown associated with the discovery
that a partner is transsexual. This may lead to loss of a parent, and
other relatives may also be rejecting. How does this affect a child
who is left with the experience of the remaining parent having sex
reassignment? This involves changes in the parental role and experiencing physical changes in the parent.

- *Parenting*

The lack of fit between mind and body is a central concern and
may result in moodiness and self-absorption. Sex reassignment is
stressful and raises issues about body image. How does this affect
parenting? What reaction might children have to a parent having
these experiences?

• *Development*

A child's development depends on the parents being able to attend to him or her. Is it possible for this to be a paramount consideration when other issues are causing so much stress and are so central? There is a question about whether the other issues are primarily about the lack of fit between mind and body and the process of change, or whether there are other concerns, the gender identity issue being only a part of this.

• *Identity*

Does a parent's change of gender role affect the child's gender identity? Richard Green's study (1978) would indicate that it does not, but how does a child who is growing and changing cope when the parent is also changing? What effect is there on a girl who sees her mother reject the female gender and wish to be a male? What effect do the medical procedures necessary have on the child's view of the parent and her own self-image?

• *Social factors*

Transsexualism can be embarrassing to talk about and may call forth ridicule and unsympathetic curiosity from others. It is an unusual condition, not well understood, and without positive status in our society. How does a child cope with this, and what are the social effects on the child?

Referral

Frances was 13 years old when she was referred to the clinic. The referral came from Frances's head teacher, who wrote that Frances was distressed, having nightmares, and difficulty in sleeping following her mother's decision to live as a man and undergo sex-reassignment surgery. Her learning was delayed, and she behaved like a younger child.

Frances' mother

Frances came with her mother for the first appointment. Frances's mother had always tended, as a child, to want to be with boys and had masculine interests.

The maternal grandparents had been disapproving of her mas-culine preferences and behaviour, and the relationship with them had been difficult. She had a brother, and he and his wife were supportive. She met Frances's father and became pregnant. Their first child was a boy, and Frances was born two years later. The marriage then broke up. Frances's father left, taking the first child with him, and he made a relationship with a new partner.

Frances

When Frances first came she was a slim, dark-haired, not very tall 13-year-old girl. There was concern about her delayed learn-ing. There had been increasing worry about her progress from teachers at school. Frances said almost nothing at the initial assess-ment interview, though she was alert and listening intently. She stated that she knew that her mother wanted to change into a man and then hid her face in her hands. Her mother, now called David, said that Frances had become most distressed when she had heard that this change would involve surgery.

Educational functioning

School reported that an educational psychologist had assessed Frances. There were concerns about her emotional and cognitive development. She was very immature, and her learning was well below average for her year. Her appearance was often untidy, and teachers thought that her clothes might have been bought in jum-ble sales. She had difficulty in concentrating and absorbing infor-mation, and it was felt that she spent a lot of time in a fantasy world. School staff commented on feeling protective towards her.

Method of treatment

It was decided to see Frances individually so that she had the opportunity to explore her worries and feelings in a neutral space. Clinical resources in the Gender Identity Development Unit were limited, and it was agreed to offer an hour's session on a monthly basis. She was seen over a period of nearly three years.

The method of work was non-directive counselling, focusing particularly on her feelings about her mother's situation and change and on Frances's own development. Her mother was also seen for counselling, and joint interviews were arranged when necessary.

First impressions

The first impression of Frances was of a much younger child. It was difficult to think of her as a 13-year-old. She seemed about 8 or 9 years old, or perhaps younger. Her voice sounded babyish, her drawings were immature, and she held her pen in an awkward, childish grip which made writing slow and difficult. She was not using "joined-up writing" and she had difficulty in spelling quite simple words, struggling over the task. She eagerly played with the toys in the room as if she were a younger child.

She made a very rapid and positive attachment to me, and the second time that she came she was able to pick me out at quite a distance down a crowded corridor, when I was walking in the opposite direction, and she ran up to me. She could recognize my footsteps when I was coming to collect her from the waiting-room and would run out to meet me. She would hold my hand walking up the corridor and sometimes put her arms around me to greet me or to say "goodbye".

At her first session, she encouraged her mother to leave, keeping at a distance until her mother had gone and then coming close to me. At a later stage in the contact, an appointment had to be cancelled and Frances ensured that her school telephoned to make another appointment as soon as possible.

Issues

• *Separation and loss*

A continuing theme throughout the contact was Frances's biological father's failure to keep in touch or remember her. When she had her birthday, she asked: "Why doesn't my father remember me?" She had reminded him about her birthday, but he had not sent her anything. She had made him a card for Father's Day during her session. An absent father is an experience that many other children share, but for her it was made more poignant by the fact that her brother and half-siblings were with him and Frances was growing up with a distressed single parent and coping with issues that are unusual and hard to manage.

She experienced four moves of home during the contact with the clinic. This would not be unusual for children whose parents need to move in connection with jobs or where families are unstable. However, in this case it seemed to be related to her mother's condition and her wish not to stand out socially as she became more masculine.

The reason for referral was the fears that Frances had about the changes to her mother and nightmares about what was happening to her mother physically. She asked whether her mother would grow hairs on her chest. She had anxieties about the physical treatments and being given instead a hairy monster, physically strange to her. There was a demand to adjust to a changing picture and the feel of her mother, who was becoming physically male. She described David's newly acquired facial hair and the rough, prickly sensation instead of the previously smooth face when she snuggled up to him. This process seemed similar to that of a baby getting to know the parents physically.

She showed anger about fathers when playing with the dolls' house figures, throwing the father figure roughly on one side and holding the mother figure gently and admiring her dress. She found the loss of being able to call her mother "Mum" very difficult and spoke sadly of how hard she found it to call him "David" but that she had to do it otherwise he was embarrassed when they were in public. Later, David wanted her to make a further change: Frances now calls him "Dad" and calls her biological father by his first name.

• *Parenting*

When she played with the family figures, she chose a figure with trousers as the mother doll. The children in her play were abandoned by their parents and left in the care of an auntie figure. This mirrored her experience of being looked after by various adults because of David's difficulties.

On one occasion she brought balloons with her, filled one with water, and spent some time snuggled in the armchair drinking the water as if she were drinking from a baby's bottle.

In a later session, she became very upset because David had "thrown a wobbly", had hurt himself, and was bleeding. She said that David sometimes throws "wobblies". She had looked after him, "putting him to sleep", and had lain beside him all night, keeping awake to make sure that he was all right. She then huddled up in the chair in the room with her eyes shut. I said perhaps she would like to rest now and offered to cover her with the blanket that was in the room. She smiled at this and snuggled under it, but she could not rest long because she was still worried about David and wanting to get home.

On another occasion she related how she and David had been in a taxi that had to keep stopping so that David could be sick. She explained that he had been drinking.

Her role as a "parenting" child was confirmed when she said that David was about to have his operation and she would be looking after him.

She was fortunate in that the uncle and aunt were supportive, stable figures for her, and she claimed that she was her uncle's favourite niece. Some of the material in the sessions suggested that she was yearning to be a baby in an ideal family with two parents. Her early attachment to me seemed to indicate that she was rather a deprived child, but also she had a need for an adult maternal figure who could be interested in her growing up into a woman.

• *Development*

Her development was delayed. About six months after she was first seen, she had her fourteenth birthday. She said that she did not want to be older: people expect more. They ask what she is going to do, and she does not know. She had difficulty with spelling and practised it in the session.

In the sessions with her, I looked for indications of her feelings about David and the issue of transsexualism. If the subject was raised directly, she became quiet and serious, and she responded rather flatly. Prior to Father's Day, she spent a long time making a card for her father. She spelt father as "Farther" and then said:

"When I give David a card, I will not give it to him on Mother's Day or on Father's Day, but in-between."

The nightmares from which she suffered at first quickly ceased, and there was evidence of her becoming more assertive and less anxious. I talked to her about the fact that she became quiet when she was asked about David, and I wondered whether Frances thought that I would think she was naughty if she said that what was happening to David was upsetting. She seemed embarrassed but listened carefully, swivelling in her chair. She stopped and looked at herself in the mirror. She stood rubbing her cheeks and seemed to be checking to see how attractive and likeable she was. She complained that teachers at school wanted her to hold her pen between her fingers instead of in her fist. I showed her how she could move the pen if she held it in her fingers. She was delighted with this, and after complaining that it felt "funny", was immediately able to write rapidly, joining the letters together.

In a later session, she talked about tummy pains and the beginnings of her periods. She brought teenage magazines to the sessions and pointed out her favourite pop stars. She spoke about wearing make-up and said that she wore it in school, though you were not supposed to do that.

When she walked along the corridor with me, she compared heights saying that she was nearly as tall as I was now. She was interested in teenage clothes and was becoming quite an elegant young lady. She spoke with pride about having the front-door key and being allowed to travel alone. She began to think about a career.

Her schoolwork was progressing very well, and her head teacher spoke of a "tremendous improvement". Frances herself attributed the change to being able to hold her pen differently and said that she was lucky because for her things were getting easier. She came one day with a long list of questions all about David's treatment. She said that this was homework, and she had to answer these questions for a project. She asked if I would help her. I answered the questions as directly as I could in a way that Frances could understand, letting her know about possible difficulties but reassuring her about her own gender development. I asked her at the end if she thought that she could talk to David about all this. She said immediately that she could not possibly do that. Speaking to me about the subject openly in this way seemed to be a great relief to her.

She began to show interest in boys, but from a distance. She had no boyfriends but was thinking about it and curious about friends who had.

• *Identity*

If David did not value the role of mothering, what effect did this have on Frances and her view of herself as likeable and on her self-esteem? She herself was changing physically, but she was having problems about the process of maturing. She should be growing into someone like her mother, but her mother was not staying constant so that Frances could do it. This had implications for her valuing growing up into womanhood.

Sometimes, in early sessions, she would come wearing clothing borrowed from someone else at school, as if she were testing out someone else's identity. She came in shoes borrowed from another child and in shoes given to her by another child. It was as if she was wondering what it would be like to be in "someone else's shoes".

A persistent theme through early sessions was a concern with disability and damage. Frances's earliest memory of her mother was of herself being pushed in a pushchair by her mother, who had her leg in plaster after a motorbike accident. In the clinic waiting-room, there was a walking-frame and sticks. Frances used the walking-frame walking slowly and painstakingly up the corridor with it and then practised using it in the session. She said she wished she could be in a wheelchair: "You get everything you want, if you are in a wheelchair." The next time, she came in with her left foot bandaged in toilet paper and using the two sticks. It was a realistic performance. She said that she had been knocked down by a car in the school car park and described various injuries including a bump on her head. The school staff had looked after her, but she felt that she had not had as much attention as she would have liked. The theme of injury continued, with accounts of people with broken limbs and concern about her own minor injuries—for example a blister on her foot. At the next session after the accident, she limped in saying that there was something wrong with her knee. She drew a picture of a knife in her leg to show what was wrong. Then she spoke about David's injections and that he said he would be married after the operation. I was concerned that the accident indicated that she had had a lapse in alertness, which might imply self-destructive feelings. There seemed to be a wish to be looked after, being pushed like a baby in a wheelchair, and that she was looking for emotional support (the sticks and the walking-frame). Was she identifying with a damaged mother whom she remembered having a broken leg, and was her concern that her mother was going to inflict further damage on herself through the operation? Perhaps the knife inside her also represented some pubertal sexual wonderings, which were quite frightening.

A child can use models other than the parents, and the uncle and aunt were in touch and fond of Frances; however, the fact that the model presented by her mother was changing from female to male had led to confusion and a standstill in her own development.

As sessions progressed, she developed a more positive view of herself. She enjoyed contact with peers. She felt herself to be attractive and became fashion-conscious. She has a feminine identity.

• *Social factors*

Frances had a great fear when she first came to the clinic that other children might find out about her mother changing into a man, but she felt unable to keep this to herself, as it was such a major preoccupation for her. She avoided other children's questions about her parents because she found it difficult to know what to say and felt embarrassed and feared teasing.

It was clear that she would not be able to keep her great concern a secret from other children at school, and she had already told two of the other children about what was happening to her mother. This had served to raise her anxiety more, and she described herself as "big mouth". After it was agreed with David and Frances, a meeting was arranged with her teacher to discuss talking to the other children about what was happening to her mother so that Frances did not have to keep it to herself, but also would not be subjected to teasing. The issue was handled well by the school, and Frances later confirmed that no one had teased her and that the other children had been very sympathetic and supportive, apart from one boy, whom the others had "beaten up".

Conclusion

The main issues raised by this case were separation and loss, parenting, development, identity, and social factors. Frances experienced a number of losses, including loss of contact with relatives, home moves, and physical and role changes in her mother. Although these changes were not as frightening as she expected, she was angry about the changes in her mother and sad about the losses in her life.

There was some role reversal in the relationship with her mother, and she felt responsible for her. It was helpful that her mother's brother and his wife were interested adults and stable figures for her. This assisted her to develop, and it was important to her that she felt that she was "special" for them.

During the course of my contact with her, she made great strides in her maturity, and her schoolwork strikingly improved. She was able to remain in the same school, which was a source of stability for her. The sessions at the clinic helped her to express and understand her emotions and experiences, and to integrate these.

She showed some doubts about herself and her identity, though there was no question about her femininity. Her view of herself improved as she matured. She showed considerable fear about the possible reactions of others to her situation, and it was important that this was addressed and handled sensitively.

Aspects of these issues as described are not unique to the child of a parent who is undergoing sex reassignment. It would be helpful for there to be further case studies to discover whether features of her experience are common to other children who continue to live with parents in this situation.

GLOSSARY

David Freedman & Bernadette Wren

This glossary explains some of the terms used in this book. The explanations are aimed at the lay and non-specialist reader: as some of the terminology can be controversial and complex, for brevity we have given somewhat basic explanations.

amnesia: The inability to retrieve particular events or feelings into conscious thought. This can serve as a defensive function if the memories are upsetting or threatening.

anatomic dysphoria: unhappiness with one's own sexual body.

androgen: steroid hormone produced by the adrenal cortex in both sexes (when known as adrenal androgens) and also by the testes (then known as testosterone) in the male. Androgens promote masculinization and, in both sexes, contribute to pubic hair formation during puberty.

anxiolytics: medicines that reduce anxiety.

atypical: not typical, diverging from a commonly known presentation.

borderline: term used to describe psychological troubles that lie on the border between neurosis and psychosis.

287

chromosome: a linear thread of **genes** present within the nucleus of every cell in the body. Normally, each cell has 23 pairs of chromosomes, making a total of 46. One of these pairs, the sex chromosomes, determines the sex of the foetus. A boy normally has an X and a Y sex chromosome (46 XY) and a girl two X chromosomes (46 XX).

chromosomal: pertaining to the chromosome e.g. chromosomal analysis.

co-morbid: the presence simultaneously of two or more medical or psychological problems.

countertransference: the therapist's emotional response to the individual patient, family, or group.

denial: an unconscious mechanism whereby a painful experience or wish or aspect of the personality is denied.

depersonalization state: a state in which an individual experiences the self or the body as unreal or "dead".

depressive position: Melanie Klein's term to describe a mental state in which infants and adults are able to experience both love and hate towards the same object. In infancy, this object is the mother or her substitute. Within this mental state there is a wish to protect the object from the damage that the negative feelings might do. In infancy it is a phase of better mental integration beginning at about 4 months, following the **paranoid–schizoid position**. After infancy, the individual may oscillate between these two mental states (positions) in particular circumstances.

dimorphic/dimorphism: exhibiting or occurring in two distinct forms; in the case of this book, male and female.

DSM: *Diagnostic and Statistical Manual of Mental Disorders,* published by the American Psychiatric Association. The fourth edition was published in 1994. The defining criteria for gender identity disorders as described in DSM-IV are used by most clinicians.

displacement: the process by which emotional investment is shifted from its original "object" onto other objects. This may lead the individual to avoid or neglect dealing with important personal issues.

dissociation: a process by which aspects of mental functioning are disconnected from each other; for example, a person who disconnects from the perception of a painful external reality while concentrating on other internal experiences or phantasies. Dissociation is common in traumatic experiences, especially in young children, and in psychotic states.

ego-syntonic: a term used to describe acts and wishes that are felt to be an integral part of the individual's ideals and standards of behaviour; there will be no motivation on the part of the individual to change them, in spite of social pressures. The phenomenon of a gender identity disorder can be viewed as largely ego-syntonic.

encopresis: the repeated passage of faeces into inappropriate places with or without constipation.

enzyme: a protein molecule that catalyses the chemical conversion of one substance to another without itself undergoing any change during the process. Most hormones are produced by a series of different enzymes that convert a precursor substance through a number of progressively modified precursors until the active hormone is produced.

Eros: Greek god of love or sexual love. Used by Freud in his later works to represent the life instincts. (See also **Thanatos.**)

fugue state: the mental state of an individual who loses awareness of who she or he is or where she or he belongs and engages in uncharacteristic behaviour while away from home or customary place.

gender (vs. sex): in recent years, this has come to be used as the term for the subjective and social categorization of an individual as being either male or female, within a particular historical and cultural context. Colloquially, it is used synonymously with "sex".

gene: a segment of a DNA molecule that contains all the information required for synthesis of a product. It is the biological unit of heredity and is transmitted from parent to progeny. Each gene has a specific position (locus) on the chromosome map.

genetic: determined by genes.

gonad: most often refers to ovaries in women and testes in men.

hermaphrodite: individual with some characteristics of both male and female sex organs and characteristics.

Hollingshead's social class classification: this is based on the occupation of the Head of Household, using five categories: I = very senior management; II & III = middle-class occupations; IV = skilled worker; V = semi-skilled and unskilled labourer.

hyperarousal: a state of excessive emotional and sensory responsiveness.

hypothalamus: an important anatomical area within the brain which influences a number of essential behavioural and functional aspects of the body (including temperature and sleep regulation, hunger and thirst, emotional behaviour, and memory). The hypothalamus also serves as the main "communication centre" for the pituitary gland, to which it is connected by the pituitary stalk. Hormonal signals from the hypothalamus control the release of hormones from the pituitary gland, which in turn signals to other glands and organs in the body. The role of the hypothalamus is thus one of controlling activity, and it plays a major part in growth, reproduction, control of emotions, etc.

iatrogenic: disease or illness caused by the process of medical intervention.

internalized breast: a psychoanalytic term from the work of Melanie Klein used to mean the infant's mental representation of the mother's breast, which can be perceived as nurturing (gratifying/good) or frustrating (persecutory/bad). These representations can be very split (e.g. in the paranoid–schizoid position), whereas in more mature mental states (depressive position) they are integrated and the breast can be perceived as having both qualities.

introjection: a mental process by which external objects and their characteristics are assimilated into the internal world and consequently become available as a part of mental life.

karyotype: description of the full chromosome set of the nucleus of a cell (e.g. normal male karyotype, 46 XY, normal female, 46 XX).

kindling: a concept in which brain areas will develop spontaneous seizures after a period of continuous but below-seizure-threshold stimulation. It is a concept that is currently being used to explain how some disorders appear to develop with initial stresses and then with subsequent bouts need little stress to be triggered (e.g. bipolar illness).

latency period: in the psychoanalytic theory of development, this is the period covered between the end of the oedipal phase and conflicts (4 to 5 years old) and the onset of puberty (see **Oedipus complex**). During latency there is a general decrease in impulses including sexual impulses, and it is described as a period of relative tranquillity and attenuated conflicts.

manic flight: a psychological defence mechanism where the individual flees from a problem and reality by developing a grandiose and omnipotent way of thinking, which may be acted out.

medial zone: area near to the mid-line of a body or structure or statistical distribution.

narcissism: from the Greek myth about Narcissus, the youth who fell in love with his own reflection in the water. Narcissism refers to an excessive preoccupation with the self, with a concomitant disinterest in others.

Oedipus complex: from Sophocles' Greek tragedy. In classic psychoanalytic theory of development, it refers to a triangular relationship between the infant, the mother, and the father, characterized by a cluster of powerful feelings. Put at its simplest, in the typical situation the infant develops an attraction towards the parent of the other sex with concomitant rivalry and fear of retaliation by the parent of the same sex. The resolution of the conflicts is partly achieved through an identification with the parent of the same sex. In the atypical situation, the infant develops an attraction towards the parent of the same sex and fears retaliation or intrusion by the parent of the other sex. In this case, the rivalry is with the parent of the other sex. Within this framework, gender identity disorders can be associated with an atypical Oedipus complex.

oestrogen: sex hormone produced mainly from the ovary, which develops and maintains female characteristics of the body.

object choice: in psychoanalytic theory, this refers to the selection of a particular gendered person as a love object; it is equivalent to sexual orientation. The term "choice" has been contested by some because the selection is not a voluntary act but is determined by largely powerful unconscious forces. In this context, "choice" may refer to the acceptance or suppression of the particular attraction.

object relations (theory): psychoanalytic school that sees the fundamental predisposition of humans to develop meaningful relations with others and establish in the internal world images of these people. These internal images can be distorted by **projections**.

paranoid–schizoid position: a term first used by Melanie Klein to describe a mental state characterized by a primitive state of mental functioning. This includes the massive use of **projective identification** and **splitting processes** to cope with unmanageable anxieties. In this state, both oneself and others can acquire either totally positive or totally negative characteristics. The capacity for symbolic thought is very limited and the individual can feel very persecuted having projected his or her aggressive and destructive feelings into others. It is a state of poor mental integration, and these features would be characteristic of a psychotic way of functioning. Although, according to Klein, this functioning is typical of the earliest months of life, she called it a "position" to highlight that this is also a mental state to which people can return during the course of their development. Bion later suggested that individuals can oscillate between the **paranoid–schizoid position** and the **depressive position** in particular circumstances—for example, in a large group or crowd, individuals who are under particular pressures may lose their ability to think clearly and start functioning within a paranoid–schizoid mode.

paraphilia: "The essential features of a paraphilia are recurrent, intense sexually arousing fantasies, sexual urges, or behaviors generally involving 1) nonhuman objects, 2) the suffering or humiliation of oneself or one's partner, or 3) children or other nonconsenting persons, that occur over a period of at least 6 months" (Criterion A, DSM IV: APA 1994). These conditions include exhibitionism, fetishism, paedophilia, sadomasochism, transvestic fetishism, etc.

part-object: the infant's internal representation of parts of the body (initially the mother's), such as the breasts, the eyes, the face, the penis, etc., and their functions. Part-object relationships are characteristic of the **paranoid–schizoid position.**

phallic stage or phase: psychoanalytic term, first used by Freud, to describe the developmental stage or phase during which boys are preoccupied with the penis. This phase comes after the oral and anal phases. Psychoanalytic theory does not offer a unified view for girls on this phase.

phenotype: the entire physical, biochemical, and physiological make-up of an individual as determined both genetically and environmentally.

proband: individual possessing a particular characteristic who is the starting point of a study of genetic inheritance.

projection: a psychoanalytic term that describes a defence mechanism against anxiety where the individual cannot accept an aspect of herself or himself and locates it in another person or thing, who is then perceived as possessing this quality.

projective identification: a term first introduced by Melanie Klein for a defence mechanism used in the **paranoid–schizoid position**. It refers to the phantasy of entering another person with split-off parts of the self, leading to a sense of confusion between the self and the other. People at the receiving end of projective identifications may feel controlled or engulfed in these interactions. Wilfred Bion saw it as a primitive and normal form of communication between the infant and the primary care-giver.

pseudo-hermaphroditism: a condition in which the gonads (sex organs) are of one sex but some morphological features of the opposite sex are present.

psychopathology: the study of abnormal mental processes.

psychosis: a form of serious psychological disturbance characterized by the experience of psychic disintegration and confusion accompanied by the development of delusional beliefs and hallucinations in full consciousness. In the acute phase of a psychotic process, insight into the illness and reality testing are usually lost.

pulsatile: a hormone that is secreted in a pulsatile manner appears in the blood stream as a series of peaks and troughs such that the amount of circulating hormone varies throughout the day.

repression: the process by which a thought, memory, or impulse that is felt to be unacceptable is pushed into the unconscious and cannot be easily retrieved.

sex (vs. gender): the assignment of a person as either male or female on the basis of key biological characteristics: for example, **chromosomes**, external genitals, internal sexual apparatus (prostate, uterus), testicles or ovaries, secondary sexual characteristics (breasts, beard, etc.), and brain.

somatization: this usually refers to the development of bodily symptoms in the place of a psychological and/or emotional response.

splitting/splitting processes: a defence mechanism by which the self and the other are split into two or more parts, in order to cope with primitive anxiety or fear of annihilation. The split-off part of the self can then be projected into the other object. For instance, the self can be split into "good" and "bad", and the bad aspects of the self are then projected into the other, who is then perceived as perse-cutory and attacking; extreme forms of this mechanism are present in psychotic states.

Thanatos: Greek god of death used by Freud to personify the "death instinct".

transference: psychoanalytic term to describe the process by which the patient unconsciously transfers onto the psychoanalyst feelings and perceptions that originated in earlier experiences, usually in relation to the parents or significant others. It is through working on the transference in therapy that understanding and change are believed to occur.

transitional object: psychoanalytic term first used by D. W. Winnicott to describe a material object (e.g. a blanket, a doll) to which an infant becomes deeply attached and which assists her or him as she or he begins to separate from the mother/care-giver to become more autonomous. This is a normal part of the infant's matura-tional process.

virilization: the induction or development of male secondary sexual characteristics, especially the induction of such characteristics in a female (e.g. clitoral enlargement, growth of facial and body hair, development of a male hair line).

Weltanschauung: world view.

APPENDIX A

Introduction to
"Gender Identity Disorders in Children and Adolescents Guidance for Management"

Professor Peter Hill
Formerly Chair of the Executive Committee of the Child and Adolescent
Psychiatry Section of The Royal College of Psychiatrists

The child who presents with an insistent wish to be a gender other than their biological sex is a challenging experience for clinicians. Demands may be made for treatments or operations which have adverse, as well as desired, effects or which may be frankly dangerous. As the child matures through adolescence such demands continue and the young teenager may appear quite desperate, even to the extent of self-harm. At this point, or even earlier, the parents may also join the chorus, demanding or opposing radical treatment interventions.

It has been apparent that different clinicians and different clinical centres differ somewhat in their responses to such demands and in their willingness to offer surgical or endocrine treatment. This is sometimes known to patients and their families who may therefore manage to get themselves referred to a centre or individual who offers a favoured approach. Sometimes this results in considerable expense for the families concerned.

With these children and their families in mind, a group of experienced clinicians who have a specialist interest in the area of gender identity have met and formulated guidance for the management of gender identity disorders in the young. This has been supported by the Executive Committee of the Child and Adolescent Psychiatry Section of the Royal College of Psychiatrists and it is hoped that it will lead to good practice across services in various countries. Much thought and discussion have gone into its preparation so that there is unanimity among those who have contributed to it. For this reason it is to be taken most seriously. Its ultimate aim is to benefit the clinical management of children and young teenagers with disturbances of gender identity by ensuring that they receive optimal management and avoid short cuts.

GENDER IDENTITY DISORDERS IN CHILDREN AND ADOLESCENTS GUIDANCE FOR MANAGEMENT

Council Report CR63   January 1998

© 1998 The Royal College of Psychiatrists

The authors are Domenico Di Ceglie, Claire Sturge and Adrian Sutton, and the guidance was drafted on behalf of the Executive Committee of the Child and Adolescent Psychiatry Section of The Royal College of Psychiatrists.

The following professionals participated in an informal consultative meeting about this guidance following an international conference **'A Stranger In My Own Body - Atypical Gender Identity Development and Mental Health'** in November 1996.

Domenico Di Ceglie, (Chairman) GIDU Portman Clinic, London

Susan J. Bradley, Clarke Institute, Toronto, Canada

Caroline Brain, St George's Hospital, London

Susan Coates, Columbia University, New York, USA

Peggy Cohen-Kettenis, University Hospital, Utrecht, The Netherlands

Richard Green, GIC Charing Cross Hospital, London

Peter Hill, St George's Hospital, London

Bern Meyenburg, Frankfurt University, Germany

Don Montgomery, GIC Charing Cross Hospital, London

Friedemann Pfafflin, Ulm University, Germany

Claire Sturge, Northwick Park Hospital, London

Katherine Weinberg, Harvard Medical School & Children's Hospital, Boston USA

Peter Wilson, Young Minds, London.

INTRODUCTION

Gender identity disorders in children and adolescents are rare and complex conditions. They are often associated with emotional and behavioural difficulties. Intense distress is often experienced, particularly in adolescence.

Gender identity disorders can be seen as states in which, in the course of the young person's psychosexual development, there is an atypical gender identity organisation. The young person experiences their phenotypic sex as incongruous with his or her own sense of gender identity.

This predicament, which is commoner in boys, is characterised by:

- A desire to be the other sex
- Cross-dressing
- Play with games, toys and objects usually associated with the other sex and avoidance of play normally associated with their sex
- Preference for playmates or friends of the sex with which the child identifies
- Dislike of bodily sexual characteristics and functions

It is important to consider these states as different from those seen in adults because:

(a)   A developmental process is involved (physical, psychological and sexual).
(b)   There is greater fluidity and variability in the outcome, with only a small proportion becoming transsexuals or transvestites, the majority of affected children eventually developing a homosexual orientation and some a heterosexual orientation without transvestism or transsexualism.

Similarly, pre-pubertal and post-pubertal groups need to be differentiated. There is greater fluidity and likelihood of change in the former.

Phenomenologically there is a qualitative difference between the way such children and young people present their predicament from presentations involving delusions or other psychotic symptoms. Delusional beliefs about the sexual body or gender can occur in psychotic conditions but they can be distinguished from the phenomena of a gender identity disorder as outlined in this paper.

There are issues of nosology because current classification systems seem to suggest that gender identity disorders in childhood are equivalent to those in adulthood and that the one inevitably leads to the other. This is not the case.

MANAGEMENT
Psychological and Social Interventions

In terms of management, we propose the following broad guidance:

1. A full assessment including a family evaluation is essential as other emotional and behavioural problems are very common and unresolved issues in the child's environment are often present e.g. loss. Separation problems are particularly common in the younger group.

2. Therapy should aim to assist development, particularly that of gender identity, by exploring the nature and characteristics of the atypical organisation of the child's or adolescent's gender identity. It should focus on ameliorating the comorbid problems and difficulties in the child's life and in reducing the distress being experienced by the child (from his or her gender identity problem and other difficulties).

3. Recognition and acceptance of the gender identity problem and removing the secrecy can bring considerable relief.

4. Decisions about the extent to which to allow the child to assume a gender role congruous to his or her sense of gender identity are difficult and the child and family need support in tolerating uncertainty and anxiety in relation to the gender identity development and how best to manage it.

    This includes problems of whether to inform others of the child's disorder and how others e.g. schools, in the child's life, should respond to the child (for example, if the child wishes to attend school using the clothing and name of the other sex). Professional network meetings can be very useful in finding appropriate solutions to these problems.

In all the above, therapeutic intervention as early as possible in a child's life is indicated and an optimistic approach to improving the child's life and, in some cases, altering secondarily the gender identity development.

The role of the child and adolescent mental health services may be three-fold:

■   Direct assessment and treatment of the mental health difficulties of the child/adolescent.

■ Where children or adolescents meet the criteria of a gender identity disorder under DSM-IV or ICD-10, there should be a referral for assessment and/or treatment in a multi-disciplinary gender identity specialist service which includes the input of child and adolescent mental health professionals.

■ Provision of consultation/liaison arrangements with a paediatric endocrinologist for the purpose of physical assessment, education about growth and endocrinological issues and involvement in any decision about physical interventions.

Physical Intervention

This should be addressed in the context of adolescent development. Identity issues and beliefs in adolescents are complex. They may become firmly held and strongly expressed. This may give a false impression of irreversibility; more fluidity may return again at a later stage. For this reason, i.e. the possibility of change of outcome, and because the effect of early physical and hormonal treatments are unknown, physical interventions should be delayed as long as it is clinically appropriate.

Before any physical intervention is considered, extensive exploration of the issues to do with the psychological, family and social network aspects should be undertaken.

Pressure for physical interventions because of an adolescent's level of distress can be great and in such circumstances, a referral to a child and adolescent multi-disciplinary specialist service should be considered.

In order for adolescents and those with parental responsibility to make properly informed decisions, it is recommended that they have experience of themselves in the post-pubertal state of their biological sex. Where, for clinical reasons, it is thought to be in the patient's interest to intervene before this, this must be managed within a specialist service with paediatric endocrinological advice and more than one psychiatric opinion.

Broadly, physical interventions fall into three groups which can be thought of as stages:

(a) *Interventions which are wholly reversible* – these include hypo-thalamic blockers which result in suppression of oestrogen or testosterone production. They can suppress some aspects of secondary sexual characteristics.

(b) *Interventions which are partially reversible* – these include hormonal interventions which masculinise or feminise the body. Reversal may involve surgical intervention.

(c) *Interventions which are irreversible* – these are the surgical procedures.

The decision to move to physical interventions should be made, whenever possible, within the context of a multi-disciplinary specialist service including a child and adolescent psychiatrist, a paediatric endocrinologist and other child and adolescent mental health professionals.

The staged process recommended here is considered safe as it keeps options open through the first two stages. (A small minority of patients eventually come to regret gender reassignment). Moving from one stage to another should not occur until there has been adequate time for the young person fully to assimilate the effects of intervention to date. Interventions which are irreversible (surgical procedures) should not be carried out prior to adulthood at age 18. As adulthood is reached, any referral on should be to an adult gender identity specialist service. Any surgical intervention should not be carried out prior to adulthood, or prior to a real life experience for the young person of living in the gender role of the sex with which they identify for at least two years. The threshold of 18 should be seen as an eligibility criterion and not an indicator in itself for more active intervention as the needs of many adults may also be best met by a cautious, evolving approach.

Summary

Gender identity disorders in children and adolescents:

- Are rare
- Are commoner in boys
- Are developmental
- Involve psychological, biological, family and social issues
- Have an outcome that cannot be easily predicted
- Require early and careful assessment and attention to emotional and developmental needs
- The approach to requests for physical interventions should be cautious, involve extensive psychological, family and social exploration, take into account adverse effects on physical growth, and be undertaken only within specialist teams

A large element of management is promoting the young person's tolerance of uncertainty and resisting pressures for quick solutions.

Surgical intervention cannot be justified until adulthood.

Suggested reading list

American Psychiatric Association (1994)
Diagnostic and Statistical Manual of Mental Disorders, (4th edn)
(DSM-IV).Washington DC: APA.

Coates, S. Friedman, R.C. & Wolfe, S. (1991)
The aetiology of boyhood gender identity disorder: A model for integrating temperament, development and psychodynamics.
Psychoanalytic Dialogues, **1**, 481-523.

____ & Person, E.S. (1985)
Extreme boyhood femininity: Isolated behaviour or pervasive disorder?
Journal of the American Academy of Child and Adolescent Psychiatry, **24**, 702-709.

Cohen-Kettenis, P.T. and van Goozen, S.H.M. (1997)
Sex reassignment of adolescent transsexuals: A follow-up study.
Journal of the American Academy of Child and Adolescent Psychiatry, **36**,
263-271.

Di Ceglie, D. (1995)
Gender identity disorders in children and adolescents.
British Journal of Hospital Medicine, **53**, 251-256.

____ (ed.) (1998)
*A Stranger in My Own Body - Atypical Gender Identity Development and
Mental Health*. London: Karnac Books, 1998.

Green, R. (1974)
Sexual Identity Conflict in Children and Adults.
New York: Basic Books.

____ (1994)
Atypical psychosexual development. In *Child and Adolescent
Psychiatry: Modern Approaches* (3rd edn) (eds M. Rutter, E. Taylor
and L. Hersov), pp. 749-758. Oxford: Blackwell Scientific.

Money, J. (1994)
The concept of gender identity disorder in childhood and
adolescence after 39 years.
Journal of Sex and Marital Therapy, **20**, 163-177.

Zucker, K. & Bradley, S. (1995)
*Gender Identity Disorder and Psychosexual Problems in Children and
Adolescents*.
New York and London: Guilford.

APPENDIX B

The Gender Identity Development Unit at the Portman Clinic, London

The Gender Identity Development Unit, at the Portman Clinic, provides a national specialist service within the Tavistock and Portman NHS Trust. The Trust is a national and international mental health training centre, providing training, clinical services, research, and organizational consultancy. The Unit is staffed by a multidisciplinary group of professionals, with contributions from child and adolescent psychiatry, psychotherapy, clinical psychology, social work, and paediatric endocrinology. It offers integrated, comprehensive, multidisciplinary assessment and therapeutic programmes to children and adolescents up to the age of 18 years with gender identity problems and intersex disorders. It also offers counselling to children and families where a parent presents with a gender identity disorder, and it provides expert advice to the courts.

The Gender Identity Development Clinic was founded by Dr Domenico Di Ceglie in 1989 in the Department of Child Psychiatry at St George's Hospital in London, following a regular workshop on gender identity problems that had been held at the Croydon Child and Family Psychiatric Clinic from 1986 until the St George's clinic opened. The service transferred to the Tavistock and Portman NHS Trust in January 1996. The number of referrals has continually increased since the formation of the service, and to date the service has seen about 150 children and adolescents.

In addition to offering a service, the Unit aims to provide training and research in this area. It contributes to professional education through running seminars, teaching in professional training courses, and organizing national and international conferences. It has collaborated with the media in programmes that help to promote a better understanding in society of gender identity problems in children and adolescents, and to reduce the stigma and taboo that surround these unusual experiences. The Unit works with schools and other social agencies in trying to integrate these children and teenagers into their social networks.

Through the clinical experience accumulated over the years, the Unit has contributed significantly to the drafting of The Royal College of Psychiatrists' "Guidance For the Management of Gender Identity Disorders in Children and Adolescents".

The Unit is well integrated within the Trust, and its staff participate in various multidisciplinary training events within the Trust. A self-help organization, called "Mermaids" (see Appendix C), grew out of groups run for the parents of the young people seen by the service.

Contact address:

Gender Identity Development Unit, Portman Clinic, 8 Fitzjohns Avenue, London NW3 5NA, U.K.

Tel: 44+ 171 794 8262;   Fax: 44+ 171 447 3748
email: GIDU@Tavi-Port.demon.co.uk

APPENDIX C

Mermaids

"Mermaids" is a support group formed by a group of parents, all bringing a child to the Gender Identity Development Unit, initially at St George's Hospital, London, and currently at the Portman Clinic, who were brought together as a result of their children's long-standing gender identity issues. They have been able to support each other and their children through the difficulties and trauma that gender issues commonly bring to families. They have identified a need to form a support group to aid other families, children, and teenagers in similar situations.

Mermaids' aim is simple:

• We aim to support children and teenagers who are trying to cope with gender identity issues.

In support of this aim, we also intend to:

• offer support to parents, families, carers, and others;
• raise awareness about gender issues amongst professionals (e.g. teachers, doctors, social services, etc.) and the general public;
• campaign for the recognition of this issue and the increase in professional services.

Mermaids can be contacted initially by writing to: BM Mermaids, London WC1N 3XX, U.K. (an SAE would be appreciated).

REFERENCES

Achenbach, T. M., & Edelbrock, C. (1983). *Manual for the Child Behavior Checklist and Revised Child Behavior Profile*. Burlington: University of Vermont, Department of Psychiatry.

Achenbach, T. M., & Edelbrock, C. (1986). *Manual for the Teacher's Report Form and Teacher Version of the Revised Child Behavior Profile*. Burlington: University of Vermont, Department of Psychiatry.

Ainsworth, M., Blehar, M., Waters, E., & Wall, S. (1978). *Patterns of Attachment: A Psychological Study of the Strange Situation*. Hillsdale, NJ: Lawrence Erlbaum Associates.

Allen, L. S., Hines, M., Shryne, J. E., & Gorski, R. A. (1989). Two sexually dimorphic cell groups in the human brain. *Journal of Neuroscience, 9*: 497–506.

APA (1987). *Diagnostic and Statistical Manual of Mental Disorders* (3rd ed., rev.). Washington, DC: American Psychiatric Association.

APA (1994). *Diagnostic and Statistical Manual of Mental Disorders* (4th ed.). Washington, DC: American Psychiatric Association.

Armstrong, C. N., & Marshall, A. J. (Eds.) (1964). *Intersexuality in Vertebrates Including Man*. London/New York: Academic Press.

Bailey, J. M., & Pillard, R. C. (1991). A genetic study of male sexual orientation. *Archives of General Psychiatry, 48*: 1089–1096.

Bailey, J. M., & Zucker, K. J. (1995). Childhood sex-typed behavior and sexual orientation: a conceptual analysis and quantitative review. *Developmental Psychology, 31*: 43–55.

Baker Miller, J. (1976). *Towards a New Psychology of Women*. Harmondsworth: Penguin.

Bancroft, J. (1989). *Human Sexuality and Its Problems*. London: Churchill Livingstone.

Beebe, B., & Stern, D. (1977). Engagement-disengagement and early object interactions. In: A. Siegman & S. Feldstein (Ed.), *Communicative Structures and Psychic Structures* (pp. 35–55). Hillside, NJ: Lawrence Erlbaum Associates.

Beitchman, J. H., Zucker, K. J., Hood, J. E., Dacosta, S. A., & Akman, D. (1991). A review of the short term effects of child sexual abuse. *Child Abuse and Neglect, 15*: 537–556.

Beitchman, J. H., Zucker, K. J., Hood, J. E., Dacosta, S. A., Akman, D., & Cassavia, E. (1992). A review of the long term effects of child sexual abuse. *Child Abuse and Neglect, 16*: 101–118.

Bell, A. P., Weinberg, M. S., & Hammersmith, S. K. (1981). *Sexual Preference: Its Development in Men and Women*. Bloomington, IN: Indiana University Press.

Bentler, P. M. (1976). A typology of transsexualism: gender identity theory and data. *Archives of Sexual Behavior, 5*: 567–584.

Bettelheim, B. (1982). *Freud and Man's Soul*. London: Fontana.

Bion, W. R. (1957). On arrogance. In: *Second Thoughts*. New York: Jason Aronson, 1967.

Bion, W. R. (1959). Attacks on linking. *International Journal of Psycho-Analysis, 40* (Parts 5–6).

Bion, W. R. (1962). A theory of thinking. *International Journal of Psycho-Analysis, 53*.

Birkenfeld-Adams, A. (1998). "Quality of attachment in young boys with gender identity disorder: a comparison to clinical and nonreferred control boys." Unpublished doctoral dissertation, York University, Downsview, Ontario.

Birkstead-Breen, D. (1996). Phallus, penis and mental space. *International Journal of Psycho-Analysis, 77* (4): 650–651.

Bleiberg, E., Jackson, L., & Ross, J. L. (1986). Gender identity disorder and object loss. *Journal of the American Academy of Child and Adolescent Psychiatry, 25* (1): 58–67.

Bleier, R. (1984). *Science and Gender: A Critique of Biology and Its Theories of Women*. Oxford: Pergamon Press.

Blumenthal, S. J., & Kupfer, D. J. (1989). Overview of early detection and treatment strategies for suicidal behavior in young people. In: M. R.

Feinleib (Ed.), *Report of the Secretary's Task Force on Youth Suicide, Vol. 3: Prevention and Interventions in Youth Suicide* (pp. 239–252). US Department of Health & Human Services. DHHS Pub. No. (ADM) 89–1623. Washington, DC: U.S. Government Print Office.

Bowler, C., & Collacott, R. A. (1993). Cross-dressing in men with learning disabilities. *British Journal of Psychiatry, 162*: 556–558.

Breen, D. (1993). *The Gender Conundrum. The New Library of Psychoanalysis.* London: Routledge.

Brent, D. A. (1997). Practitioner review: the aftercare of adolescents with deliberate self-harm. *Journal of Child Psychology and Psychiatry, 38*: 277–286.

Briggs, J. (1986). "Expecting the unexpected: Canadian Inuit training for an experimental life-style." Paper delivered to the 4th International Conference on hunting and gathering societies, London School of Economics.

Britton, R. (1989). The missing link. In: R. Britton, M. Feldman, & E. O'Shaughnessy, *The Oedipus Complex Today, Clinical Implications,* edited by J. Steiner. London: Karnac Books.

Britton, R., Feldman, M., & O'Shaughnessy, E. (1989). *The Oedipus Complex Today, Clinical Implications,* edited by J. Steiner. London: Karnac Books.

Burgess, A., & Hartman, C. (1993), Children's drawings. *Child Abuse and Neglect, 17*: 161–168.

Burns, A., Farrell, M., & Brown, J. C. (1990). Clinical features of patients attending a gender-identity clinic. *British Journal of Psychiatry, 157*: 265–268.

Butler-Sloss, E. (1988). *Report of the Inquiry into Child Abuse in Cleveland.* London: HMSO.

Byne, W. (1994). The biological evidence challenged. *Scientific American* (May): 26–31.

Carlson, V., & Cicchetti, D. (1989). *Child Maltreatment: Theory and Research on the Causes and Consequences of Child Abuse and Neglect.* Cambridge: Cambridge University Press.

Case of X, Y and Z v. United Kingdom (1977). European Court of Human Rights (75/1995/581/667) , Strasbourg.

Cass, V. C. (1979). Homosexual identity formation: a theoretical model. *Journal of Homosexuality, 4*: 219–235.

Centrepoint (1996). *Annual Statistics Centrepoint Projects 1995–1996.* London: Centrepoint Soho.

Chasseguet-Smirgel, J. (1985). *Creativity and Perversion.* London: Free Association Books.

Children Act (1989). London: HMSO

Coates, S. (1985). Extreme boyhood femininity: Overview and new research findings. In Z. DeFries, R. C. Friedman, & R. Corn (Eds.), *Sexuality: New Perspectives* (pp. 101–124). Westport, CT: Greenwood Publishing.

Coates, S. (1992). The etiology of boyhood gender identity disorder: an integrative model. In: J. W. Barron, M. N. Eagle, & D. L. Wolitzky (Eds.), *Interface of Psychoanalysis and Psychology* (pp. 245–265). Washington, DC: American Psychological Association.

Coates, S., Friedman, R., & Wolfe, S. (1991). The aetiology of boyhood gender identity disorder: a model for integrating temperament, development and psychodynamics. *Psychoanalytic Dialogues, 1*: 481–523.

Coates, S., & Person, E. (1985). Extreme boyhood feminity: isolated behavior or pervasive disorder? *Journal of Academic Child Psychiatry, 24*: 702–709.

Coates, S., & Wolfe, S. (1995). Gender identity disorder in boys: the interface of constitution and early experience. *Psychoanalytic Inquiry, 15*: 6–38.

Cohen, J. (1957). The factorial structure of the WAIS between early adulthood and old age. *Journal of Consulting Psychology, 21*: 283–290.

Cohen, L., de Ruiter, C., Ringelberg, H., & Cohen-Kettenis, P. T. (1997). Psychological functioning of adolescent transsexuals: personality and psychopathology. *Journal of Clinical Psychology, 53*: 187–196.

Cohen-Kettenis, P. T., & van Goozen, S. H. M (1997). Sex reassignment of adolescent transsexuals: a follow-up study. *Journal of the American Academy of Child and Adolescent Psychiatry, 36*: 263–271.

Collaer, M. L., & Hines, M. (1995). Human behavioral sex differences: a role for gonadal hormones during early development? *Psychological Bulletin, 118* (1): 55–107.

Cotgrove, A., & Kolvin, I. (1996). Child sexual abuse. *Hospital Update* (September): 401–406.

Crisp, A. H. (1967). Anorexia nervosa. *Hospital Medicine, 1*: 713–718.

D'Augelli, A. R., & Hershberger, S. L. (1993). Lesbian, gay, and bisexual youth in community settings: personal challenges and mental health problems. *American Journal of Community Psychology, 21*: 421–448.

Davidson, R. J., & Fox, N. (1982). Asymmetrical brain activity discriminates between positive versus negative affective stimuli in human infants. *Science, 218*: 1235–1237.

Davies, D. (1996). Working with young people. In D. Davies & C. Neal (Eds.), *Pink Therapy: A Guide for Counsellors and Therapists Working with Lesbian, Gay and Bisexual Clients* (pp. 131–148). Buckingham: Open University Press.

Diamond, M. (1997). Sexual identity and sexual orientation in children with traumatised or ambiguous genitalia. *Journal of Sex Research, 14* (2): 199–211.

Di Ceglie, D. (1996). Atypical gender identity development. *Young Minds Magazine, 26* (July): 14–16.

Di Ceglie, D. (1991). La richiesta di cambiare sesso: la curiosita del terapeuta. In: *Problemi di Identita Sessuale nell' Adolescenza*. Bologna: Editrice Clueb.

Di Ceglie, D. (1995). Gender identity disorders in children and adolescents. *British Journal of Hospital Medicine, 53* (6) 251–256.

Doerner, G., Rohde, W., Stahl, F., Krell, L., & Masius, W. (1975). Neuroendocrine condition, a predisposition for homosexuality in men. *Archives of Sexual Behavior, 4*: 1–8.

Eaton, W., & Von Bargen, D. (1981). Asynchronous development of gender understanding in preschool children. *Child Development, 52*: 1020–1027.

Ekman, P. (1983). Automatic nervous system activity distinguishes among emotions. *Science, 221*: 1208–1210.

Emch, M. (1944), On the "need to know" as related to identification and acting out. *International Journal of Psycho-Analysis, 25*: 13–19.

Epstein, A. W. (1960). Fetishism: a study of its psychopathology with particular reference to a proposed disorder in brain mechanisms as an etiological factor. *Journal of Nervous and Mental Disease, 130*: 107–119.

Erikson, E. H. (1955). The problem of ego identity. *Journal of the American Psychoanalytic Association, 4*: 56–121.

Erikson, E. H. (1963). *Childhood and Society* (2nd. ed.). New York: W. W. Norton.

Exner, J. E. (1990). *A Rorschach Workbook for the Comprehensive System* (3rd ed.). Asheville, NC: Rorschach Workshops.

Fedoroff, J. P. (1988). Buspirone hydrochloride in the treatment of transvestic fetishism. *Journal of Clinical Psychiatry, 49*: 408–409.

Fedoroff, J. P. (1992). Buspirone hydrochloride in the treatment of an atypical paraphilia. *Archives of Sexual Behavior, 21*: 401–406.

Fonagy, P., Steele, M., Moran, G., Steele, H., & Higgett, A. (1990). Measuring the ghosts in the nursery: an empirical study of the relation between parents' mental representations of childhood experiences and their infants' security of attachment. *Journal of the American Psychoanalytic Association., 41*: 957–989.

Fonagy, P., Steele, M., Steele, H., Leigh, T., Kennedy, R., Mattoon, G., & Target, M. (1995). Attachment, the reflective self, and borderline states: the predictive specificity of the adult attachment interview and pathological emotional development. In: S. Goldberg, R. Muir, & J. Kerr (Ed.), *Attachment Theory* (pp. 233–278). Hillsdale, NJ: Analytic Press.

Fraiberg, S. (1982). Pathological defenses in infancy. *Psychoanalytic Quarterly, 51*: 612–635.

Fraiberg, S., Adelson, E., & Shapiro, V. (1975). Ghosts in the nursery: a psychoanalytic approach to the problem of impaired infant–mother relationships. *Journal of the American Academy of Child Psychiatry, 14*: 387–422.

Freud, A. (1958). Adolescence. *Psychoanalytic Study of the Child, 13*: 255–278.

Freud, S. (1905d). *Three Essays on the Theory of Sexuality. Standard Edition, 7.*

Freud, S. (1905e). A fragment of an analysis of a case of hysteria. *Standard Edition, 7.*

Freud, S. (1909b). Analysis of a phobia in a five-year-old boy. *Standard Edition, 10.*

Freud, S. (1920a). The psychogenesis of a case of homosexuality in a woman. *Standard Edition, 18.*

Freud, S. (1931b). Female sexuality. *Standard Edition, 21.*

Gaensbauer, T., & Harmon, R. (1982), Attachment behavior in abused/neglected and premature infants: implications for the concept of attachment. In: R. Emde & R. Harmon (Eds.), *The Development of Attachment and Affiliate Systems* (pp. 263–280). New York: Plenum Press.

Garden, A. S. (1998). *Paediatric & Adolescent Gynaecology*. London/Sydney/Auckland: Arnold.

Garfinkel, H. (1967). *Studies in Ethnomethodology*. Englewood Cliffs, NJ: Prentice-Hall.

George, C., Kaplan, N., & Main, M. (1985). "The Berkeley Adult Attachment Interview." Unpublished manuscript, Department of Psychology, University of California, Berkeley.

Ghent, E. (1990). Masochism, submission, surrender: masochism as a perversion of surrender. *Contemporary Psychoanalysis, 26*: 108–136.

Ghent, E. (1994). Empathy—whence & whither? Commentary on papers by Kiersky & Beebe, Hayes and Kiersky & Beebe. *Psychoanalytic Dialogues, 4*: 473–486.

Gibson, P. (1989). Gay male and lesbian youth suicide. In: M. R. Feinleib (Ed.), *Report of the Secretary's Task Force on Youth Suicide, Vol. 3:*

Prevention and Interventions in Youth Suicide (pp. 110–142). US Department of Health & Human Services. DHHS Pub. No. (ADM) 89–1623. Washington, DC: U.S. Government Printing Office.

Glasser, M. (1996). Masculinity, femininity and internalisation in male homosexuals. *The British Psycho-Analytical Society Bulletin, 32* (11): 3.

Goffman, E. (1963). *Stigma.* Englewood Cliffs, NJ: Prentice-Hall.

Goggin, M. (1993). Gay and lesbian adolescence. In S. Moore & D. Rosenthal (Eds.), *Sexuality in Adolescence* (pp. 102–123). London: Routledge.

Golombok, S., & Fivush, R. (1994). *Gender Development.* Cambridge: Cambridge University Press.

Gonsiorek, J. C. (1991). The empirical basis for the demise of the illness model of homosexuality. In: J. C. Gonsiorek & J. D. Weinrich (Eds.), *Homosexuality: Research Implications for Public Policy* (pp. 115–136). London: Sage.

Gonsiorek, J. C., & Weinrich, J. D. (1991). The definition and scope of sexual orientation. In: J. C. Gonsiorek & J. D. Weinrich (Eds.), *Homosexuality: Research Implications for Public Policy* (pp. 1–12). London: Sage.

Gooren, L. J., van Kessel, H., & Harmsen-Louman, W. (1984). Estrogen positive feedback on LH secretion in transsexuality. *Psychoneuroendocrinology, 9 (3):* 249–259.

Green, R. (1974). *Sexual Identity Conflict in Children and Adults.* London: Duckworth; New York: Basic Books.

Green, R. (1978). Sexual identity of 37 children raised by homosexual or transsexual parents. *American Journal of Psychiatry, 135:* 692–697.

Green, R. (1987). *The "Sissy Boy Syndrome" and the Development of Homosexuality.* New Haven, CT: Yale University Press.

Green, R. (1992). *Sexual Science and the Law.* Cambridge, MA: Harvard University Press.

Green, R., Williams, K., & Goodman, M. (1982). Ninety-nine "tomboys" and "non-tomboys": behavioral contrasts and demographic similarities. *Archives of Sexual Behavior, 11:* 247–266.

Green, R., Williams, K., & Harper, J. (1980). Cross-sex identity: peer group integration and the double standard of childhood sex-typing. In: J. Samson (Ed.), *Childhood and sexuality* (pp. 542–548). Montreal: Editions Etudes Vivantes.

Greenberg, M. T., Speltz, M. L., DeKlyen, M., & Endriga, M. C. (1991). Attachment security in preschoolers with and without externalizing behavior problems: a replication. *Development and Psychopathology, 3:* 413–430.

Hamer, D. H., Hu, S., Magnuson, V. L., Hu, N., & Pattatucci, A. M. L. (1993). A linkage between DNA markers on the X chromosome and male sexual orientation. *Science, 261*: 321–326.

Hammer, E. (1958). *The Clinical Application of Projective Drawings*. Springfield, IL: Charles C Thomas, 1980.

Harry, J. (1983). Parasuicide, gender, and gender deviance. *Journal of Health and Social Behaviour, 24*: 350–361.

Harry, J. (1986). "Adolescent suicide and sexual identity issues." Submitted to the National Institutes of Mental Health for the Secretary's Conference on Adolescent Suicide, Washington, DC, May 8–9.

Heimann, P. (1951). A contribution to the re-evaluation of the Oedipus complex—the early stages. In: M. Klein, P. Heimann, & R. Money-Kyrle, *New Directions in Psychoanalysis*. London: Karnac Books, 1989.

Herdt, G. (1996a). Introduction: third sexes and third genders. In: G. Herdt (Ed.), *Third Sex, Third Gender: Beyond Sexual Dimorphism in Culture and History*. New York: Zone Books.

Herdt, G. (1996b). Mistaken sex: culture, biology and the third sex in New Guinea. In: G. Herdt (Ed.), *Third Sex, Third Gender: Beyond Sexual Dimorphism in Culture and History*. New York: Zone Books.

Hetrick, E. S., & Martin, A. D. (1987). Developmental issues and their resolution for gay and lesbian adolescents. *Journal of Homosexuality, 14*: 25–43.

Hooker, E. A. (1957). The adjustment of the male overt homosexual. *Journal of Projective Techniques, 21*: 17–31.

Hu, S., Pattatucci, A. M. L., Patterson, C., Li, L., Fulker, D. W., Cherny, S. S., Kruglyak, L., & Hamer, D. H. (1995). Linkage between sexual orientation and chromosome Xq28 in males but not in females. *Nature Genetics, 11*: 248–256.

Hurry, A. (1977). "My ambition is to be dead." The analysis of motives and reasons for suicide behaviour in an adolescent girl, with particular reference to the relationship between the adolescent process and suicide. Part I: Case study. *Journal of Child Psychotherapy, 4* (3): 66–83.

Hurry, A. (1978). "My ambition is to be dead." The analysis of motives and reasons for suicide behaviour in an adolescent girl, with particular reference to the relationship between the adolescent process and suicide, Part II: Past and current findings on suicide in adolescence. Part III: Discussion. *Journal of Child Psychotherapy, 4* (4): 69–85.

Huxley, P. J., Kenna, J. C., & Brandon, S. B. (1981). Partnership in transsexualism, Part I: Paired and non-paired groups. *Archives of Sexual Behavior, 10*: 133–141.

Imber-Black, E. (Ed.) (1993). *Secrets in Families and Family Therapy.* New York: W. W. Norton.

Imperato-McGinley, J., Peterson, R. E., Gautier, T., & Sturla, E. (1979a). Androgens and the evolution of male gender identity among male pseudohermaphrodites with 5-alpha-reductase deficiency. *New England Journal of Medicine, 300*: 1233–1237.

Imperato-McGinley, J., Peterson, R. E., Stoller, R., & Goodwin, W. E. (1979b). Male pseudohermaphroditism secondary to 17-hydroxy-steroid dehydrogenase deficiency: gender role change with puberty. *Journal of Clinical Endocrinology and Metabolism, 49* (3): 391–395.

Ipp, H. R. (1986). "Object relations of feminine boys: a Rorschach assessment." Unpublished doctoral dissertation, York University, Downsview, Ontario.

Isay, R. A. (1989). *Being Homosexual: Gay Men and Their Development.* London: Penguin.

Isay, R. A. (1990). Psychoanalytic theory and the therapy of gay men. In: D. P. McWhirter, S. A. Sanders, & J. M. Reinisch (Eds.), *Homosexuality/Heterosexuality: Concepts of Sexual Orientation* (pp. 283–303). Oxford: Oxford University Press.

James, A. (1993). *Childhood Identities: Self and Social Relationships in the Experience of the Child.* Edinburgh: Edinburgh University Press.

James, A. (in press). Embodied being(s): understanding the self and the body in childhood. In: A. Prout (Ed.), *The Body, Childhood and Society.* London: Macmillan.

James, A., Jenks, C., & Prout, A. (1998). *Theorising Childhood.* London: Polity Press.

James, A., & Prout, A. (1990). *Constructing and Reconstructing Childhood.* Basingstoke: Falmer.

Jenks, C. (1982). Constituting the child. In: C. Jenks (Ed.), *The Sociology of Childhood—Essential Readings.* London: Batsford.

Jost, A. (1947). Recherches sur la differenciation sexuelle de l'embryon de lapin. III Role des gonades foetales dans la differenciation sexuelle somatique. *Archives d'Anatomie Microscopique et de Morphologie Experimentale, 36*: 271.

Jukes, A. (1993). *Why Men Hate Women.* London: Free Association Books.

Kerbeshian, J., & Burd, L. (1991). Tourette syndrome and recurrent paraphilic masturbatory fantasy. *Canadian Journal of Psychiatry, 36*: 155–157.

Kinsey, A. C., Pomeroy, W. B., & Martin, C. E. (1948). *Sexual Behavior in the Human Male.* Philadelphia, PA: Saunders.

Kitzinger, C., & Wilkinson, S. (1995). Transitions from heterosexuality to lesbianism: the discursive production of lesbian identities. *Developmental Psychology*, 31: 95–104.

Klagsbrun, M., & Bowlby, J. (1976). Responses to separation from parents: a clinical test for young children. *British Journal of Projective Psychology*, 21: 7–21.

Klein, M. (1932a). The effects of early anxiety-situations on the sexual development of the girl. In: *The Psycho-Analysis of Children* (pp. 194–239). London: Hogarth Press, 1975.

Klein, M. (1932b). The effects of early anxiety-situations on the sexual development of the boy. In: *The Psycho-Analysis of Children* (pp. 240–268). London: Hogarth Press, 1975.

Klein, M. (1936). Weaning. In: *Love, Guilt and Reparation and Other Works*. London: Hogarth Press, 1975.

Klein, M. (1945). The Oedipus Complex in the light of early anxiety. In: *Love, Guilt and Reparation and Other Works*. London : Hogarth Press, 1975.

Klein, M. (1946). *Envy and Gratitude and Other Works 1946 to 1963*. London: Hogarth Press.

Klein, M. (1961). Narrative of a child analysis. In: *The Writings of Melanie Klein, Vol. 4*. London: Hogarth Press.

Kohlberg, L. A. (1966). A cognitive-developmental analysis of children's sex-role concepts and attitudes. In: E. E. Maccoby (Ed.), *The Development of Sex Differences*. Stanford, CA: Stanford University Press.

Kolers, N. (1986). "Some ego functions in boys with gender identity disturbance." Unpublished doctoral dissertation, York University, Downsview, Ontario.

Kruesi, M. J. P., Fine, S., Valladares, L., Phillips, R. A., & Rapoport, J. L. (1992). Paraphilias: a double-blind crossover comparison of clomiprimine versus desipramine. *Archives of Sexual Behavior*, 21: 587–593.

Kuiper, A. J. (1991). *Transseksualiteit: evaluatie van een geslachtsaanpassende behandeling*. Amsterdam: Free University Press.

Kuiper, A. J., & Cohen-Kettenis, P. T. (1988). Sex reassignment surgery: a study of 141 Dutch transsexuals. *Archives of Sexual Behaviour*, 17: 439–458.

Laufer, M., & Laufer, M. E. (1984). *Adolescence and Developmental Breakdown: A Psychoanalytic View*. New Haven, CT/London. Yale University Press.

Lemercier, G. (1966). *Psicoanalisi in monastero: dialoghi col Cristo*. Milan: Valentino Bompiani, 1968. [First published in French as *Dialogues avec Le Christ: Moines en psychoanalyse*.]

LeVay, S. (1991). A difference in hypothalamic structure between heterosexual and homosexual men. *Science*, 253: 1034–1037.

Levin, S., Balistrier, J., & Schukit, M. (1972). The development of sexual discrimination in children. *Journal of Child Psychology and Psychiatry*, 13: 47–53.

Limentani, A. (1989). *Between Freud & Klein*. London: Free Association Books.

Lothstein, L. (1984). Psychological testing with transsexuals: a 30-year review. *Journal of Personality Assessment*, 48: 500–507.

Luteyn, F., Kok, A. R., & van der Ploeg, F. A. E. (1980). *NVM: Nederlandse. Verkorte MMPI, Handleiding*. Lisse: Swetz en Zeitlinger.

Luteyn, F., Starren, J., & van Dijk, H. (1985). *Handleiding bij de NPV*. Lisse: Swetz en Zeitlinger.

Lyons-Ruth, K. (1992). Maternal depressive symptoms, disorganized infant–mother attachment relationships and hostile–aggressive behavior in the preschool classroom: a prospective longitudinal view from infancy to age five. In: D. Cicchetti & S. Toth (Eds.), *Developmental Perspectives on Depression* (pp. 131–171). Rochester: University of Rochester Press.

Main, M. (1991). Metacognitive knowledge, metacognitive monitoring, and singular (coherent) vs. multiple (incoherent) models of attachment. In: C. M. Parkes, J. Stevenson-Hinde, & P. Marris (Eds.), *Attachment Across the Life-Cycle* (pp. 127–159). London: Routledge.

Main, M., & Hesse, E. (1990). Parents' unresolved traumatic experiences are related to infant disorganized attachment status: is frightened and/or frightening parental behavior the linking mechanism? In: M. T. Greenburg, D. Cicchetti, & E. M. Cummings (Eds.), *Attachment in the Preschool Years* (pp. 161–185). Chicago, IL: University of Chicago Press.

Main, M., & Solomon, J. (1990). Procedures for identifying infants as disorganized/disoriented during the Ainsworth strange situation. In: M. T. Greenburg, D. Cicchetti, & E. M. Cummings (Eds.), *Attachment in the Preschool Years* (pp. 121–161). Chicago, IL: University of Chicago Press.

Marantz, S., & Coates, S. (1991). Mothers of boys with gender identity disorder: a comparison of matched controls. *Journal of the American Academy of Child and Adolescent Psychiatry*, 30: 310–315.

Marcus, D., & Overton, W. (1978). The development of cognitive gender constancy and sex role preference. *Child Development*, 49: 434–444.

Masand, P. S. (1993). Successful treatment of sexual masochism and transvestic fetishism associated with depression with fluoxetine hydrochloride. *Depression*, 1: 50–52.

Mason, A., & Palmer, A. (1996). *Queer Bashing: A National Survey of Hate Crimes against Lesbians and Gay Men*. London: Stonewall.

Mate-Kole, C., Freschi, M., & Robin, A. (1988). Aspects of psychiatric symptoms at different stages in the treatment of transsexualism. *British Journal of Psychiatry, 152*: 550–553.

Mauss, M. (1938). Techniques of the body. In: B. Brewster (Ed.), *Sociology and Psychology*. London: Routledge & Kegan Paul, 1979.

McConaghy, N., Armstrong, M. S., Birrell, P. C., & Buhrich, N. (1979). The incidence of bisexual feelings and opposite sex behavior in medical students. *Journal of Nervous & Mental Disease, 167*: 685–688.

Mead, M. (1935). *Sex and Temperament in Three Primitive Societies*. New York: Norton.

Meigs, A. (1990). Multiple gender ideologies and statuses. In: P. R. Sanday & R. G. Goodenough (Eds.), *Beyond the Second Sex*. Philadelphia, PA: University of Pennsylvania Press.

Meltzoff, A., & Moore, M. K. (1977). Imitation of facial and manual gestures by human neonates. *Science, 198*: 75–78.

Minghelli, M. (1996). *Santa Marina la travestita*. Palermo: Sellerio editore.

Mitchell, J., & Rose, J. (Eds.) (1982). *Feminine Sexuality*. Harmondsworth: Penguin.

Money, J. (1955). Hermaphroditism, gender, and precocity in hyperadrenocorticism: psychologic findings. *Bulletin of The Johns Hopkins Hospital, 97*: 253–264.

Money, J. (1976). Letter to the editor. *Science, 191*: 872.

Money, J. (1988). *Gay, Straight and In-Between*. Oxford: Oxford University Press.

Money, J. (1995). *Gendermaps: Social Constructionism, Feminism, and Sexosophical History*. New York: Continuum.

Money, J., & Ehrhardt, A. A. (1972). *Man and Woman, Boy and Girl*. Baltimore, MD: John Hopkins University Press

Money, J., Hampson, J. G., & Hampson, J. L. (1955). An examination of some basic sexual concepts: the evidence of human hermaphroditism. *Bulletin of the Johns Hopkins Hospital, 97*: 301–319.

Moore, M. S. (1990). Understanding children's drawings: developmental and emotional indicators in children's human figure drawings. *Journal of Educational Therapy, 3*: 35–47.

Moore, M. S. (1994). Reflections of self: the use of drawings in evaluating and treating physically ill children. In: A. Erskine & D. Judd (Eds.), *Psychodynamic Therapy with Physically Ill Patients* (pp. 113–144). London: Whurr Publishers.

Moore, M. S. (1997). How can we remember but be unable to recall? The complex function of multi-modular memory. In: V. Sinason (Ed.), *Memory in Dispute*. London: Karnac Books.

Morris, J. (1991). On the sadness of living abroad. *The Independent Magazine* (19 October).

Murray, L. (1991). Intersubjectivity, object relations theory, and empirical evidence from mother–infant interactions. *Infant Mental Health Journal*, 12: 219–232.

Murray, L., & Trevarthen, C. (1985). Emotional regulation of interactions between two month olds and their mothers. In: T. Field & N. Fox (Eds.), *Social Perception in Infants* (pp. 177–187). Norwood, NJ: Ablex.

Nanda, S. (1990). *Neither Man Nor Woman: The Hijra of India*. London: Wadsworth.

Nanda, S. (1996). Hijras: an alternative sex and gender role in India. In: G. Herdt (Ed.), *Third Sex, Third Gender: Beyond Sexual Dimorphism in Culture and History*. New York: Zone Books.

Nathanson, D. L. (1986). The empathic wall and the ecology of affect. *Psychoanalytic Study of the Child*, 41: 171–187. New Haven, CT: Yale University Press.

Nelki, J., & Sutton, A. (1998). Emotional aspects of gynaecological problems presenting at birth. In: Garden A. S. (Ed.), *Paediatric and Adolescent Gynaecology* (Chapter 6). London/Sydney/Auckland: Arnold.

NHS Health Advisory Service (1995). *Together We Stand: The Commissioning Role and Management of Child and Adolescent Mental Health Services*. London: HMSO.

Nichols, M. (1990). Lesbian relationships: implications for the study of sexuality and gender. In: D. P. McWhirter, S. A. Sanders, & J. M. Reinisch (Eds.), *Homosexuality/Heterosexuality: Concepts of Sexual Orientation* (pp. 350–364). Oxford: Oxford University Press.

O'Shaugnessy, E. (1964). The absent object. *Journal of Child Psychotherapy*, 1 (2): pp. 34–43.

Perilstein, R. D., Lipper, S., & Friedman, L. J. (1991). Three cases of paraphilias responsive to fluoxetine treatment. *Journal of Clinical Psychiatry*, 52: 169–170.

Perry, B. D., Pollard, R. A., Blakely, T. L., Baker, W. L., & Vigilante, D. (1995). Childhood trauma, the neurobiology of adaptation, and "use-dependent" development of the brain: how "states become traits". *Infant Mental Health Journal*, 16 (4, Winter): 271–289.

Phillips, A. (1988). *Winnicott*. London: Fontana Press.

Piaget, J. (1954). *The Construction to Reality in the Child*. New York: Basic Books.

Pilkington, N. W., & D'Augelli, A. R. (1995). Victimization of lesbian, gay, and bisexual youth in community settings. *Journal of Community Psychology*, 23: 33–56.

Pincus, L., & Dare, C. (1978). *Secrets in the Family*. London: Faber & Faber.

Plante, E., Boliek, C., Binkiewicz, A., & Erly, W. K. (1996). Elevated androgen, brain development and language/learning disabilities in children with congenital adrenal hyperplasia. *Developmental Medicine and Child Neurology, 38*: 423–437.

Radke-Yarrow, M., Cummings, E. M., Kuczynski, L., & Chapman, M. (1985). Patterns of attachment in 2- and 3-year olds in normal families and families with parental depression. *Child Development, 56*: 884–893.

Reiner, W. G. (1996). Case study: sex reassignment in a teenage girl. *Journal of the American Academy of Child and Adolescent Psychiatry, 35* (6): 799–803.

Rekers, G., Bentler, P., Rosen, A., & Lovaas, O. (1977). Child gender disturbances. *Psychotherapy: Theory, Research and Practice, 14*: 2–11.

Remafedi, G., Farrow, J. A., & Deisher, R. W. (1991). Risk factors for attempted suicide in gay and bisexual youth. *Pediatrics, 87*: 869–875.

Robins, C., Blatt, S., & Ford, R. (1991). Changes in human figure drawing during intensive treatment. *Journal of Personality Assessment, 55*: 477–497.

Ross, M. W. (1980). Retrospective distortion in homosexual research. *Archives of Sexual Behavior, 9*: 523–531.

Rotherham-Borus, M. J., Hunter, J., & Rosario, M. (1992). "Suicidal behavior and gay-related stress among gay and bisexual male adolescents." Unpublished manuscript, Columbia University.

Rutter, M., Graham, P., Chadwick, O. F. D., & Yule, W. (1976). Adolescent turmoil: fact or fiction. *Journal of Child Psychology and Psychiatry, 17*: 35–56.

Sales, J. (1995). Children of a transsexual father: a successful intervention. *European Child and Adolescent Psychiatry, 4* (2): 136–139.

Sander, L. (1977). Regulation of exchange in the infant-caregiver system: A viewpoint on the ontogeny of "structures." In: N. Freedman & S. Grand (Eds.), *Communicative Structures and Psychic Structures* (pp. 13–35). New York: Plenum Press.

Sander, L. (1987). Awareness of inner experience. *Child Abuse and Neglect, 2*: 339–346.

Savin-Williams, R. C. (1994). Verbal and physical abuse as stressors in the lives of lesbian, gay male, and bisexual youths: associations with school problems, running away, substance abuse, prostitution, and suicide. *Journal of Consulting and Clinical Psychology, 62*: 261–269.

Savin-Williams, R. C. (1995). Lesbian, gay male, and bisexual adolescents. In A. R. D'Augelli & C. J. Patterson (Eds.), *Lesbian, Gay, and*

Bisexual Identities over the Lifespan: Psychological Perspectives (pp. 165–189). Oxford: Oxford University Press.

Schachtel, E. (1959). Memory and childhood amnesia. In: *Metamorphosis* (pp. 279–322). New York: Basic Books.

Schechter, M., & Roberge, L. (1976). Sexual exploitation. In: R. Helfer & C. Kempe (Eds.), *Child Abuse and Neglect: The Family and the Community* (pp. 127–142). Cambridge, MA: Ballinger.

Schneider, S. G., Farberow, N. L., & Kruks, G. N. (1989). Suicidal behavior in adolescent and young adult gay men. *Suicide and Life-Threatening Behaviour, 19*: 381–394.

Schowalter, J. E. (1995). Normal adolescent development. In: H. I. Kaplan & B. J. Sadock (Eds.), *Comprehensive Textbook of Psychiatry, Vol. 2* (6th ed., pp. 2161–2167). Baltimore, MD: Williams & Wilkins.

Segal, H. (1957). Notes on symbol formation. *International Journal of Psycho-Analysis, 38*: 391–397.

Shaffer, D., & Piancentini, J. (1994). Suicide and attempted suicide. In: M. Rutter, E. Taylor, & L. Hersov (Eds.), *Child and Adolescent Psychiatry. Modern Approaches* (3rd ed., pp. 407–424). Oxford: Blackwell.

Shilling, C. (1993). *The Body and Social Theory*. London: Sage.

Slade, A. (1987). The quality of attachment and early symbolic play. *Developmental Psychology, 23*: 78–85.

Slimp, J. C., Hart, B. L., & Goy, R. W. (1978). Heterosexual, autosexual and social behavior of adult male rhesus monkeys with medial preoptic-anterior hypothalamic lesions. *Brain Research, 142* (1): 105–122.

Sreenivasan, U. (1985). Effeminate boys in a child psychiatric clinic: prevalence and associated factors. *Journal of the American Academy of Child and Adolescent Psychiatry, 24*: 689–694.

Steiner, B. W., Sanders, R. M., & Langevin, R. (1985). Crossdressing, erotic preference, and aggression: a comparison of male transvestites and transsexuals. In: R. Langevin (Ed.), *Erotic Preference, Gender Identity and Aggression in Men: New Research Studies* (pp. 261–275). Hillsdale, NJ: Lawrence Erlbaum Associates.

Steiner, J. (1993). *Psychic Retreats*. London: Routledge.

Steiner, J. (1996). Discussion paper at Mrs. Birkstead-Breen's presentation. *The British Psycho-Analytical Society Bulletin, 32* (4): 22.

Stern, D. (1985). *The Interpersonal World of the Infant*. New York: Basic Books.

Stern, M. (1952). Free painting as an auxiliary technique in psychoanalysis. In: G. Bychowski & J. Despert (Ed.), *Specialized Techniques in Psychotherapy* (pp. 65–83). New York: Basic Books.

Stoller, R. (1964a). A contribution to the study of gender identity. *International Journal of Psycho-Analysis, 45*: 220–226.

Stoller, R. (1964b). The hermaphroditic identity of hermaphrodites. *The Journal of Nervous and Mental Diseases, 139* (5): 453–457.

Stoller, R. (1968a). Male child transsexualism. *Journal of American Academy of Psychiatry, 7*: 193–201.

Stoller, R. (1968b). *Sex and Gender, Vol. 1*. New York: Science House.

Stoller, R. (1975). *Sex and Gender, Vol. 2*. London: Hogarth Press.

Stoller, R. (1986). "Gender identity development and prognosis: a summary." Paper presented at conference of the International Association for Child and Adolescent Psychiatry and Allied Professions (ESCAP), Paris, France, 21–25 July.

Sutton, A. (1990). "A case study of psychoanalytic psychotherapy with a 15 year old patient with incomplete testicular feminisation." Proceedings of the 9th Congress of the European Society of Child and Adolescent Psychiatry, London.

Swaab, D. F., & Fliers, E. (1985). A sexually dimorphic nucleus in the human brain. *Science, 228*: 1112–1115.

Tayler, P. J., Burton, K., & Kolvin, I. (1992). Suicidal behaviour in children and adolescents. In: K. Granville-Grossman (Ed.), *Recent Advances in Clinical Psychiatry, Vol. 7* (pp. 1–13). Edinburgh: Churchill Livingstone.

Taylor, D. C., & Eminson, D. M. (1994). Psychological aspects of chronic physical sickness. In: M. Rutter, E. Taylor, & L. Hersov (Eds.), *Child and Adolescent Psychiatry: Modern Approaches* (3rd ed., Chap. 42, pp. 737–748). Oxford: Blackwell Scientific.

Terr, L. (1983). Play therapy and psychic trauma: a preliminary report. In: C. E. Schaefer & K. J. O'Conner (Eds.), *Handbook of Play Therapy* (pp. 308–319). New York: Wiley.

Terr, L. (1988). What happens to early memories of trauma? A study of twenty children under age five at the time of documented traumatic events. *Journal of the American Academy of Child and Adolescent Psychiatry, 27*: 96–104.

Terr, L. (1990). *Too Scared to Cry*. New York: Harper & Row.

Thorne, B. (1993). *Gender Play: Girls and Boys in School*. New Brunswick, NJ: Rutgers University Press.

Trevarthen, C. (1985). Facial expressions, emotion, mother–infant interaction. *Human Neuro-Biology, 4*: 21–32.

Troiden, R. R. (1979). Becoming homosexual: a model of gay identity acquisition. *Psychiatry, 42*: 362–373.

Tronick, E., & Cohen, J. (1989). Infant–mother face-to-face interaction:

age and gender differences in coordination and miscoordination. *Child Development, 59*: 85–92.

Trowell, J. (1997a). Child sexual abuse. In: Hon. Mr Justice Wall (Ed.), *Rooted Sorrows: Psychoanalytic Perspectives on Child Protection, Assessment, Therapy and Treatment*. Bristol: Jordans.

Trowell, J. (1997b). The psychodynamics of incest. In: E. Welldon & C. Von Velsen (Eds.), *A Practical Guide to Forensic Psychotherapy*. London: Jessica Kingsley.

Turner, B. (1992). *Regulating Bodies: Essays in Medical Sociology*. London: Routledge.

Udwin, O. (1993). Annotation: children's reactions to traumatic events. *Journal of Child Psychology and Psychiatry and Allied Disciplines, 34*: 115–127.

Ussher, J. M. (1991). Family and couple therapy with gay and lesbian clients: acknowledging the forgotten minority. *Journal of Family Therapy, 13*: 131–148.

van der Kolk, B. S. (1987). *Psychological Trauma*. Washington, DC: American Psychiatric Press.

Wagner, B. M. (1997). Family risk factors for child and adolescent suicidal behaviour. *Psychological Bulletin, 121*: 246–298.

Wallander, J. L., & Varni, J. W. (1998). Effects of paediatric chronic physical disorders on child and family adjustment. *Journal of Child Psychology and Psychiatry and Allied Disciplines, 39* (1): 29–46.

Wellings, K., Wadsworth, J., & Johnson, A. M. (1994). Sexual diversity and homosexual behaviour. In: A. M. Johnson, J. Wadsworth, K. Wellings, & J. Field (Eds.), *Sexual Attitudes and Lifestyles* (pp. 183–224). Oxford: Blackwell Scientific.

Winnicott, D. W. (1935). The manic defense. In: *Through Paediatrics to Psycho-Analysis* (pp. 129–144). New York: Basic Books, 1975.

Winnicott, D. W. (1960). Ego distortions in terms of true and false self. In: *The Maturational Processes and the Facilitating Environment*. London: Hogarth Press, 1965.

Winnicott, D. W. (1971). Transitional objects and transitional phenomena. In:*Playing and Reality*. London: Tavistock Publications.

Wohl, A., & Kaufman, B. (1985). *Silent Screams and Hidden Cries*. New York: Brunner/Mazel.

Woodman, N. J., & Lenna, H. R. (1980). *Counselling with Gay Men and Women: A Guide for Facilitating Positive Lifestyles*. San Francisco, CA: Jossey-Bass.

Zachary, A. (1996). Contribution to the discussion on homosexuality. *The British Psycho-Analytical Society Bulletin, 32* (11): 15.

Zhou, J., Hofman, M. A., Gooren, L. J. G., & Swaab, D. F. (1995). A sex difference in the human brain and its relation to transsexuality. *Nature, 378* (November): 68–70.

Zucker, K. J., & Bradley, S. J. (1995). *Gender Identity Disorder and Psychosexual Problems in Children and Adolescents.* New York: Guilford Press.

Zucker, K. J., & Bradley, S. J. (in press). Adoptees are overrepresented among clinic-referred boys with gender identity disorder. *Canadian Journal of Psychiatry.*

Zucker, K. J., Bradley, S. J., & Lowry Sullivan, C. B. (1996). Traits of separation anxiety in boys with gender identity disorder. *Journal of the American Academy of Child and Adolescent Psychiatry, 35*: 791–798.

Zucker, K. J., Bradley, S. J., & Sanikhani, M. (1997). Sex differences in referral rates of children with gender identity disorder: some hypotheses. *Journal of Abnormal Child Psychology, 25*: 217–227.

Zucker, K. J., & Green, R. (1992). Psychosexual disorders in children and adolescents. *Journal of Child Psychology and Psychiatry and Allied Disciplines, 33*: 107–151.

Zucker, K. J., Wild, J., Bradley, S. (1993). Physical attractiveness in boys with gender identity disorder. *Archives of Sexual Behaviour, 32*: 449–463.

Zucker, K. J., Wilson-Smith, D. N., Kurita, J. A., & Stern, A. (1995). Children's appraisals of sex-typed behavior in their peers. *Sex Roles, 33*: 703–725.

Zucker, L. (1948). A case of obesity: projective techniques before and after treatments. *Journal of Projective Techniques, 12*: 202–215.

INDEX

327

332   INDEX

Hershberger, S. L., 98, 105, 106
Hersov, L., 304
Hesse, E., 47, 48
Hetrick, E. S., 104, 105
Higgett, A., 51
hijras of India, as third sex/gender,
        82–84, 86
    see also sex, third, occurrence of in
        various societies
Hill, P., xiv, 295, 297
Hines, M., 70, 71, 72, 74
Hofman, M. A., 15
Hollingshead's social class
        classification, 29, 31, 32, 289
homoerotic sexual interest, first
        awareness of, 97, 99, 102–105,
        116
homophobia, and sexual identity
        decisions, 98–99
homosexual, identification as, 99–
        109
homosexuality, passim
    developmental trajectories
        towards, mental health
        implications of, 95–108
    and gender identity and role, 11
    genetic factors in, 14–15, 75–76
    hereditary factors in, 14–15
    hormonal factors in, 75
    neuroanatomical/structural factors
        in, 72–74
    during adolescence, 95–109
Hood, J. E., 155
Hooker, E. A., 107
hormonal factors, in homosexuality,
        75
hormonal imbalance, 7
hormonal sex, 64–67
hormones, influences of, on gender
        identity, 11, 12, 15, 69–77, 84,
        174
Hu, N., 14
Hu, S., 14
Hua of New Guinea, cross-cultural
        practices in, 86
Hunter, J., 127
Hurry, A., 134, 135
Huxley, P. J., 127
hyperarousal response, 290
    sensitized, to trauma, 15

identification:
    introjective, and child sexual
        abuse, 165
    projective, 18, 19, 60, 156, 189, 224,
        241–243, 291, 293
    and child sexual abuse, 165, 166,
        168
identity formation, sexual,
        identification of, 99–107
Imber-Black, E., 269
imitation, in search for knowledge, 51
Imperato-McGinley, J., 12, 69, 70, 176,
        177
Incomplete Testicular Feminization,
        240
integration, development of, 5
intersex disorders, 3, 63, 64, 66, 68–71,
        78, 85, 87, 238, 239, 245–248
    "Agnes", 88, 93–94
    in childhood and adolescence,
        173–184
    gender identity development in,
        176–178
    "Lesley", 237–249
    management of, 181–184
    multidisciplinary approach to,
        190–191
    "Laura", 191
intersexed individuals, vs.
        transsexuals, 177, 178
intersexuality, concept of, 64
introjection, 290
    and child sexual abuse, 165
Inuit, cross-gender child-rearing of,
        12, 79–80
    see also sex, third, occurrence of in
        various societies
Ipp, H. R., 27
Ironside, L., xiv, 198–215
Isay, R. A., 101

Jackson, L., 187, 191
James, A., xiv, 12, 79, 88, 92, 93
Jenks, C., 92, 93
Johnson, A. M., 96
Jost, A., 64
Jukes, A., 168

Kaplan, N., 47
karyotype, 290